End of an Innings

END OF AN INNINGS

DENIS COMPTON

Introduction by Benny Green

THE PAVILION LIBRARY

First published in Great Britain 1958

First published in the Pavilion Library in 1988 by
PAVILION BOOKS LIMITED
196 Shaftesbury Avenue, London WC2H 8JL
in association with Michael Joseph Limited
27 Wrights Lane, Kensington, London W8 5TZ

Series Editor: Steve Dobell

British Library Cataloguing in Publication Data
Compton, Denis
End of an innings.
1. Compton, Denis   2. Cricket players—
England—Biography
I. Title
796.35'8'0924   GV915.C65

ISBN 1-85145-269-9 Hbk
ISBN 1-85145-270-2 Pbk

Printed and bound in Great Britain by
Billing & Sons Limited, Worcester

Cover photograph reproduced by kind permission of the
Hastings and St Leonard's Observer

INTRODUCTION

Judging from the memoirs of reliable witnesses, it is by no means unusual for young impressionable men to see in some gifted athlete qualities which the athlete himself might be surprised to learn he possesses. Perhaps on occasion the surprise is justified, and the athlete no more than a reservoir into which his idolater has poured his own fantasies of longing, imbuing the object of his worship with virtues which never existed outside his own head. But even in the most extreme cases of self-delusion, there must always be some spark of inspiration within the athlete, for how else would the flame of his admirer's adoration ignite the forest fires of hero-worship we all know exist? It is instructive that Neville Cardus, on his own confession, received his initiation into the heady rites of Romanticism neither from Byron nor Delacroix nor Beethoven, but from the imperious front-foot play of the Lancashire batsman A.C.MacLaren, whom Cardus, in a pardonable excess of rapture, described as 'The Noblest Roman'. The prolific bookman E.V.Lucas was more inclined to collapse in ecstasy before the men of Hambledon than over Hazlitt or Lamb, and even H.G.Wells was proud enough of his father's bowling feats to advertise the family's permanent niche in the Records section of *Wisden*. When the dying poet Francis Thompson mourned the death of his own bright promise, the symbol he chose was the opening batting partnership once renowned at Old Trafford between Hornby and Barlow, whose sad mortality Thompson took for the transience of all things, in particular the perishable nature of boyish dreams of innocence, of aspiration, of idealism, and whatever else which renders adolescence itself so intensely romantic an experience. The reader, first encountering these and copious other instances of the potential power of cricket to influence what used to be called the soul, and had now better be called the psyche, is inclined to shuffle nervously and wonder if some old man is not making a fool of himself. I experienced these very misgivings myself on first reading, in Cardus's *Autobiography*, that MacLaren 'lighted a fire in me never to be put out', that his batting 'thrilled my blood, giving shape and reality to things I had till then only vaguely felt and dreamed about of romance'. Was not Cardus, in the words of the streets of my boyhood, coming it a bit strong?

And yet I have before me, always, the irrefutable evidence of my own youth, and its link with the sporting genius of one of the greatest players of ball games ever produced by the English. My first exposure to the sorcery of Denis Compton had nothing to do with cricket at all. It was in the winter of 1942–43, leaning against the icy rusting stanchions of White Hart Lane, that I first witnessed the revelation of Compton in full flow. It remains one of the more crushing ironies of the sporting life that Compton's peak years as an outside left, years in which there was no rival who remotely approached him, should have coincided with the war, which means that to this day a certain element of tinsel attaches to his reputation as an international footballer simply because during the war caps were not awarded for England appearances. And yet greatness remains greatness no matter what the context, and Compton out on the wing at White Hart Lane in those mid-war years was one of the supreme sights of English life (White Hart Lane rather than Highbury because throughout the war the Arsenal club, its home ground commandeered by ARP, was obliged to become a sitting tenant of its great rival club, Tottenham Hotspur). In that season of 1942–43, it seemed there was nothing Denis could not do with the ball at his feet, or rather foot, because, as he has always been fond of admitting, his right boot was merely decorative when measured against the great thunderbolt of his left – although I can still see him on the screen of recollection, right-footing a ball past the West Ham goalkeeper to give his side a 3–1 win in some long-forgotten Southern cup-tie. In the semi-final, he performed even more prodigious feats, running the QPR defence ragged at Stamford Bridge, scoring one of the great goals of my experience by dribbling the ball along the goal-line, past one defender after another and, while the crowd bayed and screamed for him to push the ball back to one of the oncoming forwards, consummating this brilliant episode by hooking the ball past the goalkeeper into the net with the sort of stylish nonchalance which left the entire opposition desolate. Arsenal went on to win the final against Charlton Athletic by a cricket score, after which they played the Northern cup-winners, Blackpool, a club which, because of the chance siting of RAF headquarters, was able to field weekly a side which was virtually a Great Britain eleven in disguise. The match was played at Stamford Bridge and was assumed to be a set-piece starring the Blackpool winger Stanley Matthews. Denis, who was Stanley's fellow-winger for England at the time, stole the day with a most astonishing one-man exhibition. After taking an early two-goal lead, Arsenal were at last outplayed by the opposition, lost 2–4 and took away with them the consolation of Compton's unforgettable virtuosity on the left wing.

Years later I had the chance to remind Denis of this match. He remembered it well, reacting to my recollections as a man would who has kept the memory fresh in his own mind but is surprised to find that anyone else has. Moments adhere to the memory for no apparent reason, and as we reminisced I asked him if he could recall the trouble he was having with his face. He looked at me in genuine astonishment. He remembered, but why should I, or indeed anyone? But the young keep a very close watch on the welfare of their gods, and I can never erase the image of the Arsenal side posed for a team photograph before the game began. I can see Denis now, looking round in the moments before the camera clicked, seeking out one of the club's back-room boys, finally catching the eye of one, and then, in vigorous pantomime, rubbing the stubble on his cheeks. To see Denis with stubble was a unique thing, but all was explained a few moments later when the club assistant returned with a pot of cream, which Denis immediately rubbed into his cheeks. I was instantly smitten with anxiety. Would a mild bout of dermatitis reduce Denis's shooting power, or flatten the arc of his body swerve? In the event he played better than ever, putting on the sort of show which later prompted two England captains, Joe Mercer and Billy Wright, to name him in their memoirs as the best left-winger of their epoch.

But then, without warning, a catastrophe hit our world. Denis disappeared from it. The army required his services in India, where he scored prodigious runs for Holkar and reduced maharajahs to goggling delight. To say we missed him at White Hart Lane would be like saying that Captain Hook missed his hand. The terraces were bereft without those dribbles and those thunderbolts, and we prayed for his swift return. There at last came the Saturday afternoon of his comeback. We arrived at the ground two hours before the kick-off, took up our positions high in the stand and awaited the second coming of the god. He was greeted with a great crashing roar of welcome, and when, after a few seconds play the ball came to him the entire stadium erupted in triumph and anticipation of joy. Denis took the ball up to the full-back, showed it to him and ran round him. But somehow the back caught him, dispossessed him and kicked the ball upfield. I can never forget the deep pang of dismay which went through me with the realisation that the unthinkable had happened. The god had been rendered mortal. The episode in India had minutely thickened his waist, slowed him down, only fractionally but enough to render him human and his art fallible. His career continued for several years, and encompassed the glories of another England appearance, a League championship medal and a cupwinner's medal. But life was never quite the same, at any rate in winter.

The summer was a different matter altogether. If Denis's footballing ability was obscured by the clouds of war, nobody, except possibly the occasional demented Yorkshireman, ever questioned his genius as a cricketer. Although during the war there was no county championship, there was regular cricket at Lord's on Saturdays and Bank Holidays, and it was here that Denis, without suspecting what he was doing, demonstrated the subtle differences between conceptions of match fitness at football and at cricket. The young man who danced down the wing had lost a yard in pace he was destined never to find again, whereas the young man at the crease remained the embodiment of gilded youth, easeful in his mastery, handsome in his attitudes, the very paragon of the sporting virtuoso. It came as no surprise to his followers when, after the war, he began smashing records all over the place, setting marks which nobody will ever approach now that the cricketing calendar of England has been so sadly dismantled in the name of financial expediency. At last, with his eminence so irresistible, the god was formally anointed. With Brylcreem. Denis was the first cricketer to be taken up by the advertising industry, to become a brand image, to be deemed to have attained a fame so widespread that the entrepreneurs judged, quite rightly, that his face beaming down from the hoardings, from magazines, from the backs of buses, would convey its message even unto those who knew nothing of cricket.

The apotheosis of the god came in 1947, when Denis, partnered by Bill Edrich, laid the bowlers of England to waste with a style and insouciance which was breathtaking. All through that balmy summer men listened to the radio telling the lunchtime scores up and down the country, received the message that Denis was not out and going strong, and hailed taxis to whisk them to St John's Wood in time to partake of the feast. Denis took six centuries off the South African tourists that year, four of them for England. Between 12 July and 17 September he scored 2,074 runs, including twelve centuries, for an average of 109.01. And just to crown the joke, there was the business of the Middlesex–Surrey match at the Oval just after the August Bank Holiday. After scoring a not-out century on the opening day, Denis bowled so bewildering a gallimaufry of spin as to mesmerise the opposition, taking six wickets for 94 runs in the first innings and six for 80 in the second, helping to swell his final figures for the season of 73 wickets at just over 28 runs each. I saw much of all this, although never quite contriving to witness the breaking of Jack Hobbs' record of sixteen centuries in a season. It seemed the deed would be done in a match at Lord's against Northants, when Denis, after scoring 60 in the first innings, reached 85 in the second before being clean bowled by a quite ordinary, normal man called Broderick. But I did see the greatest innings of my life that season, again at Lord's, a few days after the rout of Surrey. Middlesex had to score 400 in the last innings of the match in order to defeat Kent. The task was palpably beyond them because of Douglas Wright, who had run through them in the first innings, taking seven wickets, including Denis, clean bowled, for less than a hundred. The required batting rate was over 90 an hour, and with Brown, Robertson, Edrich and Robins gone with the score at 135, the end seemed a formality. I was sitting high in the Mound Stand, where I had had the misfortune to fall into the hands of some relations who never normally attended sporting rites. But even their tongues were silenced by what followed. F.G. Mann held an end up while Denis set about the job of dismembering the Kent attack, which he did with a flair so brilliant and an improvisatory fluency so extraordinary that next day, in *The Star*, Wright wrote a piece confessing the sheer impossibility of knowing what and how to bowl at Denis on such rampant occasions. Denis hit nineteen boundaries even though, as *Wisden* confirms, 'most of the Kent fieldsmen were placed on the boundary'. So long as Denis was there, victory was feasible. When he had made 168 and it was beginning to look as though Middlesex might pull off an incredible win, he mishit a leg-break from Wright and was bowled. The last five wickets fell within half an hour, but I was gone by then, nursing the recollection of an innings which, by its wit and beauty, had already divorced itself in my mind from the circumstances which had given rise to it. I went home truculent and delighted that such an afternoon in my life could go so well, even down to the last flourish of a lost cause. I vowed I would never forget it, and I never have.

But what had it to do with me? I had never met Denis. I knew nobody who knew him. I did not aspire to the sort of virtuosity he so casually displayed. My cricketing horizons were marked by the railway bridge and the underground station on Sunday afternoons. Nor had I ever aspired to any considerable footballing heights. My own ambitions, to do with music and literature, were not remotely connected with anything Compton did. And yet, in defiance of the incongruity, my dreams of Lester Young and H.G.Wells became curiously commingled with my vision of Denis dancing down the pitch to stroke some hapless off-spinner to the Tavern boundary, where the arrival of the ball would be announced with beery cheers from shirtsleeved young votaries. Everyone in the ground was rendered rapturous by what was going on out there on the grass. At peak moments, like the last innings of the Kent match, Denis actually seemed to have transcended human limitations and to be soaring up on to some new plane of being. And as this metamorphosis was precisely what I was dreaming about in secret every time I commenced my daily instrumental practice, or picked up one of Wells's social comedies, it is perfectly understandable to me now that my own sensibilities should have become so confused with the batting style of a professional cricketer.

This equating of an athlete's grace with one's own potential is nothing new. We have been well instructed by Cardus in how MacLaren's imperious ways confirmed a boy's dawning suspicion that there were, in this mundane world, pockets of dazzling self-expression if only you could find them. And it comes back to me that I once read a book by the Australian writer Philip Lindsay, who, having arrived in London in 1930 in search of literary success, quickly found himself faced with destitution. As the weeks went by and the sentences refused to form, one thing alone sustained young Lindsay in his struggle to carry on. It so happened that all through the summer of 1930, when he was sleeping rough and going hungry, another young Australian aspirant was conquering the Old Country with a terrible relentless power. Lindsay writes in his confessional that had it not been for Bradman's reassertion of faith on behalf of a whole generation of young Australians, he might have been tempted to give up the ghost and reject his own literary ambition once and for all as a foolish vanity. It was Bradman alone, Bradman who had never heard of him, who never suspected his existence, who gave him the strength of will to fight on to stay artistically alive. To be frank, Lindsay's state of mind throughout that summer seems in retrospect to have been a riot of confusion in which national pride, literary vainglory and run-of-the-mill youthful excess all collided to form a melange of hyper-romantic illusion. None of that mattered. The truth is that for all its outlandishness, its illogicality, its sheer gaseous folly, Lindsay's exalted condition in the depths of privation and failure was one more demonstration among many of how the casual virtuosity of a great player of games can fire the imagination, stiffen the will of some young man totally unknown to the object of his idolatry to continue on his pursuit of the impossible. When on those gilded afternoons I arrived breathless at Lord's with the sound of my own instrumental labours still ringing in my ears, a copy of *Tono Bungay* or *The Great Gatsby* hanging out of my pocket, all things seemed to fuse into a single vision of triumphant self-mastery.

As it had been for Lindsay watching Bradman, for Cardus watching MacLaren, for Hazlitt watching Cavanagh, so it was for me in the summer of 1947, living through the turmoils and uncertainties, the bravura and the bewilderment, the despairing fears and the wild hopes inevitable for any young man aspiring to professionalism in some demanding craft. Painfully aware that the last few months of my teens were slipping away, half eager to be rid of them, and yet too sentimentally in love with them to part company from them once and for all time, feeling at once young and old, mortified with shame at the pitiful ineptitude of my own work, convulsed with laughter at the contemplation of the vast abyss between ambition and achievement, yet still crazily resolved to become a musician and a writer, horrified at the speed and apparent ease with which my contemporaries, my long-standing comrades on cricket and football fields, were suddenly contemplating marriage, earning money, starting careers, while I was still at the beginning of everything, I must have been in a condition of nervous receptivity just as Lindsay had been, and Cardus before him, and so on right back to John Nyren, whose hero-worship of the players in his father's Hambledon side had inspired him, for one brief moment, to the supreme virtuosity of *The Cricketers of My Time*. The matchless beauty and originality of a paragon like Denis Compton dazzled the imagination and lifted the spirits every time he trotted down the pavilion steps and strode briskly out to the business of the morning, purposeful yet blithe, with that odd, very slightly hobbled gait, and took guard at the crease. You knew that today he would play a great innings, and you felt a little sorry for the bowlers. And yet you feared disaster from the very first ball and could hardly bring yourself to watch. Cardus has described those precise contradictory reactions when watching Reggie Spooner as a boy. So committed was Cardus to Spooner's glorious success that he later wondered if he had ever seen Spooner actually playing the ball, so tightly were his eyes screwed up against the chance of catastrophe. It was like that for me with Compton. Day after day I sat there, high in the Mound Stand, willing him to spirit the ball from his presence, praying for a century, basking in the expectation of an undisturbed flow of miracles and, most miraculous of all, getting them. In that summer of 1947, after a merely goodish start, Denis came on with a burst of glory never before seen on English cricket grounds.

I saw then that the world was a better place for his being in it, as he refined the sensibilities of tens of thousands of men through the practice of his art. And it followed that this same world would be immeasurably diminished once he strode off the green for the last time. It was this fearful thought whose shadow gradually crept across the Lord's turf as the seasons plick-plocked into *Wisden* and the past. But there was no need to fret over the prospect of a Comptonless world for a long time yet. As I strolled home through Regent's Park in the early evening of the great innings against Kent, past the very house in which my other great hero, H.G.Wells, had died in the previous summer, I exulted in the thought that Denis was still only twenty-nine, a mere lad when compared with the likes of Wilfred Rhodes, who had played for England at forty-nine and for Yorkshire at fifty-two; of Herbert 'Dainty' Ironmonger, first capped for Australia when approaching his forty-sixth birthday; of Frank Woolley, still drawing the crowds when past fifty, and who, at the age of fifty-two, earned my displeasure by dismissing Denis in a wartime match at Lord's in August 1940; of J.C.Clay, the comic Methuselah of the Glamorgan dressing-room, still a county cricketer in his fifties; above all of Jack Hobbs, the master whose records Denis was now poised to surpass. Of the 197 centuries to the credit of Hobbs, half had been made after the age of forty, so surely Denis had years and years of profligate run-getting before him. Somehow this confirmation of great reservoirs of time still untapped was a great solace to me, although how I equated Denis's expectations with my own I was unable to explain. One day it came to me suddenly why I retained this curious vested interest in the well-being of a man I had never met. It was simply that Compton had come to stand in my mind for my own carefree adolescence, and that so long as he endured, then so did my own youth. Later on I was to encounter a whole generation of men who felt the same, if not about Compton, then about someone in the same line of business: Ted Drake, perhaps, or Eddie Hapgood, or Walter Hammond. Every time he walked out to bat, Denis carried with him the hopes and fears of those of us who had invested so much emotional capital in him and adopted him as a talisman, as a surety of sweet youth, above all as a cast iron, copper-bottomed guarantee against the infirmities of old age.

The worm, however, had already found its way into the bud. The strain of playing professional sport at the very highest level for fifty-two weeks a year, although it had not the slightest effect on the man's temperament, had done its work on his body; to be precise, to his knee, which now began to plague him in ominous fashion, sometimes in mid-match. In one of the last matches of 1947, for Middlesex against the Rest of England, even as he slaughtered the opposition for a remarkable double century, he was obliged to do the slaughtering on one leg. The years of dashing down the wing, of riding tackles, of swerving and half-turning at full speed, had taken their toll. There were those, although I was not among them, who cursed Denis's football career, wished it had never existed, wondered aloud how so great a cricketer could have chosen to put his art at risk for so graceless an affair as soccer. Quite apart from the fact that with his talent Denis could hardly have helped himself, the football career brought with it rich consolations, notably a family double unprecedented in all the realms of English sport, a double so outlandish that even to think of it ever being approached is pure madness. In 1947 Denis and his brother Leslie were members of the winning side in the County Championship. In the football season which followed, they were members of the winning side in the First Division of the Football League. And if not all the moments were quite so exalted, some of them were much funnier. In a wartime match at Lord's, Leslie achieved the piquant distinction of appearing as wicketkeeper for the West Indies. Even more freakish were the events of 28 August 1943, when both brothers were selected to play for the combined Middlesex and Essex eleven to play Kent and Surrey at Lord's. Rain fell all morning, making the possibility of play so remote that at lunchtime the Comptons received permission to respond to a call for help from the Arsenal club playing at Charlton on the first day of the football season. The Comptons departed, the rain stopped, the cricket began, too late for the brothers to be snatched back from the Valley.

Such demands, of playing both games, season after season, year after year, finally brought about a situation where Compton's Knee eclipsed Jenkin's Ear as the most renowned item of anatomy in the annals of the English. The fallibility of the god began to dawn on us with sickening clarity. Although 1948 proved to be another triumphal processional, with Denis holding the bridge single-handed against the Australians, the ecstasies of 1947 were destined never quite to return, even though there were still marvels to come. There was, in December 1948, an innings at Benoni in South Africa so brilliant that it is clear that *Wisden* found words inadequate:

Compton made his first hundred in sixty-six minutes, his second in seventy-eight and his third in thirty-seven. Often he walked down the pitch before the bowler released the ball, and he mixed orthodoxy with a bewildering assortment of unclassified strokes which went from the middle of the bat at a lightning speed. He whipped balls pitched outside his off stump to the mid-wicket boundary and he stepped away in order to cut leg-breaks pitched outside the wicket.

Five years later at Nottingham Denis made his highest Test score, 278 against Pakistan, and the period between was punctuated by countless batting banquets around the counties. There was even the melodrama of a debacle, in Australia in 1950–51, when inexplicably he averaged over fifty with the bat except in the Test matches, where he scored only fifty-three runs in eight innings.

But I recall these years with nothing like the same immediacy. The necessity of making my own career finally caused me to neglect Compton's. As the 1950s opened, I lost touch with the world of cup-ties and averages and analyses. Sport, which had been the dominant theme in my life, suddenly faded away. My football boots, once as vital to me as my instruments, ended up in a cardboard box under my bed, where they lay for an eternity before my mother discovered them one morning with the dried mud of some municipal field still caked around the studs, and presumably gave them away or threw them out with the rubbish. Whatever became of those bizarre suede shinpads, a gift from an uncle who had won a sackload of medals while wearing them? By what mysterious agency did my punchball and my boxing gloves become consigned to the limbo of lost causes? Exactly when did I retire from Sunday cricket? And when did I stop stealing afternoons at Lord's? For all these lapses I can only plead extenuating circumstances, more pressing business to be attended to, like dozing the miles away in touring band coaches, munching sandwiches in scattered provincial bandrooms, staying up half the night in order to study some virtuoso of a very different profession.

One day in 1953 I rose at noon, dressed and sauntered down to the offices of a musical weekly whose editor was in the habit of publishing my occasional pieces on the jazz life. After handing over my copy, I found myself wandering eastward along Shaftesbury Avenue, where a great crowd was blocking the pavement, intent on some unseen spectacle. As I approached, I saw that the focus of their rapt attention was the shop window of an electrical emporium. On the screen of a television set placed centre stage behind the glass there flickered the black-and-white images of a cricket match. It took me no more than one wild glance to grasp the context. There was Denis Compton at the crease, and there at the other end was Bill Edrich. This was not Lord's but the altogether more plebeian Oval, and what the assembled congregation was following with such religiosity was the final act of the final Test in the struggle for the Ashes. I had happened across this shop window at the very moment when, after a lapse of twenty years, England were about to regain the Ashes. So they had done it after all, after years which encompassed all of my sentient life. And of all living cricketers it was Compton who was about to strike the last ceremonial blow. It could hardly have been more adroitly stage-managed had I been God Almighty. I watched in a curious confusion of emotions as my old hero smacked the ball to the boundary, thought back to my teens as the field became a shifting mosaic; the thousands ran over the grass to congratulate the cricketers, to express their exaltation, to apotheosise a moment in their lives which they would still remember when they were old men. How, I marvelled, could I ever have allowed myself to lapse so utterly, so regrettably, to have denied myself access to the paradise so close at hand? I resolved to pick up the threads immediately.

But something impeded my resumption of the sporting life. There was always something, although I forget now what it was. Usually the circumstances of the musical life kept dumping me in places far removed from my favourite cricket grounds. Three years after the apocalypse in Shaftesbury Avenue, Denis, now a veteran with a gammy leg, made his England comeback in the most dramatic circumstances. In the previous November, after years of evasive action, his right knee-cap had been removed. Throughout that summer he played in only eight matches for Middlesex, but here were the selectors, heroically plumping for true class in an attempt to buttress the England batting. With his immaculate sense of theatre, Denis batted in the old style, scoring 94 and 35 not out at the Oval. Here is *Wisden*:

> Gradually, Compton unfolded all the familiar strokes of his golden days. The special leg-sweeps of his own brand, and the most delicate of late cuts, as well as peerless cover drives took him and England to prosperity.

I watched every ball of that match, but only on the television screen of a holiday camp in the Isle of Wight. Not until 1958, beginning the long process of disengaging myself from the music business, was I able to return to Lord's, by which time Denis's career had almost run its course. On those afternoons, I watched him bat once again, watched him reconstructing the backdrop of my adolescence, and each time I hardly dared breathe in case this might be the very last innings I would ever see him play.

And what if it were? What could it matter to men still young that one more professional cricketer should depart from the scene? It matters not at all, any more than growing old matters, or losing that first fine careless rapture matters, or forgetting the addresses and telephone numbers of faithful old friends matters, or hearing of the death of some girlfriend from the remote past matters. Since Denis's retirement I have been fortunate enough to make his acquaintance at cricket dinners, at odd charity matches, on a few grand cricketing occasions. During last summer I sat with him under the plaque to Lord Harris in the garden behind the Lord's pavilion and conducted a crosstalk for the benefit of the cameras. In the course of our chat a fact emerged which I had forgotten, or possibly made a subconscious resolve not to notice. Soon Denis would be seventy years old. I would rather have denied the accuracy of this rumour, but there was no arguing with the figures. It then occurred to me that we might as well make a feast out of it, so I asked Denis if he welcomed the idea of republishing the book he had written originally in 1957, telling his story from the end of the war to the end of his career. He agreed with delight and some surprise, and I was delighted too, because the publication of the book would give me the opportunity I had wanted to express my thoughts on the subject. He is the most charming of men, everybody's friend, as the saying goes, and I have yet to encounter the curmudgeon who disagrees.

I have never so much as mentioned to him any of the things in this confessional for fear of being thought some sort of lunatic. I wonder what he would make of it if I confessed that now, whenever I regard the receding images of my own adolescence, he is one of its leading characters, along with Shaw and Wells, Lester Young and Benny Goodman, Lewis Carroll and Charles Dickens, Groucho Marx and George Gershwin. Today he remains accessible still, but what of the rest of my companions who shared my idolatry? Where is Albert O, who spent hours, days, weeks, with a tennis ball at his feet, running over the cobbles of Warren Street in a vain attempt to defy nature and acquire Denis's body swerve? Where is Siggy B, who split himself down the middle, amoeba-like, loving Denis in the summer for sustaining Middlesex, hating him in the winter for not sustaining Tottenham Hotspur? And where is Lionel W, who was so stricken by the tragedy of 1950–51 that in later years when he saw it mentioned in the book he happened to be reading, he would close his eyes against the print and turn the pages till he reached the safe harbour of some other season, as though by refusing to contemplate the disaster he might at last erase it from the record books? Some of the young bloods who shared my idolatry all those years ago are pushing old age now. Others have not been so lucky. But on behalf of all of them, I enter the defence, which is the same one which William Hazlitt once offered for his worship of another great English player of ball games, John Cavanagh, the Fives champion of England. Hazlitt delights in Cavanagh's style, saying:

> He did his work with the greatest ease, never took more pains than was necessary, and while others were fagging themselves to death, was as cool and collected as if he had just entered the court. His style of play was as remarkable as his execution. He had no affectation, no trifling.

So much for the style, which reads as much like an appreciation of Denis Compton as of John Cavanagh. But how much does any of it matter when weighed in the scales against the more portentous issues of this world? Hazlitt had been scoffed at by his contemporaries for attaching so much significance to a game, for investing so much affection in a player of games – to which he delivered the riposte which serves for all like occasions:

It may be said that there are things of more importance than striking a ball against a wall. There are things indeed which make more noise and do as little good, such as making war and peace, making speeches and answering them, making verses and blotting them, making money and throwing it away.

It is a dangerous game trying to follow Hazlitt, and I would never dream of attempting it.

Benny Green, 1988

END OF AN INNINGS

by

DENIS COMPTON

For those who play and
watch Cricket

CONTENTS

PREFACE

BEFORE I start I want to clear the ground a little.

I have wanted very much to write this book. As I write, I shall attempt to say what I really thought and felt throughout my career. Of course, I shall try to write it fairly, and I hope as kindly as honesty will permit—but I do want to set down what I did in fact think: not what people may think that I thought, or have said that I have thought, or even perhaps think that I ought to have thought. At the same time, I shall not be critical or destructive just for the sake of making a noise or a headline—that, I think, is the worst approach of all.

If I were to adopt any other attitude I don't think this book would be worth writing.

D. C. S. C.

CHAPTER I

NEW BEGINNINGS

When I had come back to England from India on demobilisation, like many another I had gone up to Olympia and been given my suit—quite a good suit it was too, I remember. Certainly in the spring of 1946 it was a good suit. Then you were lucky to be able to get one at all.

Almost immediately I had gone round to Lord's, where it seemed as if in a distant past an exciting and successful life had once been developing before me. Some time in that past I had got into uniform as everyone else had done. Now, in my new suit, I came into Lord's by the back entrance at the nursery end, just as I used to after I left school. Then I was usually in a state of high delight because though I was small and unknown, I was nevertheless a member of the Lord's ground staff. I was coming back in 1946 to take up where I had left off in 1939, hopeful, I suppose, but a little apprehensive. Apart from games in India, it was more than six years since I had played in a first-class cricket match. I might have changed a lot since then.

I stood by the ground where I had so often bowled and been bowled to, in the nets, and looked over at the back of the stands. It wasn't much of a view really, but the principal thing was that it had hardly changed. Everything seemed to be the same; a little worn, and shabby, but substantially the same—almost as if I had never been away, and was taking up my career again in the ordinary way in the year after the West Indies tour of 1939.

I walked slowly towards the tunnel which leads under the stands on its way round to the pavilion, past the building in which was the room—not much changed, I noticed, and still packed with the miscellaneous gear of the ground staff—where I used to have tea at a deal table with the other chaps. If I was being nostalgic perhaps I could be forgiven. I suppose my time on the ground staff had its times of unhappiness as well as happiness, but at that moment of return I was seeing it very rosily indeed. I do remember that it was for me very much a time of hope and ambition, and deliberate disciplining of myself to play cricket. I may not have been the most efficient member of the staff so far as the ground was concerned, but I doubt if there was anyone who had been more keen to learn how to hold a bat and bowl a ball. As I passed the printing shop near the deserted bars a picture came into memory with sudden vividness, of sunshine, mostly on Saturday afternoons, when I used to go in and collect the next card, and then, if Surrey were playing Middlesex, and Hobbs was batting, or if Patsy Hendren was batting in any game, I would rush out and get to a place where I could study their stroke play as I handed over the match cards and took the spectators' money. We were pretty good at selling match cards: we used to club together and pool takings, and on a good afternoon, with energetic salesman-ship, we could hope to make as much as £5 apiece in a Test Match.

I could see some of the machines through the windows now, black and crowded together. Someone recognised me and gave me a smile of welcome. It felt good to be back, but I didn't want to talk, not for the moment anyway; I wanted to get round to the pavilion, to look out towards the middle.

When I got there it didn't look any different from what I had so often remembered while I was away. It was smaller perhaps, and less green, and everything was shabbier—but really unchanged. Father Time was there still, crouched waiting for the new season to begin, it seemed; the hands of the clock were moving round towards noon, and over on my right the Tavern had the same appearance of rather casual welcome. The stands were bare and empty, a bit lonely look-ing, though as I stood there I could imagine them peopled with spectators in the sun, as they were that day in 1938 when I was sent out at a crucial moment in our second innings against the Australians. It was the Second Test, and we hadn't many runs on the board, and I felt a bit apprehensive as I walked out over the green grass to the middle. I was just twenty and very hopeful, playing in my third Test Match. I got 76 runs—I shall never forget the number—not out, and they were badly needed runs and may have saved the game for us. It's an innings which I will always remember with a good deal of satisfaction.

I started to walk out to the middle now, over the green grass, with the empty stands all round about me.

It was here at Lord's that my life as a professional cricketer had begun, was to flourish, vary, and come to an end.

Without doubt I have been lucky most of my life, right from the start. To begin with, my father fostered my interest in cricket and football from the time when I was very young indeed. He gave me all the equipment and the books he could afford, and unlimited encouragement and attention. If I wanted to go to the Oval to see Jack Hobbs play he would usually find a way of ensuring that I got there. I am not sure at the beginning when I began to show that I wanted to make a career in sport that my mother was so keen. She probably thought there were safer and more secure ways of earning a living, and it was very natural that she should; but as time went on she did approve—very much, in her quiet kind of way, and I don't suppose anyone turned up on the field with shirts and trousers better cared for than mine.

Then there were the masters at school who helped me along all they could, without allowing me, I am now thankful to say, to neglect the other things I had been sent there to learn. They were pleased when I played for the Elementary Schools against the Public Schools and made a century at Lord's. And, of course, there was my elder brother Leslie, equally keen on sport, who preceded me to Arsenal, and I am sure did a lot to make the way there a good deal easier for his younger brother.

It was to Highbury I went when I left school in 1933, to go on the Arsenal ground staff. I was fifteen and small for my years, undergrown even; it was just about then that I began to grow and reach anything like a decent size. Tom Whittaker was the trainer, and in the years following he looked after my training and that of the other youngsters there with the same care that he gave to the great and numerous stars who made Highbury in those days such a brilliant place—people such as Cliff Bastin, David Jack, Alex James, and so on: they were great players, and it was a pleasure and a thrill for one young person at least to know that he belonged to the same club. It meant, of course, that it was many years before I had even a hope of getting into the Arsenal team, though, no doubt because of the greatness of those who were the team, I can never remember feeling impatient or frustrated about it. While I was there I played for some other teams, in particular for Nunhead, and I still have one of the match programmes in a scrapbook. I may have been small, and I probably looked a bit insignificant, but I never lacked the ambition or the determination to play soccer and cricket well.

It was not until the war broke out that I really began to play regularly in top-class football, and in the time before I went abroad to India in 1944 I played in fourteen war-time internationals for England. Then, and potentially at least until 1945 or 1946, was my best period for football. I was very fit—never fitter perhaps than after a six weeks' course in 1940 at the Army School of Physical Training in Aldershot, during which I remember so often dragging myself stiffly and creakingly to bed and wishing that I could get back to the relative ease and comfort of ordinary football training. My knee never troubled me and I never thought it would again. It had been injured in the 1938-9 football season when I was playing against Charlton and the diving goalkeeper and my right leg swung hard at the ball collided. I had the cartilage removed; but in those active war-time years it seemed as good as it had ever been. Although soccer was then my game my greater ambition had always been for cricket. Each summer I went from Highbury to Lord's, from ground staff to ground staff. Whatever system for the finding and training of young players may take its place—and as yet I don't see anything definite—I have no doubt that it would be difficult to find anything more effective than the training I had during those early years at Lord's. Apart from anything else the atmosphere of being in close contact with great players like Patsy Hendren and Jack Hearne was so very important to me. It acted as a spur, the more so when I found, as I soon did, that I was to get so much help and to have it given with so much intelligence and understanding.

I say that because my style of play was soon discovered to be "unorthodox"—though I might some day take the trouble to inquire precisely what that word is supposed to mean. Anyway, whatever it means, I was not "orthodox"; that fact was very obvious indeed, and I suppose has remained so for the whole of my life in cricket.

I had first come to the notice of the powers that be by scoring runs in matches that I played for the Nippers, a ground-staff Sunday side which George Fenner, the coach, organised. If you made runs for the Nippers it quickly had an effect on your standing at the Lord's ground, and soon you found people watching you as a hopeful prospect. George Fenner always took a special interest in me, and before very long he had me playing for the Middlesex Second XI.

After that I began to get even more coaching; and then the cricket shrewdness of those who were looking after me began to show itself. I would go into the nets and practise, playing my usual shots, in my usual style, including my leg sweep which even then I was using, sometimes with considerable efficiency, and advice and hints and instructions would be given to me—but no attempt was ever made to change my style: the whole effort was directed towards developing and stylising the talents which I had been given, in the form in which they first appeared. Those are the important words: in the form in which they first appeared. Basically, my batting style never varied throughout the whole of my career, though, of course, the technical execution of my shots developed and became more assured. But my method of play remained the same. For that I shall always be intensely grateful to George Fenner and Archie Fowler, who, quietly and intelligently, made sure that I developed my cricket along the lines natural to me.

George Fenner, the head coach, was most helpful. I know now that at quite an early stage in my life on the ground staff, he picked me out as a promising-looking player. At every available opportunity he used to get me off to the nets for a couple of hours' practice, and many a time in those young days I bowled to the great Patsy Hendren. George Fenner pushed me as much as he could into day games for the M.C.C., and saw that I got as much practice as he could make available.

I practised hard and constantly and diligently. I was a familiar figure in the nets, getting all the bowling and as much variety of it as I could. Sometimes, during a career in cricket which has extended over twenty years, I have had the impression from cricket writers that my ability to play cricket has been something just natural to me, God-given, as it were, spontaneous, effortless. Anyone who saw me in those early years would have realised how very far from being the truth that impression is. Natural gifts, of course, I had; no cricketer could get anywhere without them; but in years of practice I developed them by sheer hard work to a stage at which I thought they were as good as I could make them. Everything I did depended on that first substratum of training and discipline. Even those of my shots that cricket writers most like to describe as unorthodox—for instance, my habit of walking or running down the pitch to spinners —have been practised hour after hour, day after day, in the nets. I left as little as possible to chance. I was too keen to succeed in both cricket and football to leave more to chance than was absolutely necessary.

Of course there is no doubt that on occasions, on the days when things go well and every shot you attempt is a winner, I have been carefree and spontaneous and even seemingly effortless; but I could have been none of these things if it had not been for the arduous and painstaking hours spent at the nets when I was very young: when I was still in the process of formation and still on the ground staff at Lord's.

I first played for Middlesex in 1936, when I was just over eighteen years of age, and I got 989 runs in my first season. Some of the first things that happened to me were humorous. Two incidents I remember were concerned with Bill Reeves, a famous cricket wit, without too much respect for persons or things. He used to umpire games at Lord's. In May of 1936 Middlesex were playing Sussex at Lord's and, having originally been due to go in higher up, I was gradually demoted in the order until, very young and new, I found myself walking out to the wicket at No. 11, to join Gubby Allen, then at the height of his power and fame, in a situation where Middlesex needed some number of runs for first-innings lead.

Gubby was determined to get them. Maurice Tate was bowling, and Gubby came up to me and told me to play forward to him: "Play forward," he said, "and stick there." For some reason I played back, twice, and was nearly out. Eventually I was given out l.b.w. by Bill Reeves when I was 14, though by then we had secured our first-innings lead.

Gubby was quite satisfied that I was in fact not out, and that Bill should not have given me out.

He went to Bill afterwards, and remonstrated in clear terms.

"Bill," he said, "you're a so-and-so cheat. . . . Young Compton wasn't out, and well you know it."

Bill was quite unperturbed.

"I know he wasn't, sir," he answered, "but you had your

first-innings lead, and I was dying to spend a penny. . . . So I gave
him out."

Perhaps his language was a little bit more colloquial than the
words I've used here.

On another occasion Bill was umpiring and R. W. V. Robins—
Robbie—went on to bowl. To begin with, before starting an over
he removed his Middlesex sweater, with its badge of three scimitars,
and gave it to Bill, who added it to the others around his waist, and
when the over was finished he took it from him again and put it on.
After the third or fourth over, however, he didn't take his sweater,
and as he was walking away from the wicket Bill called out to him:

"Mr. Robins," he said, "don't you want your sweater?"

Robbie turned round and looked at him for a moment.

"No," he said then. "No, I don't . . . and you know what you
can do with it."

Bill, quick as a flash, came back with: "What! Swords and all,
sir?" And, Robbie, perhaps not in a very good temper before, and
everyone else within hearing, burst into laughter.

In the 1937 season I played in my first Test Match. It was in the
last Test, against the New Zealanders, at the Oval—where I was
to play my *last* Test Match in this country. I got the news of
my selection, as afterwards I was to get similar news, from a
bulletin on the wireless. I was a very happy young man indeed,
although by the time I was on my way to the ground with my
father, I was taut and very nervous. I scored 65 runs before, charac-
teristically, being run out. My brother Leslie was at the ground to
see me play, and so was my mother—for her it was a very great day
indeed.

One other thing about the 1937 season was that in it a young man
called Leonard Hutton made his mark for the first time in international cricket. He played in all three Tests against the New
Zealanders, and in his first he scored a century exactly. His career
started in its fullness a little earlier than mine, but our lives were to
run parallel for many years in the future.

I really arrived in Test cricket in the Australian series in 1938.
With Len Hutton I was one of the young players who looked as if
they might have some of the stuff of Test cricket in them, and no

doubt many people saw us as the men eventually to take the places of such seasoned players as Charles Barnett, Walter Hammond, Eddie Paynter and others whose great careers were now drawing near to their conclusions. Looking back, I can see that that was exactly how it was.

I played at Nottingham in the First Test. For me it was, and will always remain so, one of the great experiences of my life. It was all very well the previous season to have got 65 against the New Zealanders; but to prove yourself, you had to play good cricket against the Australians. In those days that was how you judged a batsman—could he make runs against the Australians? If he could, well then, the probability was that he was a cricketer.

For me the approach to that game was one of many different moods and feelings. First of all, it was the biggest and severest trial I had yet had. If I came through it well it would be a very big step forward; again, I was going to play against a side which was being captained by the great Don Bradman whom, it seemed only a few years ago, I had been hero-worshipping from afar with schoolboy enthusiasm. Now I was going to play against the great man himself. Inevitably I asked in my own mind—and I could see it in the un-spoken hopes of those closest to me—could I not only do well, but very well, and make a century in my first Test Match against the Australians, in the classical style of those who are, as I was, bent on success.

It was an exciting and fascinating game, and I made my Test century, sure enough, in my first innings against the Australians. I suppose my father and I were just about two of the most pleased people in the world that day.

As so often, I was lucky. Before I had scored, I was dropped off O'Reilly by the great Don himself, and I can still remember how I sighed with relief. Then I went on to make my hundred, 102 to be precise, and was caught on the boundary. Overnight when I had been going well with 65 to my credit, Walter Hammond, my cap-tain, said that when I got my first century I was to take a fresh guard and go on and make a second. But I was so exhilarated by the time I made my hundred that I forgot all about a fresh guard, or about any guard, and it wasn't long before I was out. The Press con-gratulated me; I had telegrams and letters and messages of congratulation—but Hammond, quite rightly, ticked me off for not getting that second century. I remember well the look on O'Reilly's face that day as I passed him on my way to the wicket. It said, as plainly as if he had written it out and handed it to me, that here at least was one easy wicket for him—and how nearly he was right. He showed me no mercy, and I expected none.

Tiger O'Reilly, as we called him, was probably the greatest bowler of all time. He had everything: he had flight, he had spin, he was tremendously accurate, and he could bowl a wonderful fast ball and disguise it from you. He could make the ball bounce like a tennis ball, especially his googly off which he got so many people caught at short leg. The curious thing about him was that to watch him, he seemed to do everything in the wrong way according to the cricket book. With his hunched shoulders as he ran up to the wicket, and his failure to use his great height, even though he bounced the ball so much when he delivered, he never seemed to "do it right".

When he was bowling he had a great loathing for batsmen, as if they were enemies to be challenged and immediately defeated—and the angrier he got the better he bowled. Some bowlers when they get angry lose their ability—but not O'Reilly; if he just missed your wicket that might anger him, and back he would come and bowl an absolute fizzer.

He had a wonderful volatile fighting temperament; perhaps, like his name, it was Irish. For me it was a great experience to play against him in that 1938 season, and to find him so genial and kindly and helpful off the field to a young player like myself.

I was selected to play in all five Tests of that series, although in fact we played four only, as the Manchester Test was completely washed out by rain. In the Fifth Test at the Oval when England made 903 for 7 declared and Len Hutton scored the 364 runs which until very recently stood as a world record, Eddie Paynter and I laid a bet. Padded up, we had been waiting to go in for two and a half days—which in those conditions is a very long time indeed. We were sitting in the pavilion watching the game and the inexorable scoring of runs out in the middle, nodding off to sleep occasionally, when Eddie Paynter turned to me, and said in his northern accent: "Denis," he said, "I bet we don't make ten runs between the pair of us."

"I'll have a pound we do," I answered.

Then Hammond was out, and Eddie went in, and a few minutes later he was out, bowled O'Reilly. Now it was my turn; I got one off O'Reilly and was down at the other end to face Mervyn Waite, who had had a very mediocre tour; but he bowled me first ball, and I was back in my well-used place in the pavilion, paying over a pound to Eddie Paynter.

Arthur Wood of Yorkshire went in some time later at No. 7, when the score was 770, and rubbed it into the Australians, the poor Australians, by making 53 runs in about an hour and a half's exhilarating cricket.

As he walked back from the wicket up the steps of the pavilion between the applauding members, he turned to them and said:

"I'm just the man for a crisis."

When the Australians returned home that autumn, having again won the series, there was much about which I was both pleased and grateful, for though not yet twenty-one I had joined the ranks of the established Test cricketers. I had gained a great deal in the essential cricketing virtue of confidence and come to know more keenly something which every cricketer must know: the absolute necessity of consistent concentration when you are batting. I was finding too, as I found in making that 76 not out at a vital time in the second innings of the Lord's Test, that when I was placed under pressure I seemed the more easily to find my closest concentration. That was something for which I was particularly grateful.

Next year, in 1939, the West Indies came over. They were not then the formidable cricketers they were later to become and as which we now know them, and we won the series fairly comfortably. They had one outstanding player, Learie Constantine, and in all-round capacity he may be one of the greatest ever. I saw him in action for the first time in the M.C.C. game at Lord's before the First Test Match.

Learie Constantine was an opening bowler who could bowl very fast and also could bowl spinners; he was a tremendously effective fielder—certainly the best fielder I have ever seen—and a great hitter of the ball: so that if he wasn't bowling perhaps at his best, he was giving an exceptional fielding performance, and if he was doing neither of these things, he'd almost certainly be doing well with the bat. Often he would do all three things well at the same time. At all times you were very conscious of him indeed. He was always in the game.

I got a century in that game at Lord's against bowling which included Martindale and Constantine, and so I went into the First Test Match, on the same ground, with the kind of psychological lift which I have found to be so important an element in batsmanship. In that Test, Hutton and I had our first great stand together—he got 196 and I got 120. We made 228 when we were at the wicket together. I have said the first great stand, though in fact it was one of only two stands that we have had together—all the time that we have played in the same sides we have had only two stands: that one in 1939 and the stand of 93 at Nottingham in 1948. It sounds difficult to believe, but if you check the records you'll find it's true.

When I arrived at the wicket that day Hutton was 91. He had got the runs rather slowly, playing with the care and concentration which was so characteristic of him. For me it was one of those days when I middled the ball from the start and was fluent in my stroke play. Suddenly the disease, as it were, seemed to infect Len, and very soon both of us were opening up all round the wicket and scoring very fast indeed, Len producing the finest and most attractive shots and showing the style of open cricket which perhaps we did not later see from him sufficiently often. It was a Saturday afternoon at Lord's, with the sun shining, the ground full of spectators in bright dresses or shirtsleeves, and the ball racing to the boundary from English bats with comforting regularity. It was one of my last and certainly one of the most vivid memories of cricket in those days which now seem so far away. Then the war came and county cricket ended and until my last year in India I, naturally, like everyone else, had to concentrate on other things.

In the months before I came home, in the spring of 1946, I played a lot of cricket in India, some of it of quite a high standard, though not of the dazzling quality of the play which was seen in the Victory Tests, before the Australian Army finally left England to go back home.

On their way back the Australians played a game against an Indian team in Calcutta and, perhaps because I was so tanned by the Eastern sun that I was browner than any Indian, I was the only Englishman included in that Indian side. The Australians won quite easily, but the game remains in my memory because of the riot. I have told the story before, but it will bear telling again.

I was at the wicket and had made 94. Keith Miller was fielding somewhere near, in the slips, I think, and Lindsay Hassett wasn't far away. All of a sudden we heard a tumult of yelling voices, and before long the ground had become the scene of a political demonstration with shouting and banner-carrying Indians parading round the boundary as if a revolution were in progress. Not surprisingly, we stopped playing. Then the incident took place.

The leader of the revolutionaries detached himself from his circling supporters and started to walk out to the middle, soon followed, though at a distance, by a number of his companions. We waited, wondering what was to come next. I felt perhaps a bit more secure than most, because I had a bat in my hand and stumps with steel-pointed ends within reach.

The leader advanced firmly towards us. I remember thinking as he came closer that he looked more sophisticated than I expected of a leader of rioters.

He stopped within a few yards of me. Out of the corner of my eye I was conscious of Keith Miller's close interest in what might happen very soon and very suddenly.

Then suddenly the sophisticated rioter said:

"Mr. Compton, you very good player, but the game must stop," and burst into a howl of white-toothed laughter. I wasn't sure that I saw the joke, but Keith Miller obviously did, and for years afterwards when I came out to bat he would repeat the words to me menacingly.

After the game restarted I went on to score a century, just to show my smiling Indian that he had described me correctly.

It wasn't very long afterwards that I went to Delhi, and from there I returned home to be demobilised, and to go to Olympia to collect my new suit.

On that day of return to Lord's I must have stayed out in the middle for fifteen or twenty minutes, pausing and looking at the wicket, or walking up and down at the side of it, speculatively, wondering what it would really be like to play on it again in the

1946 season which soon would be beginning. The speckled pigeons, I noticed, were still there, moving in their usual ragged formation about the ground, probably the same ones as had been about when I was last there six years ago. Everything was pleasantly familiar and usual and unchanged.

I started to walk back slowly towards the pavilion. There was a little heat on my back from the spring sun which was reflected in the big windows ahead of me and from the smaller windows to the right of the pavilion. There was the special gate, from where for most of the time the professionals in county games went out to bat and to where they returned when they were out. The amateurs walked down the steps, from the main door of the pavilion. I remember wondering if distinctions such as that would remain.

Faintly, as I drew nearer the white railings, thoughts of the future ran through my mind, of the fresh starts, the new beginnings, as it were, that I would have to make both in football and in cricket. If nothing else it was at least an exciting and probably a hopeful prospect.

Then I was at the pavilion rails. I had completed once again a journey I was to make, out and back, on many occasions in the ten variable years that were ahead of me.

CHAPTER II

OLD MAESTROS

I DIDN'T start well.

In fact, I had a spell from late May when in six county innings and a Test Match innings I had scores of 10, 0, 7, 0, 8, 0 and 1: a total of 26 runs in seven innings. For the first time I lost all my confidence, more totally than I was ever to lose it again. Indeed for a time I doubted my ability ever to play cricket well again, the result I suppose of six years, more or less, away from the first-class game.

I was really concerned about myself and even began to think that I wouldn't be able to play the game properly again. I realise now that I should not have allowed myself to get into that state: I should have shrugged it off with as much cricket philosophy as I could muster; to have told myself that it happens to every cricketer, some time in his life. But it was my first time, and I had a good deal to learn yet.

Instead of doing that I went to the nets and practised hard, thinking that perhaps I had lost something which I could find again if I really got down to it at the nets; but the more I practised the worse I seemed to get. The climax was at Lord's, on my own ground, in my first post-war Test. The adjective horrible is perhaps not too strong to apply to my experience: the long and uncertain walk out to the middle, taking guard, looking round to see how the field is placed, and then being bowled, first ball, as I was; after that, the long walk back to the pavilion. Indeed, the classic nightmare of the batsman was my daytime experience.

In the end the turning-point came, against Warwickshire at the end of June at Lord's. I went out to the wicket hardly knowing which end of the bat to hold, and with my confidence absolutely nil. To a delivery from Hollies I tried to play what I thought was a correct stroke, edged the ball, and with a strange kind of fascination saw it roll gently on to the wicket. That, I said to myself a bit grimly, is another nought. But it wasn't: the ball touched the stumps all right and the bails shook, but didn't fall. My fortunes had finally turned.

After that I decided I'd throw the bat at the ball. I did so to the next delivery, made contact beautifully and saw it go sailing into the grandstand balcony. I went on to make 122 and at the end of the innings was a man with confidence in himself fully restored. I knew then that I'd come through my bad patch, "a trot" as the Australians call it. Now I could go forward with more assurance. The first post-war obstacle had been traversed.

The experience (and I remember hoping—quite vainly as it turned out—that I would never have to go through it again) taught, or began to teach, me one of the essential lessons of the fascinating and unpredictable game that is cricket. Everyone, no matter who he is, will have lean times—batsmen who can get no runs, bowlers who can bowl no one out. When such times come they must be viewed objectively and philosophically, without needless gloom or despair —and so viewed will usually come to an end before very long.

Any other attitude may be disastrous, and there have been fine cricketers who have allowed themselves to become so despairing in a bad patch that they have never been able to get back their true form again. It is, in part, a question of temperament: in part, I believe, of trying to be completely objective about things when you are failing consistently. If you play cricket, you must accept the fact that there will be times when you will fail.

We won that series against the Indians without great difficulty, and our thoughts and those of the cricketing public were turned then to the prospect of the Australian tour in the winter of 1946-7. When the Test Matches were resumed again with the Australians, you could really feel justified in saying that post-war life was getting back to normal. That continuing battle, where fortune has varied so much over the generations, was to be joined once more. It was like old times again.

In some ways the tour that followed was not altogether satisfactory. I don't criticise the decision which the M.C.C. made to send out a team: I think that was the right decision. I know there were many who said that it was too soon after the war, and that the nation generally was too exhausted, not sufficiently well fed, having too many other important things to do, to justify sending out a side to Australia at that moment.

I don't agree; in my view the decision had the kind of boldness and foresight which made it exactly right.

But what I do criticise was the composition of the team which went out. In the first place, there were too many old-timers. They had had great careers in cricket, and still it may be had a lot of good cricket left in them, but they should not have been taken on the tour. The primary object should not in my view have been to try to win the series—no one, in any event, thought there was much possibility of that—or to play safe, but should rather have been to blood young players who had been showing promise during the cricket that had been played in England since the war had ended.

Walter Hammond, of course, was the obvious person to captain the side: there could not reasonably have been any other choice. However, as things turned out, primarily perhaps because of the tension which sprang into being between him and Bradman, his captaincy came in for a great deal of criticism. Hammond was then at the end of his tremendous career in cricket—my own view is that he was the greatest all-rounder ever—and it may be that he did not quite retain all his great gifts in their earlier fullness. Indeed, it sometimes, unhappily, appeared that he was failing to communicate to the side the fruits of his own gifts and experience, or to give them the feeling of enthusiasm for the game—a talent which I had seen in him before the war.

He tended to be individualistic and uncommunicative; worse still, he didn't seem to be part of the side. He had been given a present, a Jaguar—and most deservedly if I can be allowed to say so—but unhappily he used it to transport himself and the manager from game to game, while his team travelled by train. There was an absence of that sense of community and all being in it together which is an important element in keeping up the spirit of a side, and to which of course the captain has the most vital contribution to make. Worst of all, we seemed to go into each Test without a plan and without a sense of urgency.

With Bradman captaining the Australians it was more essential to have schemed carefully to make the best possible use of the cricketing ability available than against any other captain. The Don was then thirty-nine years of age, and though I think it is true to say that somewhere about this time he was tending to doubt whether, after the war-time interval of six years and indifferent health, he still had all his old flair and ability, yet no one could ever have been in doubt that he retained his old tactical skill as a cricketer, his knowledge of the game and of individual players and of their strength and weaknesses, and perhaps above all the relentlessness with which he approached and played the game. He was the best captain that I ever played against.

Yet if a decision in the First Test at Brisbane when Bradman was 28 had been given the other way, things might have turned out very differently both for him and for the two Test teams. I remember the incident very well. Up to that point Bradman had been only a shadow of his old self and appeared, uncharacteristically, to be feeling his way, almost sadly so. Had we set a more attacking and hostile field he would have been out before he had reached even his modest 28. Then something happened which is cricketing history and will probably be argued and written about while the game is played.

I was fielding at long leg, and Voce was bowling to Bradman, who played a bad shot into the slips. I had no doubt at all that he was caught by Ikin. Very much to my surprise, and I think to the surprise of everyone on the field, including Hammond, who appeared to be very angry as well, Bradman remained at the crease. He just stood there, and waited for the decision of the umpire.

After an interval of silence, which I suppose was quite short but seemed very long, there was a confident appeal by the English players, to which the umpire returned what to my mind was one of the most extraordinary decisions I have ever heard. To everyone's astonishment he gave Bradman "not out", and the game continued. Bradman went on to make 187 runs, to find nearly all his old confidence and to shed the uncertainty from which he had been suffering as to whether he would retire or go on playing. He would go on playing, and with a vengeance.

It was, if you like, one of the key moments in the post-war history of cricket as Bradman shaped to play the next ball after that decision.

I don't want to go into any more detail about the decision itself, except to say that I'm sure it was wrong and that I'm equally sure that Bradman was out. But the more important thing is this—I believe that if Bradman's innings had ended there his career in cricket would have ended there also, and we would have gone into the next Test against an Australian team captained by someone else. I'm pretty sure that Bradman, had he been faced with a total of 28 very shakily made, would have decided that the time had come for him to retire.

Walter Hammond was very angry about the decision, and in my view quite justifiably. Bradman obviously realised this, and as a result the relations, never particularly cordial, between the two captains—both of them great figures in their different ways and both masters of the game—now became strained to an almost unbearable extent. I have often thought that in consequence Bradman's determination to win, already of the firmest kind, became still more resolute, and that there was now added to it the incentive not just of beating Hammond and his men, but of defeating them utterly.

As things turned out, that was almost what he did do, and his own contribution to the process was very far from negligible— as, for example, his 234 in the Second Test. But his greatest contribution was his captaincy. You were always conscious of that thoughtful, active, penetrating brain which constantly applied itself to the individual problem of getting the particular player out. Bradman knew our weaknesses and went for them with the greatest skill.

I cannot say that I felt drawn to his approach to the game of cricket, though I must admire the consistency and determination, almost the ruthlessness, of his attitude and its effectiveness. I am not sure that he brought the best out of Keith Miller. In a way we were grateful that he did not, because Keith was quite formidable enough as it was. Not that it made any difference to the result; we did not win a Test.

Although I think that the decision at Brisbane was a bad one, yet if it had the result which I think it had, I am glad that it was given, for it may have meant that one of the greatest of cricketers stayed a few years longer in the game.

On that tour I saw two sides of Bradman, the private and the public: the one I liked, the other partly admired, partly disliked.

One night during the Second Test Match at Sydney, Bradman asked me to have dinner with him at his hotel. He was most charming and friendly and very helpful, and we got on well together. We had a general discussion about cricket and about batsmanship. At one stage Bradman produced a cricket bat from somewhere, and demonstrated very carefully and very exactly how he thought certain strokes which I used should be played and which in fact I had not been playing very well. I found it all very instructive, especially from the Australian captain in the middle of the Second Test of the series.

That was typical of Bradman in private, with the people he liked. In public he would rarely express an opinion: but in private he would talk freely and tell you exactly why and how he did things. He would express his opinion quite frankly and openly about the performance of other players, both English and Australian. One thing I remember he stressed particularly to me that night—the importance of having confidence. It is a theme which runs very clearly through the whole of my own cricketing life. Bradman was confidence incarnate, deliberate steely confidence which never seemed to fail him.

But in public it was different. When you were on the stage, as it were, with Bradman, you played your part and he his, and he would make no concessions. He was there to captain the Australian side to victory, and to that every other consideration, or almost every other consideration, must be subordinate.

An incident at Adelaide in the Fourth Test illustrates the point I am making. There I got a hundred in each innings. In the second innings I was at the wicket with Godfrey Evans, and if we were to save the game it was essential that Godfrey and I should stay together, because if either of us got out there would have been little hope of saving the game. Godfrey played his part magnificently, and, though he is one of the most forcing batsmen in the game, that day he stayed at the wicket for ninety minutes without scoring a run: a most exceptional feat of self-discipline under the circumstances.

Our joint policy was to keep Godfrey away from the bowling. Bradman's policy, very naturally, in order to get at Godfrey, was to put his fielders on the boundary and to give me the single. Of course, seeing what Bradman was up to, I refused the single until the fourth or fifth ball—which made a very dull game. I was not going to play Bradman's game for him by letting Godfrey go down the other end and take the bowling.

This went on for some little time. Bradman finally came over to me, with a look of annoyance on his face.

"Denis," he said to me a bit sharply, "this is not cricket. Do you realise that all these people are here to see cricket and what you are doing is not the way cricket should be played."

"All right, Don," I answered, "perhaps you are right . . . but if you bring your fielders in and set a normal field we can put things right, can't we?"

He set a normal field then, and the first ball of the first over afterwards I hit for four.

Bradman came over to me again.

"I am not going to give you runs," he said.

"Then we go back to the same procedure," I answered.

He reset the field on the boundary regardless of whether it was cricket or not.

Not long afterwards we had another talk together. As sometimes was my practice, I had been going up the wicket to the slow bowlers, and so playing them quite effectively. I was wearing spikes in my cricket boots and naturally made some marks as I went up the pitch. It was inevitable: it was also quite permissible.

Before very long Bradman spoke to me again.

"Denis," he said, "look at this wicket . . . we've got to bat next . . . look at your spike-marks."

"That's the way I play, Don," I said, "you know that . . . you can't blame me for those marks . . . I am terribly sorry"

"Ah, but we have to bat on this," he replied.

"Well, Don," I answered, "I am *terribly* sorry . . . but I'm playing for our side."

And that was the end of our conversation.

Each time, I had the odd impression that Bradman, in some strange way, did not like what was being done and therefore seemed to think it should not be done—because it might interfere with his ruthless determination to win.

It was my first tour in Australia and I was twenty-eight years of age. I was getting my first look at the type of wicket on which cricket is played in Australia, and, more important, at the new generation of Australian cricketers, in particular the two very formidable customers called Miller and Lindwall, one of the greatest fast-bowling combinations which Australia has produced, and on their day, in short spells, perhaps the most devastating.

I was beginning to feel fully in touch again, though my first experience of these two bowlers was something quite new. In common with a number of the other players I had never faced an attack as fast as theirs before, and found it presented new problems and a new challenge to my batting technique. I won't say that I mastered them then, or ever, but on that tour I certainly learned a great deal from them and laid the foundation for the contests which I was to have with them in the years to come. That tour did me a lot of good.

I cannot say that I ever felt happy about the way Hammond seemed to think we should deal with this fine Australian attack. I thought his policy was the wrong one and I was very surprised by it, because from what I knew and had seen of him it seemed so uncharacteristic. "Occupy the crease" appeared to be his motto. I shall always remember the substance of what he used to say on this question: "It doesn't matter," he said to us, in effect, "it doesn't matter if you don't score any runs—they will come—but don't do anything stupid and don't get out."

It was the last type of instruction to suit my style of play, and I think it probably had a curiously inhibiting effect, not only on me but on other batsmen. It tended to impose a restraint on your natural way of playing, and certainly diminished any pleasure you might get from playing the game. From the beginning I have thought and still think that a batsman's function is to make runs, and that if you don't enjoy cricket you might as well give up playing it.

Perhaps I was unfortunate in my relations with Hammond. I know that at one stage of the tour I was feeling stale. I had played probably more games than anyone else in the side and at the same time I had the impression, whether rightly or wrongly, that Hammond was reluctant to give me a rest. Eventually, not being in good form and feeling the need of a lay-off, I approached Hammond and suggested that perhaps I should be allowed a few days away from the game. His reply again was uncharacteristic, or so it seemed to me: "Yes," he said, "you can have a rest—you can become twelfth man at Bendigo"; to which I replied that if that was all I was to be allowed I would rather play in the game. In the end Hammond did let me have a few days rest.

The point is this. A Test tour is a long and exacting process and cricketers get stale. When that happens they should be given a few days right away from the game, out of the atmosphere of cricket, and in my experience it very often had a beneficial effect on the player. Keith Miller is perhaps the perfect example of this. A few days off at the races during a tour seems to make a new man of him. But Hammond did not apparently think that the treatment would suit me.

Of course, there can be no doubt that it was a most difficult tour on which to captain the M.C.C. side, even taking into consideration the fact that he had such an excellent vice-captain in Norman Yardley, who, I thought, showed qualities of friendliness and leadership combined which were most helpful to the players. But Hammond's resources were slender, and any man would have found the situation difficult.

Our main deficiency was the lack of anything like a pace attack. We had nothing with which to counter the force and energy of the Lindwall-Miller blitz. Bedser was our fastest bowler, and his pace was only medium fast. He worked tremendously hard on that tour and got very little assistance from the wickets, and I think he learnt a great deal, and certainly began the process of development which in the end was to make him the destructive force who did so well in later years. But there was not a great deal of support for him, and he was then, by himself at least, far from being sufficient, no matter how willing or hard-working.

A glance at the bowling figures makes the point very clear. Norman Yardley on that tour bowled 1,859 balls and took 16 wickets. Yet he would be the last person to mind my saying that he was not a recognised bowler at all and had not been taken on the tour as such; but such were our deficiencies that in the end Hammond had to rely considerably on him, and how well he did the job! Undoubtedly Hammond had one of the most difficult assignments ever.

In one respect at least the M.C.C. had the advantage, even if only quite a slight one—we had the better of two really exceptional wicket-keepers, Godfrey Evans being in my opinion just a shade better than Don Tallon. Both were so outstanding that it was difficult to decide which had the greater talent; both seemed to have the capacity for taking what seemed impossible chances—of turning what looked like a perfectly safe stroke into a seemingly easy catch behind the stumps. I would choose Godfrey Evans because to the medium fast attack of Alec Bedser and to the very difficult type of bowling which Doug Wright bowled, he had to stand up close to the wicket, thus having less time in which to make or accept his chances, whereas Tallon could stand right back to both Miller and Lindwall. I should doubt whether in any series a more gifted pair of wicket-keepers have been seen opposed.

It was the beginning of my long association with Godfrey Evans in Test cricket, and I began to see then the tonic effect of his alertness and keenness and effervescence in the field. I also saw that in him the spectacular and the efficient were combined in an inseparable unity.

I have made a lot of criticisms about this tour, but I don't want to leave the impression that it did not have its positive and beneficial effect too. Undoubtedly, the batsmen in the side learnt a great deal which proved useful to them in future games, and at least, by the time we started back for England on the flying-boat, we had seen exactly what it was that we would have to face in the future when we were playing against Australia, even if we hadn't yet found a way to master it. As in anything else it was useful to know precisely what the question was which we faced. Now we could start trying to find the answer.

One or two things were quite obvious, and were to prove very useful indeed. For example, it was plain that the Australian batsmen greatly disliked being tied down, and Norman Yardley showed how effectively this could be done by bowling accurately on a good length to a field which he had set very deliberately. The Australians didn't like it a bit. It seemed to give them a feeling of restriction which they might attempt to break by making a stupid or hasty stroke and consequently losing their wicket. Even so good a batsman as Miller, it would seem, was prone to react in this way. It was a useful piece of information and it was duly noted, and used later on.

But of course the real answer was for England to find a fast attack, and for her batsmen to get more experience against fast bowlers.

It was many years before we could do either.

CHAPTER III

THE NARROW GRAIN

TOWARDS the end of the tour in Australia I had run into my best form, and I seemed to continue it throughout the 1947 season. It was my best season: in a way I have often thought a freak season, a phenomenal season: once I had got started everything seemed to go right for me, every kind of shot even if weird and unheard of was a surprising success. At cricket when your luck is in, it really is in.

I remember at the Oval in making my eighteenth century against Sir Pelham Warner's XI—I had already at Hastings beaten Tom Hayward's record of 3,518 runs in one season—I was playing to the bowling of Tom Goddard in the champion county game against The Rest. I went forward to play a shot, and as I did so I spiked my right foot with my left so that both feet were almost locked together and I couldn't move. All I could do was to fall forward, and as I did I waved my bat, middled the ball and it went for a four. I did not seem to be able to go very far wrong—indeed I went on to make 246. Except for one mishap, that was the kind of luck I had all through the 1947 season.

Luck you must have, all the time, in greater or lesser measure. In almost any hundred a cricketer makes there will be some element of luck; even in Bradman's centuries there was luck, though he gave fewer chances than most. In my experience it is seldom you can say of a batsman that he has scored a hundred runs and did not have one bit of good fortune. Certainly in my own case hardly any of my 122 centuries have been scored without a chance.

But in 1947 it was good fortune for me all the way—except that my right knee began to give a lot of trouble towards the end of the season. In the last games I had to have it strapped tightly so that the piece of bone which had become detached and was floating round inside would at least be kept in one place. It was uncomfortable, but my confidence was such that I was hardly affected.

Perhaps the 1947 season was the moment of relief for the reserves of cricketing energy and capacity which had built up during the six more or less cricketless years of the war, when that side of my life had marked time—in the way that any athlete after a long rest may come back to enhanced form and ability. Six years had been a long lay-off. In 1947 it may be that I reaped the benefit.

Not that I began particularly well in the May of that year. I didn't. Though I beat Tom Hayward's record of 3,518 runs in a season, I didn't, as one might reasonably have expected in such circumstances, get my 1,000 runs in May. In fact, I never got them in any season, though once I did get quite near. In the May of 1947 I got only 353 runs.

Then, of course, things started to go very much my way. The South Africans were here that year, and I got six centuries in my various games against them. Everything seemed to be right for me, even the weather, which was so hot that many of the South Africans, over here for the first time, complained of the heat. I loved it. I feel a different person, and find cricket almost a different and certainly a more pleasurable game, when the sun is shining down hotly and the perspiration begins to run down the back of my neck. That's when I really want to play cricket. The sun agrees with me. I tan deeply, going almost black; blacker, oddly enough, in a fine summer such as 1947 in this country than I ever did under the fiercer suns of India or Australia, South Africa or the West Indies.

Naturally I was pleased with my form in 1947 and I enjoyed myself making runs in the sunshine. I always wanted to enjoy the game, and usually I did—if I didn't enjoy a game I couldn't go on playing it. In that season I suppose I enjoyed myself rather more than I ever did before or since. I reached a pinnacle in my career which later I was to find a little uncomfortable, and from which no one seemed to think that it was proper or possible that I should ever descend, however slightly.

I was all the more pleased because Bill Edrich shared my success. We had appeared on the Middlesex scene together at about the same time; in fact, I played one year for Middlesex before Bill did, as at that time he was in the process of qualifying for Middlesex, being a Norfolk man. After that, for the rest of my days in cricket, Bill and I played constantly together for Middlesex and for England, and we have always been the firmest of friends.

Bill is a great fighter with a serene temperament. I have never known anything to overawe him or anything deprive him of the will or the courage to fight back, not even the hostile accuracy of Lindwall bouncers bowled over after over. He is a great batsman, very strong on the on-side and much more than a competent bowler.

He started well in cricket, and in May 1938 he got his 1,000 runs before the month was over. Then, quite suddenly, things did not seem to go well for him. Against Australia in 1938 he had a most unhappy series. O'Reilly regularly got him out and his highest score was 20. In South Africa in the following winter things were little better until the last innings of the Fifth Test at Durban when he scored 219—but that was the game that was never finished because the English players had to catch the boat home before it could be brought to an end. Anyway, Bill was not selected to play against the West Indians in 1939, and only once against the Indians in 1946.

But in 1946–7 in Australia he came into the Test form of which I for one had always felt he was capable, and I remember in particular the magnificent century he scored in Sydney. Now, in the summer of 1947, he reached his full potential, getting twelve centuries and breaking Tom Hayward's record with an aggregate of 3,539 runs in the season. The newspapers called us "The Middlesex Twins", and there was a certain aptness in the title. A lot of twins do the same things at the same time in the same way, and that was what Bill and I were doing. For each of us it was the most successful season of our careers. A lot of our runs were made at the wicket together, and I think each encouraged and stimulated the other. That was so both in county games and in Test Matches. In the Second and Third Tests we both got hundreds and we got a lot of our runs when we were at the wicket together. The only thing that didn't seem to go well with us was our running between the wickets, which became famous for its unpredictability and landed us in complicated tangles more than once. Perhaps the fault was mainly mine. No doubt it must have been if the after-dinner story sometimes told about my calling a run is correct. My first call, it has been said, is an invitation to treat; my second, a basis for negotiations; the third is too late anyway, for by then the other chap has been run out.

I made all those runs with the same bat, and others to whom I lent it during the season added to its total. It was a light bat, about

2 lb. 2 oz., with a short handle, both things which I like in a cricket bat. Also it had a narrow grain, which is not supposed to last well, though the drive in it is usually better. This one drove beautifully from the beginning and lasted the whole season: in fact, it is still in existence, in good condition with lots more runs in it, with Warsops, the firm who made it, and whose managing director, George Hunt, had himself recommended it to me at the opening of the 1947 season.

A cricket bat is a very important thing indeed. To have a bad bat, one that when you drive sends the ball gently to mid-on, is perhaps the quickest way to put a cricketer out of form. My bat that year, light, close-grained, short-handled, was so perfect that it almost lured me on to success.

In the last few weeks I made my seventeenth and eighteenth centuries of that season, with my seventeenth beating Jack Hobbs's record of sixteen in one season. Yet, almost ironically, it was at that time that my knee began to trouble me seriously again, and I played these two innings with it strapped tightly, so that to some extent my movements were restricted. I got the seventeenth at Hastings against the South Africans, and was bowled by Tufty Mann almost immediately afterwards. Tufty Mann is dead now; I remember him very kindly indeed; he was a magnificent cricketer and a magnificent person. The South Africans seemed almost as pleased as I was that I had beaten the record.

At the Oval, for Middlesex against The Rest, I got 210 runs, and it remains in my memory as one of the best innings I ever played. Right from the start I played my shots and everything I attempted succeeded, even the most wildly unorthodox strokes, including the four which I scored when falling forward. If I wanted a thing to happen it seemed to happen—just like that. It was the happiest and most exhilarating of sensations. I felt I could have batted with a stump.

Never in the years that followed was I able to play with quite such ease and zest again.

For the 1948 season Don Bradman brought over to this country perhaps the greatest of Australian sides which he captained. It was a side which had everything: great batsmen, bowlers, fielders, and a great captain. They beat us again in the series—again we didn't win

a single Test—and there was a good deal said and written that year
which was gloomy and lacking in hope. I feel that although the
Australians were a greater side than we were, we have never quite
had the fair assessment of our abilities which the England players of
that year deserved.

In the Fifth Test our batsmen failed, wretchedly, inexcusably, with
a first-innings score of 52; but in all the other Tests we made considerable totals: 441 in the second innings of the First Test, 215 and
189 in the Second and so on, and against an attack which never let
up for a moment. If you examine the figures, you will see that our
totals compare most favourably with the runs made in the 1954–5
season in Australia and in the 1956 season in this country when,
undoubtedly, we were right on top. And, perhaps most important
of all, these runs were made when the Miller-Lindwall attack was at
its greatest and most unrelenting, and was being used with consummate skill by Bradman. It was a major part of the greatest attack
Australia has ever had. If we had had a fast attack I think we could
easily have won that series.

Thinking about the Tests of that year, I have always had the
impression that we saw very little of the old ball. In England 1948
was an experimental year: it had been decided that in the Test
Matches the new ball, for the first time, should be taken after only
55 overs. I think, and have always thought, that the decision was
a stupid one—perhaps the fact that it was so quickly changed proves
my point.

Bradman, of course, made the most shrewd and intelligent use of
the new rule. When the shine was still on the ball he bowled
Lindwall and Miller, and that year he knew exactly how many overs
to bowl each of them and with exact precision how to place the
field for each individual batsman as he faced them. Then, when their
spell was over, on would come Toshack at one end and Bill Johnston
or Ian Johnson, usually in turn, at the other. Their function was to
close the game down until the new ball was due, and they closed it
down completely: right down. It was an unattractive but tactically
effective way of playing the game.

I never thought that Toshack was a great bowler, although he was
an efficient one, and was just what Bradman needed under the
circumstances. He could put Toshack on for long periods if need be,

and he would attack the leg stump with great consistency. With five men on the on-side it was very difficult indeed to get after him: in fact, we never really did get after him, and he most effectively shut up the game. Meanwhile, at the other end, Bill Johnston, a very great bowler on that tour, would be bowling left arm over the wicket, with great accuracy and quite a lot of pace, and an ability to move the ball both ways: or perhaps we'd have a spell from Ian Johnson with his off-spinners. In an unbelievably short time, the 55 overs would be up, and Don Bradman would look round, see Lindwall and Miller refreshed again and hand them the new ball with the shine on it.

As I have said, you had the impression of hardly ever seeing the old ball. You seemed constantly to be facing Miller and Lindwall with the new one. Undoubtedly the tactics were clever, and perfectly adapted to the circumstances: but they began what has since acquired the bad name of negative cricket. Negative cricket started in that season and has continued since, and seems a very difficult weed to uproot. It is somewhat ironical that Bradman, now the greatest advocate of brighter cricket, should have started it, for start it he did.

What I have just said emphasises the point I was making—that our batting that year was as effective almost as it has ever been. Indeed, to some extent the same is true of the 1946–7 tour in Australia. In 1948 none of our established batsmen failed consistently. Hutton, Washbrook, Edrich and myself, all at some time or another in the series produced good form. For myself I regard the season as one of my more successful ones because I headed the English Test averages with 62·44. If I'd never done any worse than that in my Test career I would have been most exceptionally pleased with myself, all the time.

Our batsmen that year have been criticised, for example by Jack Fingleton, for not being able to play the fast bowling. The mistake they made, it has been said, was that they played forward to the quickies when they should have played back. In my view, so far as four of the established batsmen were concerned, that simply isn't true. Hutton can and did play back against the quicks, so did Washbrook and so did I. Edrich admittedly did not, but then he has always played off the front foot to pace bowling, and for him to have tried to alter his style at that stage would have been lunacy.

It comes back to the same point again: what we really lacked then and continued for some time to lack was fast bowlers. We simply didn't have them: at that stage there seemed no likelihood that we would have them. The reason, of course, was the war and the cessation of first-class cricket in England. In a fast bowler's life six years is a long time—indeed it may be the whole of his effective career —and that means many a potential pace bowler never got his chance because of the war. Our trouble against Australia in 1948 was that we couldn't bowl them out for a reasonable total.

Jim Laker played in three Tests in that series, and his appearance in Test cricket did not give much indication of the greatness he was later to achieve. In the vital Fourth Test Match at Leeds, the wicket should have been an ideal one for him. It was a dry crumbler, and had worn considerably. On the fifth day Australia needed 404 runs to win, and even Bradman expressed the view that the Australians would be lucky to get 150 all out, and that, definitely, it would be a win for England. Admittedly we had a depleted attack, but we were confident that with a spinner of Jim's quality we could succeed.

In the result Australia got 404 runs for 3 wickets, and Jim Laker finished up with a bowling analysis of 0 for 93. At Manchester, eight years later, against the Australians, on a wet sticky, he got 19 wickets for 90 runs—which marks his development as a bowler. The dry crumbler at Leeds should in my view have been more helpful to his style of bowling than the wet sticky wicket later on at Manchester. Indeed during that series the Australians went after Laker a good deal, and his success against them was small. Even making allowances for a deterioration since then in Australian batting ability against the turning ball and the wickets of 1956 which favoured him exceptionally, it is obvious that Laker has developed most outstandingly as a bowler.

Everyone who writes about cricket writes about Sir Donald Bradman at some stage or another. I have not been and will not be an exception. Cricket and Bradman are entities which don't separate easily. I think this clearly underlines the fact that Bradman was one of the greatest cricketers—perhaps the greatest who ever played the game. He was, as it were, the most merciless of entertainers of a crowd. When I was little more than a schoolboy in the early 'thirties and he was scoring his centuries with relentless brilliance, then I hero-worshipped him and, in the years since, my admiration for him as a cricketer has hardly diminished, although it has become more informed. I want to emphasise this and wish it to be borne in mind in relation to the other things which I feel I ought to say because I experienced them.

The 1948 tour was Bradman's last, and it was his good-bye to international cricket. I think in that series we saw him at his greatest and most astute as a captain. By then his experience had extended over such a long period that he seemed to know almost all that was to be known about each individual player, and he used his knowledge with powerful effect in directing the attack and setting the field. Batting against a side captained by him always gave you the feeling that you had been carefully examined, studied and thought about, and that the attack was organised accordingly. This was never more apparent than in 1948.

He knew the game from beginning to end and had reflected on his knowledge and experience. One of the most admirable things about him, I considered, was the way in which he seemed to be able to spread his cricketing skill through his team, and so give a lift to their competence and their confidence. By 1948 I think he had mellowed a great deal in many directions. Certainly with one or two exceptions he got on very well indeed with the members of his team.

Sidney Barnes was one of the exceptions, and that may not be surprising when one remembers how strongly individualistic Sidney Barnes could be. I was not greatly attracted to him—for one thing, it always seemed to me that Barnes was always too much concerned about how Sidney Barnes was getting along, and too little about anyone else. He was, I thought, over-harsh in his judgment of the Australian players and our own, and he appeared to be a man with a chip on at least one shoulder.

He was a magnificent player, especially against the turning ball, and as a player of all types of bowling he was probably the best in the Australian side. His powerful build, especially his shoulders, enabled him to be a very forceful batsman. He played nearly everything off his back foot, and he had the most glorious square cut.

Unquestionably he was an excellent and intrepid fielder—a little too intrepid on that tour as things turned out. He fielded in a spectacular and indeed an effective position, very close to the batsman on the leg side, not more than three yards away. It was a fine piece of showmanship, apart from anything else, but I thought it unfair to the batsman because as he faced the bowler he couldn't help being conscious of Barnes almost at his elbow. You saw him out of the corner of your eye, and it hindered concentration. As you watched the bowler, Barnes came most unhelpfully into your vision as well.

He did it once too often. It was at Old Trafford and I was at the wicket with Dick Pollard, a burly Lancastrian with auburn hair who wasn't a batsman but threw the bat at everything, hopefully. He took strike, with Barnes three yards away, and I remember that Dick glanced at him with an expression that seemed to show surprise and wonderment that anyone should stand so close when he was at the wicket.

Ian Johnson was bowling and I was interested to see what might happen. After a few minutes he sent up a slow flighted delivery, and Dick Pollard drew on it tremendously with all his strength, connected for once, and hit the ball straight into Barnes's ribs, under his left arm. Barnes had had the sense to turn away as the ball struck, sensing perhaps that this was one which even he could not field.

It was a dramatic moment, though I am not sure that everyone had as much sympathy for Barnes as they might have had for somebody fielding a bit farther from the wicket. It was fortunate for him that he was struck on a fleshy part of his body and that he suffered no more than bruises. He left the field, and didn't do any more of his close-up-to-the-bat stuff.

He came out to bat, however, later on, and as he walked to the wicket you could see that his face had a look of considerable pain. However, he managed to get as far as the wicket, and to take strike, but then he collapsed on the ground, somewhat to my surprise in view of the fact that he'd got so far. Then he had to be taken off. Bradman very correctly came running out to the wicket to assist his stricken comrade from the field.

I remember one day at the Leeds luncheon table sitting beside

Barnes, who hadn't got many runs in the Tests. Perhaps understandably he seemed a bit unhappy about it, maybe even disgruntled. We had, I think, been talking about Bradman, and Barnes turned to me and said: "Mr. Bradman, he gets all the publicity, let him get all the bloody runs." There was an Australian astringency about the comment which was refreshing in a way, even if it was not entirely justifiable. Its content revealed as much about Barnes as it did about Bradman.

Bradman, to put it mildly, had some qualities which were difficult to like or admire. It is so, I think, with nearly all outstanding people. For example, one never had the impression that he forgave easily, and in one instance, at least, he hardly spoke to an opponent for twenty years after a comment, admittedly not a very kind one, but probably just, made on the field during the progress of a Test in Australia.

Basically Bradman's judgment was sound—certainly it was sound in relation to the day-to-day practice and tactics of the game; but outside that I often had a feeling that it could vary extraordinarily with how he found himself personally affected by the matter under consideration.

Take, for example, the question of body-line. There can be little doubt that Bradman has often expressed himself, not without characteristic force and point, on that much-debated question, and I am certain that he considered it a very bad thing indeed. And I agree with him. Yet I remember one occasion when something very like body-line caused him no sign of distress whatever.

It was at Nottingham in 1948 and I was at the wicket with Len Hutton. For about thirty-five minutes before half past six, Keith Miller bowled bouncers at the rate of four an over. It was in its way a wonderful piece of bowling, by someone who was very fit indeed. Keith would follow right through with a run round to cover-point, pick the ball up almost without stopping, turn and run back and come up again, with his effective, unorganised run, and deliver, probably another bouncer. It was very uncomfortable. On his day Keith could bowl a very hostile bouncer indeed.

Hutton was hit on a number of occasions, but I managed, I remember, to get out of the way. Before very long I became very conscious of Bradman at cover-point, grinning his head off. It was bad enough trying to get my head out of the way of the flying ball, but it was very, very much worse to see Bradman apparently deriving so much pleasure from my antics.

When we were leaving the field at close of play I walked alongside him.

"Well, Don," I said, probably with more than a touch of sarcasm in my voice, "I saw you enjoying yourself just now. I can't really understand why and how you were. . . . I thought you used to say that this wasn't the right way to play cricket—bouncers and all that. . . ."

He wasn't smiling any more. From his answer I had the impression that he was a little uncomfortable but, being Bradman, was very definitely not going to show it. "You've got a bat in your hand, haven't you?" he answered. "You should be able to get out of the way of them anyway. . . . I used to love it when I played against bouncers. I used to hook them. . . ."

I don't remember any more of the conversation. Equally, I can't remember Bradman, the target of bouncers in the 'thirties, ever before having expressed such tolerant and amiable views on the matter.

Another incident of the same kind occurred, also at Nottingham. Bradman, as I have said, showed himself an unparalleled expert at closing the game down. That year he became the herald of negative cricket. Norman Yardley decided, when Bradman had scored about 100 runs, that he would give him some of his own medicine. He put himself on to bowl, with five men on the on-side, and pegged away with great accuracy on the leg stump. Bradman, of course, found that even he couldn't score runs; Bradman, in fact, had himself been closed down.

It was very obvious that he didn't like it one little bit, and he made it almost equally obvious that he didn't think that it was the way to play cricket. For Bradman's side to bowl bouncers or to perpetrate negative cricket was, it almost seemed, perfectly all right; for anyone else to do so was a serious cricketing offence. I don't for one moment suppose that he really intended it that way, but in fact that was the way it appeared to me quite often to work out.

I think that Bradman's greatest and most important quality was his deliberate confidence. He seemed to know, or to believe, before he went in to bat, that he was going to make runs, and make them he usually did. And I believe that he probably predicted that he would make runs, almost an unheard-of thing for a cricketer to do. He was a most remarkable person. He had great ability and he organised it, as an outstanding general might train his troops. And in the end he seemed to be able to transmit this ability and the power to organise through his own side. Nearly everyone who played under him, especially towards the end of his career, found his ability and knowledge enhanced by the experience.

Bradman went for the essentials, and discarded the unessential. It used to be said of him that he couldn't cope on bad wickets, and to some extent that no doubt was true—but the reason was this: Bradman had decided that the great majority of the wickets on which he would play would be good wickets and he developed his style accordingly. To what he would meet most often he would give the maximum concentration; the rest he would disregard. I've no doubt that if he had wanted to, and had got down to it, he could have played just as well on bad wickets. The decision he in fact took was very typical of the man.

He was a great man and, in his way, a great entertainer. He had unyielding concentration, the kind which regards the first century merely as a cogent reason for getting down to scoring the second one. He was not considered to be orthodox in his stroke play, but he did regard the object of a batsman to be the making of runs as quickly as possible. And he made them quickly, entertainingly, in large quantities in many places, over a span of twenty years.

Bradman was a killer at the wicket. He never liked to be beaten; neither did W. G. Grace.

In May of 1948, Bill Edrich and I almost made a record. It was in the game against Somerset at Lord's when we found ourselves at the wicket together, for a third-wicket stand. By the time it was over we had made 424 runs, which was more than any other pair had made for that wicket in first-class cricket, except for a stand of 445 between W. N. Carson and P. E. Whitelaw in New Zealand in 1937. It was, if you like, a leaf out of our 1947 book.

We made 209 runs in seventy minutes after tea, and that against an attack which included Wellard and Tremlett, both England

players, and Hazell. I got 139 of them, scoring 3 sixes and 37 fours
—so *Wisden* now tells me. I suppose Bill encouraged me with his flow
of strokes, and I encouraged him. It was mutual infection. Then, too,
the Middlesex policy in a situation like that was to get all the runs
you could by half past five or a quarter to six, and then to put the
other side in and, because they were tired after a long day in the field,
hope to get a wicket or two before half past six. That afternoon we
carried out our orders.

I remember the general picture of that innings very well indeed.
Again, it was one of those afternoons out in the middle when I
seemed only to have to will a thing for it to happen. Often I've been
called unorthodox, and I suppose I was as unorthodox on that
occasion as I ever was. Yet I intended the strokes I played and played
them because I intended them. I found I had some kind of exhilarating psychological lift, which enabled me to conceive and execute
strokes in exactly the way I wanted, whether I stayed on my crease
or pranced off half-way down the wicket. Bill and I were on top of
the bowlers and we knew it, and they knew it and didn't seem to be
able to do much about it.

It confirmed what very early on I had seen about the game—
that as much of it is played out in your mind as on the pitch. The
mental approach, discipline, serenity, confidence, are all of the first
importance.

That afternoon with Bill, scoring runs seemed a natural and
nejoyable pastime.

For me it wasn't to remain so for very much longer.

CHAPTER IV

A BENEFIT AT WHIT

GEORGE MANN took the M.C.C. side to South Africa for the tour of 1948–9. The side did not include Bill Edrich, and I thought then it was a mistake to have omitted him. A great deal, I suppose, could be said about the decision. I'd like to say now that I still think it was quite wrong. He was a great cricketer in good form then—he'd had a wonderful summer against the Australians—and he should have been included.

When George Mann was named as captain there was no doubt a good deal of criticism. People asked: "Is he a sufficiently gifted or capable cricketer to be able to make a proper contribution to the side's cricketing ability?" It could at that stage have been said with some justification that Mann wasn't a bowler, that he was an enthusiastic fielder but not much more, and a reasonable kind of bat. It is doubtful whether Mann, if asked if that were true, would have minded or disagreed. He wasn't the sort of person to mind, or to exaggerate his ability.

As it turned out I think he was the most effective captain that I have ever played under.

He had those human gifts which add up to the capacity for leadership which, in a captain, is more important than the capacity to play cricket. From the start, you could almost see that he was a man determined to do well by the side, not to let it down in any way or circumstance. He worked very hard indeed throughout the whole tour, and in the end succeeded, I thought, in getting the best out of almost all the players. He had a great deal of charm, and yet in the last analysis he was a very decisive person indeed; he was very good to the players, but he was also very firm with them, as one or two instances showed. By and large the side was both happy and successful. It was to my mind the happiest side with which I ever toured.

He consulted the players before making an important or difficult decision, and yet he made the decision himself. There was never any question of his saying, or implying even, that a thing was right because he said it was right. He discussed things, thought about them, took advice, and then formed his own view. This was the case even on the field where, after he'd taken Hutton's view, or Washbrook's, or mine, before deciding on a move, he then went on to make up his own mind. It in no way decreased his efficiency.

What may not sound very important from a strictly cricketing point of view can become very important indeed on tour when fifteen or sixteen men are to be in each other's company in strenuous and public circumstances, away from home, for a period of five months. For example, the question of invitations and public functions, inevitable concomitant of any tour: badly handled, they can produce ill-feeling, a sense in some people of being rather left out, a sense even that the captain is taking all the good things for himself and leaving the less pleasant for the others. It may sound a bit stupid, even a little silly or petty, but in fact things like that can make a lot of difference to the morale of a side on tour.

George Mann handled them perfectly. Public and private functions —and I wouldn't be honest if I said otherwise—can be very boring indeed. If Mann thought that some function might be a little less than entertaining, that would be the one which he would make quite certain to attend himself and, oddly enough, attending it with him, he seemed to make it much more enjoyable than you could ever have anticipated. On the other hand, with some of the private invitations, well known to be more than usually attractive and entertaining, if there were any limitation on the numbers to go, Mann as often as not would leave himself out and ensure that someone else went in his place.

As I say, it does not perhaps sound very important, but there is no doubt that Mann's attitude on this question helped quite considerably to make the side into a happy family.

Furthermore, he seemed to have the gift of communicating his own enthusiasm to the rest of the side. This was especially so in fielding. The South Africans, now the greatest fielding side in the world, knew quite a bit about it even then; and on that tour I think the South Africans would have said that in the field we were the best side they'd ever seen. Largely it was due to our captain: he had the way of making the right comment in the right place, which was very helpful indeed to the players.

The happiness of a team on tour, of course, depends to a large extent on the sort of people who compose the team; not on whether they are good or great cricketers, but on whether they are good tourists. Bill Edrich, I always thought, was almost the ideal tourist, because of his great love of the game and his real fondness for those with whom he played. He was loyal to the game, and he was loyal to the cricketers; seldom if ever did you hear Bill say anything detrimental about another cricketer.

The bad side-upsetting tour-spoiling tourist is the self-centred tourist, the chap who wants to get as much as he can for himself out of the trip and out of the game, without regard for anyone else. He lacks the team spirit, and holds himself apart and aloof from the other players; he is mean and seeks all the advantages he can find for himself, never trying to secure his luck, if he has any, for his fellow-players too. Sometimes he doesn't even buy drinks back, and on tour there is a lot of hospitality to be returned. He is often moody and jealous of other players' success, and he bats or bowls for himself and not for the team—for example, if he is a batsman and there is a bowler off whom he finds it easy to score, he will ensure as much as possible, whatever the chap at the other end may think, that he gets and scores off that particular bowler's bowling; if he is out of form or lacking in success he gets infuriated and puts the blame on other members of the team and takes it out of them accordingly.

A bad tourist can be most upsetting to a side, and he creates a very unpleasant atmosphere all about him. Fortunately, there are not very many of them.

We had a successful tour, winning the series very comfortably, with a most successful captain who, despite the doubts expressed about his ability, got 136 not out in the last Test at Port Elizabeth, and finished up with an average for the series of 36·28. Anything over 35 I regard as a very reasonable average indeed.

George Mann, I thought, had the essence of good captaincy in him—the very human gifts of being able to communicate enthusiasm and to lead.

It was my first tour of South Africa. Before the war, in the winter of 1938–9 when the last M.C.C. team had gone there, I had in fact been asked to go, but had felt that I must refuse in order to spend the winter playing football for Arsenal, who, after all, had invested a great deal of time and quite a lot of money in developing my capacities as a footballer. So I hadn't gone. It is perhaps an interesting reflection that it was in that football season that my knee trouble began. I have often wondered whether if I'd just stuck to cricket it would ever have troubled me at all.

I liked South Africa during my first visit and have liked it ever since. Of all the countries that I have played cricket against I have always liked South Africa, and the South Africans, best, Perhaps it's something in my temperament or in theirs, but that is the way it worked out from the beginning. Of course, my wife is South African.

At that time I was still finding cricket an exhilarating and relatively easy game to play. I made eight centuries on the tour and headed the averages in all first-class matches with a figure of 84·8. It could have been said quite accurately that I was happy in my cricket. The South African sun agreed with me and I seemed to be able to score runs without difficulty.

Against North-eastern Transvaal at Benoni I scored 300 runs out of 399 in 181 minutes, making at that stage my fourth century in five innings. It was in fact the fastest treble century in history. I made the first hundred in sixty-six minutes; the second took me a little longer—seventy-eight minutes; and the third took thirty-seven. Obviously, it was an innings which I will not easily forget.

I mention it partly because it illustrates a number of cricketing points. I again had the feeling that I could do almost anything I wanted with the bat—I had that uncaring sense of confidence which seemed to help my batting to such a marked extent. I remember that particularly because when I made my first century I decided, because the game was not of the first importance, that now perhaps it was time I got out, so I started experimenting with shots, rather as I used to do at the nets, but these shots seemed to succeed better than the others. Among them I did play strokes which were both extraordinary and incredible.

Before I quite realised it I saw that I was nearing my second century, and decided that perhaps I should stay until I had reached it. So I quietened down a little, until I passed the 200 mark. Then

I started to hit everything again, but still with the same unavoidable success, in the middle of the bat each time, and in thirty-seven minutes I had added another hundred runs. Shortly afterwards I was out. I had enjoyed myself and so, I think, had most others who were there.

An innings like that acts as a kind of tonic for one's cricket and seems to spread a benign effect of heightened self-confidence over succeeding games. It has been suggested to me that perhaps so large a score might give rise to over-confidence, but I have never been aware of that danger. After you have played cricket for any length of time, you become very deeply conscious of its subtleties and intricacies and difficulties, to such an extent as to make it unlikely, for most people at least, that you should ever forget them. It doesn't matter how long you play, you can never be sure you're going to make runs. I certainly, for a while, found it easier to be confident after the Benoni innings than before, but I would not say more than that. One bad innings might destroy confidence overnight.

A big innings I have found to be a good proving ground for strokes. Then you can try shots which ordinarily you would not dare to attempt, at least not until they had been laboriously tried out at the nets and, if not perfected, at least shaped and disciplined to a fair resemblance of reliability. But in the high-scoring innings you can experiment to advantage, and come away afterwards with a new stroke or perhaps several new strokes added to your repertoire.

As I have said, we won that series in South Africa. Our opponents were not then the formidable side which in later years they were to become. One could see signs of development then, but the game seemed to arouse very little interest in the country. Before very long the whole cricketing situation there was to change very radically.

I came back to England for the 1949 cricket season to the most boring Test series that I have ever played in. All the matches against the New Zealand team were drawn; it was stalemate in three acts. I'm afraid I had the very strong impression that the policy of the New Zealand side over here (whether actually decided upon previously or only happening, as it were, as the situation developed) was not to lose at all costs. It didn't matter to them so much, so it seemed to me, whether they won or whether they didn't; but whatever happened they were not going to be defeated. I hadn't often been bored by cricket, but playing in those New Zealand Tests in the summer of 1949 really did bore me.

The situation of cricket in this country and the weather and the wickets, combined to provide the ideal conditions for stalemate. We still hadn't found any bowlers who could really bowl people out in Test Matches. The problem which had appeared so nakedly immediately after the war, on the 1946-7 tour of Australia, was still obdurately unsolved, and no solution appeared likely. What we needed was someone who could sometimes be devastating and achieve a break-through. What we had in fact were accurate bowlers who seemed to have little power of penetration on good wickets. I remember thinking as I fielded on those good wickets that year, that if we just kept on bowling, by virtue of the law of averages or lapse in concen-tration by the batsmen, we would eventually get someone out. In the result, on the beautiful wickets on which all three Tests were played, in good weather, we had tedious last days when the New Zealanders settled down to bat for a draw, and we hadn't got the bowlers to bowl them out. Our batting nevertheless had been quite entertaining. I can't say that the New Zealanders' was, although it was good enough to enable them to stay in against our bowling. It was not my idea of cricket, or of enjoyment. I am glad we don't have many tours like that one.

Perhaps the most extraordinary thing about the season was that I headed the Test bowling averages. My figures were 5 wickets for 25·2 runs per wicket in 33 overs. I have often told my friends to look at that section of the 1949 *Wisden* long and carefully, because it's something they will not see before nor since. For me, I had even proved economical as a bowler. The main inference to be drawn is one which flatters neither our bowling nor the New Zealand batting. In each Test Match, Denis Compton got at least one wicket.

My bowling has so often been the target of humorous comment, and quite rightly, but I must try to say something in its favour by telling of two occasions when it was effective and another, for the most surprising reason, when it wasn't.

In the Test Match at Cape Town I got 5 wickets for 80, which surprised everyone, myself included. In 1947 after Middlesex had won the championship and the county and myself were riding a high wave, at the Oval against Surrey I got 6 wickets for 70 in the first innings and 6, again, for 80, in the second. It would be spectacular if I could do that against today's Surrey side.

My best bowling spell yielded less than half the results it deserved, perhaps because of the surprise created by four successive opportunities of wickets coming off my bowling to the best batsmen in the world. It was at Leeds in 1948 against the Australians, on the last day, with the Australians needing 400 to win. Norman Yardley decided on desperate measures, and he put Len Hutton on to bowl; when Len had had 30 taken off him in 3 overs Norman threw the ball to me. It was a crisis decision and produced the incredible.

I started from the pavilion end, and in my second over I had Lindsay Hassett caught and bowled. Next, Arthur Morris, in tremendous form, came right up the wicket to the pitch of one I bowled him, was beaten by the spin and was left stranded about four yards up the wicket. In agony, his as well as mine, I saw Godfrey behind the stumps juggling, juggling, juggling, unable to get hold of the thing, trying desperately hard; Arthur Morris, at first starting his walk towards the pavilion, saw what was happening and ran backwards and just got back into his crease.

After that I was taken off and put on at the other end. Bradman had come in in place of Lindsay and was now facing me, and I remember thinking the probability was that I was going to get murdered. But I was wrong—for some reason Bradman couldn't tell my googly and my Chinaman apart, and I soon had him in an intricate tangle. Then he edged one gently into slips, and Jack Crapp at first slip dropped it; in the next over Bradman edged another just as gently, and poor Jack dropped it again. After that the gods favoured me no longer.

If those catches had been held I think we should have won that Test, for with Bradman and Morris back in the hutch we could somehow have got the rest of the wickets for less than 400. It was one of those things—several times over.

The New Zealand series was Alec Bedser's fifth Test series, and although he had bowled competently in most of them—and particularly effectively against India in 1946—yet at that stage he was never really giving the impression that he was anything other than a very good stock bowler. His guts and stamina were quite remark-able, but up to that time his results were not. I think the know-ledge that he would inevitably have to bowl for such long spells probably had a bad effect on him, as it made it necessary for him to conserve his energy in order to get through those long spells of bowling. Consequently there was no hostility in what he did bowl. Against the New Zealanders he obtained only seven wickets in two matches. I wonder how many people thought then that Alec would develop into the devastating seamer he later became, the world's greatest medium-pace bowler in fact?

The high point of the 1949 season was the first appearance of Trevor Bailey in Test cricket. His entrance from the wings could not have been better staged by the most perceptive dramatist. It was an important moment for the nine years to come, and I hope for much longer than that.

It was in the Second Test against New Zealand at Lord's in the first innings. I was at the wicket; five batsmen were out and there weren't very many runs on the board: only 112 in fact. England were a bit in the cart and there was a crisis. Then a new figure started the walk out from the pavilion to the middle; he was very young, lithe, absolutely serene, looking rather as if he were walking out to play an innings for Cambridge, where until then, with the addition of a few games for Essex, he had played all his first-class cricket. In a way he looked only a boy. It was, of course, Trevor Bailey coming in to bat in the kind of situation which was to become classical for him.

I watched him from the other end as he took guard and began his innings and then continued, firmly and stolidly. His expression showed none of the signs of a batsman playing on his first big occasion: on the contrary, he gave me the impression of someone who had been playing Test cricket for years. He was quite unruffled, absolutely concentrated, absolutely determined, plainly a most diffi-cult man to dislodge; not a person with a great range of stroke play perhaps, but in his mastery of defensive technique obviously some-one who was going to play an important part in English cricket and for England for years to come. He seemed in his calmness to be quite unaware that there was a crisis. Watching him, I was both very pleased and very impressed.

We stayed at the wicket together until we had put on 189 runs, and then I was out. When the England side were all out Trevor Bailey was still there, 93 not out, and the situation had been saved. In more senses than one Bailey had come to stay. It hadn't occurred to me as I watched this new player that one day not far away in the future, at Trinidad during the Colony match, Trevor would come down the wicket to me at the end of an over and say, with a humorous look in his eyes: "Denis, I don't want you to get out. Will you stay there while I make the strokes?" This was no less amusing for the fact that the situation was not really a Bailey situation, but one where quick runs were needed in a short time.

Against the New Zealanders Bailey took more wickets that year than anyone else; his figures were 16 wickets for 599. He bowled more overs, a total of 158, than any other seamer, and if it hadn't been for those beautiful batting wickets, I have no doubt that his figures would have been a great deal better. Even so, you could see his potential. He hadn't any experience then against Test batsmen, and comparatively little against county players, but all the time as he bowled you could see that he was thinking very hard indeed about the weaknesses of the particular batsman facing him and about the type of ball likely to be most effective against him. Later, as he got more experienced, the results were to show. It was the beginning of the career of a great all-rounder.

At Whitsuntide against Sussex I had my Benefit Match, before a total three-day attendance of 55,000, at Lord's. Saturday was disappointing; it rained and we couldn't get started until nearly four o'clock, and I was more than a little depressed, first as I watched the rain coming down over the ground and falling on the green grass out in the middle, and then by the late start of play. It looked as if for once my luck was right out.

But Whit Monday changed all that. It was a bright sunny day, with a cloudless blue sky over Lord's, and the ground full of gay holiday crowds—a crowd that you felt you couldn't disappoint. The gates were closed after 35,000 people had been admitted, 7,000 more than should have been allowed in. I felt I must give them what they'd very likely come to see.

I felt more taut and nervous than usual as I walked out to the wicket in the bright sunshine, with the great crowd giving me very generous applause. Usually a beneficiary gets one off the mark; but the usual thing didn't happen that day—and I make no complaint about it; plainly Hugh Bartlett, in assessing the situation, had said to himself: "This is the best chance we have of getting this chap out—and we badly want him out." The fielders crowded round me and got after me right from the start. For sixteen minutes I remained on nought, and I remember feeling that the silent crowd were very much on my side. Then I got a single, and applause; the tenseness loosened out of me, and I was started.

I got 182 runs before I finished, and I played the kind of innings which gave me satisfaction. After I got my hundred I cut loose a bit, and I think the Whit Monday crowd felt that they got their money's worth. I was all the more pleased because my elder brother Leslie was with me at the wicket for a while, and in the end he collected a very enterprising 59 not out. Perhaps the person most pleased of all was my father, then aged sixty-nine, who watched the game from the members' stand.

I was exceptionally fortunate because in the end my benefit amounted to £12,000, until then the largest benefit except for Cyril Washbrook's. A substantial sum was retained by the county and invested for me, following the principle laid down in the old days when professionals tended to squander their benefits in a very short time if the county did not step in and save them from themselves. My money was invested in Gilts, a good investment then, but not the best place to have your money the way things have turned out.

In the winter football season of 1949-50 I played my last game for Arsenal and achieved what had always been my ambition, and the ambition, I suppose, of everyone who plays the game at all seriously. It was a good way to end my career in football. It was the fulfilment of a dream of a certain smallish boy who had turned up for the first time outside the Highbury Ground, a new member of the ground staff, in the autumn of 1933.

Up to Christmas I had not been playing well; I was in the reserve side and had not been very impressive. Neither for that matter were the Arsenal first team impressive. They were going through rather a lean period; but they were good enough to get through the third and fourth rounds of the F.A. Cup, even if they were not playing very convincing football.

By then it was after Christmas. One day Tom Whittaker came over to me and said: "Denis, next Wednesday I am going to watch you playing with the reserves; if you impress me, I am going to put you into the Cup side, starting with the fifth round game against Burnley."

I said I'd do my best—Tom Whittaker was very much the sort of person for whom you would want to do your best, although I wasn't all that confident about my prospects.

However, the next Wednesday I had my first really good game of that season, the reserves winning easily, and the day afterwards Tom Whittaker called me into his office, and I knew I was in the Cup side. The following Saturday we played against Burnley, and luck seemed to stay with me, for playing on the left wing I scored the first goal after fifteen minutes, and we went on to win 2–nil. It was easily my best game of the season, and from then on I remained in the Cup side, right up to the Cup Final at Wembley.

It's very much easier on the nerves, even at a Cup Final, to run out on to the green turf of Wembley with ten others than to start the long solitary walk from say the pavilion at Lord's out to the middle. At least that was how I found it. By then I was very used to large crowds—in fact, I liked to have a large crowd watching because it seemed to provide me with an incentive to play well—but I'd never quite been able to overcome the tautness and nervousness of the walk to the wicket. Sir Jack Hobbs always said that the players who suffered from nerves were the best ones. I think all the best players did have them, even Bradman, though he pretended he didn't. I certainly used to have some very peculiar feelings on that lonely walk.

Of course, on that Cup Final day I was more nervous than I usually was before a big game of football. A lot was to be in the balance out there in the next hour and a half or so, and we were to be introduced to Her Majesty and the Duke of Edinburgh; but nevertheless I had the feeling of being one of eleven, of being all in it together, and the knowledge too that in a football game you can make mistakes and have time and opportunity to retrieve them, seemed to make it easier. In cricket, if you're batting, it's not very often that you can put a mistake right. I soon found myself with the others, after the gracious introduction and the ceremonies were over, kicking the ball from one to another down our end of the field, just as in any other game of football that we played.

I didn't have a good first half, and I came back to the dressing-room at half-time exhausted and rather gloomy about the way I had been playing. Tom Whittaker came over to me, looked at me smilingly for a few minutes, and then spoke.

"Denis," he said, "soon you're going to give up football—you've got just about another forty-five minutes left of your soccer career. . . . Now. . . ." He spoke a little more slowly as he continued. "Now . . . I want you to go out there and give it every ounce you possibly can."

"All right, Tom," I said, but not very confidently.

I felt I needed something to assist me, so I did something which I had never done before. The trainer, seeing I was tired, recommended me to take a glass of whisky. It was just what I thought I needed, and I drank it down when it was brought to me, without delay, and seemed to have additional energy as I went out on to the field, and it lasted me for the rest of the game.

I had a good second half. The full-back, who'd had the measure of me in the first half, now seemed to have his measure taken by me. I found out his weaknesses and I played a vastly better game. And when it was all over and we'd won, with the rest of the team I received my Cup winners' medal at the hands of Her Majesty. The small boy had had his dream fulfilled.

Tom Whittaker was pleased with me, and I was pleased to have pleased him. When I first turned up in Highbury that autumn long before, Herbert Chapman had been manager and Tom Whittaker the trainer of a side full of stars like James, Jack, Buchan, Drake and Bastin. Chapman was one of the greatest managers, and Whittaker one of the greatest trainers of all time. When I joined Arsenal, Tom Whittaker was there, and when I left he was still there, by then one of the greatest institutions of the game, then no longer trainer but manager.

Tom had a marvellous temperament. He was patient, tolerant and understanding, and I never saw him lose his temper, although there were often occasions when he would have been justified in doing so.

He took infinite trouble with everyone whom he considered to be his responsibility, whether famous or unknown. In my early days at Highbury I often saw him there till eight, nine or ten o'clock at night, personally working to get players or one of the players fit for the following Saturday. He'd do the work himself, and wouldn't delegate it to anyone else. He had a kind of genius for it, I think.

At that time he would also find the opportunity to give his attention to some unknown boy like myself, playing then for Nunhead or Golders Green, and after six or seven hours, perhaps, with the stars, he'd come along and say: "Well, now, my boy, let me have a look at you," and then he'd get down to the business of keeping the unknown and the unimportant fit, or personally supervising and advising on their training.

I experienced his understanding and kindness in many ways. For example, though he was himself no great cricket fan—football and the Arsenal seemed to fill his life almost completely—he nevertheless always remembered that I had a career to make in cricket too, and he never tried to get me to do any more than he felt I was easily capable of undertaking. This was especially so when my knee had given way and he took special pains not to overplay me. Indeed, when my knee was being troublesome, he would himself come down from the manager's office at Highbury and supervise the treatment it was receiving from the trainer.

I shall always feel a particular sense of gratitude and admiration for Tom Whittaker. He was a great and kindly man.

During that last season's football I had played all the time with my right knee strapped. I blame no one but myself, but I think that I played too much and imposed on it a greater burden than it could be expected to bear. The cricket season of 1950 hadn't been long in progress before it gave way completely.

A difficult time in my life was about to begin.

CHAPTER V

THE FOREIGN BODY

IT WAS during the Middlesex game against Sussex in May that I finally realised that my knee wouldn't allow me to go on and that something drastic would have to be done about it. I had felt previously that something was wrong; that there was something loose in the knee which I couldn't find because it had an odd way of disappearing into the joint. Part of the time, through some understandable wishful thinking, I used to consider that it was all imagination. There had been some swelling before the game against Sussex, but I had treatment and it seemed to be all right again, so I had played.

I went in to bat in my usual position and had reached 40, going quite well, when I had the first warning. A little piece of bone was loose in my knee and it had got between the joint. I had a sudden sharp jerk of pain which pulled me up short for a moment. I managed to get to the other end, and I then leant over and felt my knee with my hand, and could feel the little piece of bone. I carried on until I was exactly 50, perhaps foolishly running between the wickets myself, and then was out. Within an hour after my return to the pavilion my knee had blown up like a balloon, and next day I could hardly walk at all. Apparently as a result of an arthritic process the cushion between the bones of my knee had gone, so that bone bore on bone, and little pieces eventually had chipped off.

I was out of the game for the first time in my life for two months until I returned again in the Middlesex match against Surrey at the end of July and the beginning of August. I was then in my thirty-third year.

I had met Bill Tucker, the surgeon, before then, though I hadn't yet been under his care. He was becoming quite an institution among sportsmen—not only with cricketers and footballers, but with Rugby players and jockeys too. He is a big, genial, capable man, who understands sportsmen, having himself played Rugby for

England. I was glad when he took me in hand, and have remained glad and grateful every since.

About a week after the Sussex game I went to the London Clinic, and Bill Tucker operated on my knee, removing another piece of bone from it, the foreign body which had been causing the trouble. I had had operations before and had recovered from them easily, and relatively quickly, but this time it was to be different. No doubt my knee was beginning its protests against the prolonged wear and tear it had undergone since that day when I had collided with the Charlton goalkeeper.

It took me a great deal longer than before to be able to move about without help, and even when I found myself able to do so, I quickly realised that for the first time in my life my movements were going to be restricted, and for quite a long period after the operation I had the gloomy feeling that I wouldn't play cricket again. Then, when I felt that I could, I went to the opposite extreme and tried to persuade myself and others that I was physically as good as I'd ever been, and would soon, after a necessary period of convalescence, be one hundred per cent again. In some remote corner of myself I knew that this wasn't true, but it was a fact that for a time I either could not or would not face.

It was the first time that I had had to confront the fact of physical disability, permanent physical disability, and the process I found distressing and sometimes agonising even. Until then I had been very fit and very strong and to a large extent my whole way of life had been built on those factors. Now there was a possibility, a certainty even, that to a greater or lesser degree my physical effectiveness would be cut down.

I didn't react well at the beginning. Sometimes it got me down and I felt wretched and depressed; at others I would feel resentful or infuriated. People constantly asked me how I was and invariably I would reply that I was fine, as good as ever. After a while I didn't believe my own answers, and I don't think those who got them did either. At the same time I was trying to do things which I had been able to do before and now was finding that I couldn't do them.

Reluctantly I began to see that I would have to accept myself as a person with only about seventy per cent left of my old bodily strength and mobility, and to get down to the hard business of organising to the maximum what I had left. I don't know at what precise stage it happened—I think all told it took about a year—but a moment did come when I was able to say to myself that I would be content to make the most of what I'd got and get down to the problem of readjustment. It was a slow process; but once I had made that decision everything was all right again, and I began to feel more at ease with myself and with the world.

Once I thought I was on the road to recovery I began to try my knee out in one-day games for the M.C.C. against teams such as Brighton College. I found, gradually, that with some difficulty and awkwardness I was able to play again, and decided as soon as I felt I could and Bill Tucker would let me, to play in a county game.

I came back against Surrey at the Oval at the end of July, and as if the gods wanted to encourage me, I made 115 not out. It may have looked quite a good innings and, no doubt, in a way it was, and I did in fact get most of my touch back as the innings developed. But, in reality, it was a laboured performance and I was struggling a good deal in my movements.

Still it was good to be back playing again.

The West Indies side toured England during the summer of 1950. They won the Test series, and although of course I was always keen to see England win, yet in a way I was glad that victory went to the tourists, because they were such a fine side and played such attractive cricket. Also it was good for international cricket that another country should be reaching the heights of form and ability.

In that season, I think, post-war English cricket touched rock-bottom. The tide had gone far, far out for us. Up to that time our batting, at least, had been fairly reliable and in all the previous Tests since 1945 had given a good account of itself; but now even our batting became deplorably inconsistent and we seemed to have nothing left: our bowling still hadn't improved and our batting was failing.

The selectors, of course, had been making every effort to discover and bring on new talent, but that season they failed completely, or almost completely, to judge by the performances of young players who were given their chance. Parkhouse, Dewes, Insole and Sheppard were all tried in the Tests, and none of them, on their form, gave any certain promise.

I played with Sheppard in the last Test at the Oval, and although his scores in the two innings were 11 and 29 only, I was considerably impressed with the way he made his 29 runs. They took him a long time to collect, in a difficult situation, but at least, if he didn't show very much else, he showed that he had fight. By the time the game, and the Test series, were over the best the selectors were able to say was that at least they'd found one new player who showed definite promise as a Test cricketer. In the circumstances, it wasn't very much to be able to say.

The others had failed, in that series at least. I had the impression that they were all too much affected by the importance of the occasion to be able to produce their best form.

The series might aptly be called the Calypso Series. There was a brilliance and dash about the West Indian game, and colour too, both from them and from their supporters, which could justify the title. And then, of course, there was the song about Ramadhin and Valentine.

Without any doubt it was Sonny Ramadhin's tour. The little man burst on to the cricketing scene with almost magical delusion in his right wrist and fingers.

I saw him first on television—the first time I had watched a game on the screen—on a small set which had been brought in to help me pass the long hours at the London Clinic. I remember that Bill Edrich came in to see me in the afternoon, just before he left for Manchester and the First Test. He told me before he went that he considered that the dangerous player to the English batsmen in this West Indian side was Ramadhin. I hadn't played against him, or even seen him at that stage, and didn't really know much about him; but Bill plainly considered that something new and important in the way of bowling ability was about to make itself known.

The next afternoon I switched on the set and went from the racing at Ascot to the cricket at Manchester, both events in which I was taking a considerable interest. That afternoon, and all the time I was in hospital, I found television a great help, particularly in coping with the sort of restlessness which comes down on me when I have to stay in bed, no doubt because I've been used to so active a life. Apart from that, I think television is a great help to the game in that it gives millions an opportunity of a close view of the pitch and the play and, with the help of a good commentator, the chance to appreciate the finer points of a first-class game.

I couldn't, of course, on that telecast of the Test get a sufficiently close view to enable me to read Ramadhin, or even to decide whether I could read him or not, but it was nevertheless quite obvious that here was a new and difficult phenomenon. It made me all the more anxious to get back into the game again.

I watched him from the pavilion at Lord's in the Second Test, at Nottingham in the Third, and played against him at the Oval in the last Test; but in that series I did not succeed in reading him: like everyone else who batted against him in that season, I was unable to determine from watching his hands and his wrists at the moment of delivery whether it was his leg-break or his off-spinner. Later, in the clearer light of the West Indies, it was to be different.

Ramadhin bowled with his sleeve buttoned over his wrist and that may have added a little to the effect of concealment, though basically I think he achieved it by means of his quick arm action and the rapid movement of his fingers against the dark background. The trouble was that you couldn't tell his off-spinner from his leg-break.

Of course there were all kinds of theories held by the players about him; there always are. Some said he flighted the leg-break so that if you watched not the wrist and fingers but the flight of the ball you could tell when the ball was going to leave you. Others said that, on the contrary, he flighted the off-break; another view was that sometimes he flighted the leg-, sometimes the off-break; this was contradicted by the opinion that he bowled either the one or the other a bit faster. In the end you were left with mystery: that year Sonny Ramadhin remained a mystery. Even later on in 1957 when perhaps Ramadhin was not as effective as he was in the season of which I am now writing, Peter May said he still found great difficulty in reading him.

It was his best year and he achieved great results. I remember at the Lord's Test Bill Edrich said to me: "You know, when you are facing the bowling of that little man you feel exactly as if someone were throwing a handful of confetti at you." It was an indication of the puzzlement which he imposed on batsmen.

No one really succeeded in getting after him that year. I had the impression in 1950 that he had a slightly vulnerable temperament, and that if he were played aggressively it would react badly on his bowling. With some bowlers, of course, it has exactly the opposite effect, as they think it will improve their chances of getting a wicket; but as we later found out, it seemed to make Sonny Ramadhin lose his accuracy and his spirits. Not long afterwards the Australians, perhaps having received a hint on some cricketing grape-vine, tried these tactics against him and very greatly reduced his effectiveness.

Valentine was the perfect complement, bowling away with accuracy and consistency from the other end. He bowled left arm, and there was no mystery about him. He spun the ball a lot, and he could turn it on a good wicket, which most left-arm bowlers find very difficult to do. He spun the ball away from the bat. He knew exactly what he was trying to do and did it; the batsman knew too, even if he couldn't always cope with it. I thought that Valentine had a touch of genius about him. Everything he did seemed to be wrong, according to the view most cricket coaches would take; his action was very ungainly and he bowled square on to the wicket, and yet he was superbly effective. If anyone had tried to change him he would no doubt have been ruined. With Ramadhin, he was the perfect combination.

I don't suppose I will ever forget the joy and jubilation which flooded over the Lord's cricket ground when the West Indies won the Second Test. The West Indian supporters had grouped themselves in a solid block of dark faces on the top part of the stands at the Nursery End, and as I watched the game from the familiar Middlesex balcony I could see the colour and gaiety of the women's dresses and the frequent eccentricity of the men's. It was a mobile, restless section of the crowd; vigorous and witty comments sparkled out over the ground from there.

And then the unreadable Ramadhin ended the England innings and the match by bowling Alec Bedser—and the West Indians had won their first game ever at Lord's. At the Nursery End there was nothing but enthusiasm and delight. Hats were thrown in the air, people were jumping and singing and shouting with joy and pride at the victory. Suddenly there was a calypso band on the field, dancing with their followers across the turf, with the jerky, irregular music coming over towards the pavilion from the guitars and the steel drums.

I looked down at the members below me. Part of the great charm of Lord's is its formality and tradition. It is not often that there is a breaking loose from the customary and the polite. The members now were acting with their expected courtesy and restraint as the band jigged and circled round the field. There was a gentle and polite rustle of applause from the restrained clapping of hands. Then the band began a demonstration of Caribbean song and rhythm directly in front of the pavilion.

From the expressions that I saw down below me, I thought that some of the members were saying to themselves, and in their glances, to each other: "Could this possibly happen at Lord's, here, in the ancient centre of world cricket?" It was happening; so far as one could judge from the calypso band, it was going to go on happening for quite a little time yet.

Then, in a moment, everything changed, and the members were grinning with real amusement, and applauding vigorously and laughing out loud, thoroughly enjoying the West Indian performance. Lord's, in inimitable style, had gracefully added another page to a very long history.

The West Indies won that game by playing the attractive cricket which was characteristic of them and from which we had and still have a great deal to learn. The West Indian players were fast scorers, they hit the ball hard, and as a result because of the top-class entertainment they provided were an extremely popular side. There was none of the grim and dour determination to win, and not to lose, which can make the game so unattractive. They played wonderful exciting cricket and gained a victory at the same time.

I had not been on the M.C.C. tour of 1947-8 in the West Indies, and it was the first time I saw Worrell and Weekes and Walcott. As it turned out, it was the best possible time to see them because they were all on form at the same time, all producing the powerful, colourful cricket which so delighted the crowd. I think, in fact, that it was the only series when they were all on form simultaneously.

Worrell was an artistic batsman and a pleasure to watch. His execution of strokes was perfect and he was a fast scorer. All of them indeed were fast scorers. Weekes was short and stocky and a murderer of ordinary bowling: not very orthodox perhaps, but a powerful stroke-player. Walcott was a giant, enormously and very strongly built. When he came out to the wicket the bat looked like a toy in his hand; but he was an elegant stroke-player and tremendously powerful off his back foot—the most powerful I have ever seen.

They had, of course, many characteristics in common: for example, the way they used their feet in facing the slow bowlers. Indeed they were pulverisers of the slow bowling. At Nottingham, in the Third Test, we had an instance of this when, to use cricketing language, Jenkins got the most awful stick.

Jenkins had had a very good tour in South Africa and was a bowler who could flight the ball most deceptively. If you played him from the crease he would soon get you into quite a tangle. Worrell and Weekes in that game had the most aggressive intentions which didn't apparently include playing Jenkins from the crease. As soon as Jenkins had flighted the ball they would be up the crease like lightning, and would not allow it to pitch. In effect they didn't allow Jenkins to bowl and Norman Yardley could give him only 13 overs, with 73 runs scored off him, for 1 wicket, an average of more than 5 runs per over. In that innings the West Indies scored 558 runs, and Jenkins had only those 13 overs.

Hollies with his leg-spinners got much the same treatment, and got 2 for 134. Shackleton, usually a tight and accurate bowler, got 1 for 128 in 43 overs, and even Bedser had 127 scored off him in 48 overs for 5 wickets. Yardley put himself on to bowl and got 1 for 82.

Worrell scored 261 in a most beautiful innings, and Weekes 129. As someone said, there was an awful lot of stick and hammer flying about that day. Worrell and Weekes dictated policy—the bowlers bowled as well as they were allowed to by these two batsmen who were right on top, in the most gloriously entertaining cricket. On that tour the West Indies were on top most of the time, and when they are on top they are right on top. Contrariwise, if they are down, they are down at the bottom. The one is perhaps the corollary of the other.

It was a new and a very exciting chapter in West Indian cricket and was not without its effect on the fierce M.C.C. tour of the West Indies in the winter of 1953-4 when the bottles were thrown.

One evening in August of 1950, not long after the final Test at the Oval, I was listening to the nine o'clock news on the B.B.C., hoping to hear the composition of the side which was going to tour Australia in the following winter, when I heard, for the first time, that I was to be vice-captain of the team. In fact, as I listened, what had most concerned me was whether, because of my lack of fitness and all the doubts about my knee, I would be included in the side at all. It was a great honour: it was also a bolt from the blue. The next morning I had the official notification.

My first reaction was astonishment, as the secret had been extremely well kept and no hint of a rumour had reached me beforehand. I don't remember hearing any discussion among cricketers or cricket writers about the possibility or even the desirability of a professional vice-captain. Then, of course, I felt very pleased, and thought that it was one of the most pleasant surprises that I had ever had. After that it began to occur to me that I had been given a very difficult task indeed. I was a professional, but not the senior professional in the side. I remember wondering how Len Hutton and Cyril Washbrook would react. I remember thinking, too, that it would be in the way of my first experience of captaining a first-class side at cricket.

It was the beginning of a new phase of my life as a cricketer. It was also a break with a very long-established tradition that a professional should be appointed to the position.

Under Freddie Brown the side did well on the 1950-1 tour of Australia. I know we were beaten four to one in the Tests, but things were very much better than these figures seemed to show: in fact, with just a little more luck we could have won the series three to two. It is unavailing, I know, to talk of what might have been, but I think it is of interest. One of the fascinating qualities about cricket is that so many things might, but for the slightest chance, so easily have been.

The flood of fortune changed direction earlier than has been fully realised. I would say that you could have seen strong indications of it in the First Test Match at Brisbane, where, as in four of the matches, we lost the toss. For a time it almost looked as if the law of averages had been interpreted against us.

At Brisbane, the most notoriously changeable ground in the world perhaps—someone said it was more changeable even than a woman —the Australians had first use of the beautiful batsman's wicket, but nevertheless we had them all out for 228 runs. We had our tails up then, until the rain came down in torrents and we knew we would have to go out and bat on a wet sticky, the nearest thing to a morass that cricket can be played on.

A tense and fascinating battle of tactics followed. We batted as well as we could—which wasn't very well—but no longer than we had to, and when we had collected 68 runs for 7 wickets we declared, so as to avoid the follow-on, and put the Australians in again to see how they would enjoy the pitch. They didn't do very well on it either; and before long 7 of their wickets were down for 32 runs. Then Lindsay Hassett made the obvious decision and with about seventy minutes left to play, he declared and put us back in, hoping in the time remaining to get some of our wickets before the close of play on a wicket which had improved, but which he hoped would continue to be unpredictable. He had nothing to gain by not putting us in in that fashion; indeed it was plainly to his advantage to ensure that the M.C.C. had as long as possible that day on that bad wicket. It was a nice piece of retaliation. However, the wicket had by then lost practically all of its devil, and it was only the occasional ball which was doing something odd; but what followed with devastating suddenness was disaster for England: before we left the ground that evening we had lost 6 of our wickets for 30 runs.

Even then we might have saved the game if I could have produced anything like the good form which I had been showing in the State matches which led up to the First Test. The next morning, in the brilliant sunshine which at Brisbane so often follows the tropical storm, the wicket had dried out so that the batsmen had a strip of ground to play on which was almost as good as the first day. Len Hutton and I had every reason to be confident that with any luck we could get the runs we required, 163 runs to be precise.

Then I was out first ball, caught at short leg off Johnston, and though Len went on to play the most beautiful innings for 62 not out, we nevertheless lost the game by 70 runs. Plainly it was a game we might just as easily have won; equally plainly our bowlers were beginning to get the measure of the Australian batsmen, even on a perfect batsman's wicket. It was unfortunate that the new vice-captain should choose that moment to begin what proved in the end to be his worst series of Test failures. But that is the game of cricket, and I don't complain.

We came very near to winning the next Test at Melbourne. I didn't play in the game because by then my knee had begun to trouble me again, and I decided—Freddie Brown having left the decision ultimately to me—that as it was swollen there was a possibility that it might break down during the game, and therefore that there was a risk which I could not feel justified in taking. So I watched the cricket from the pavilion.

Again we lost the toss and again we bowled the Australians out for quite a modest total, this time 194 runs, on a fast green wicket. Then we made 197, getting a lead of three runs, giving the Australians their second turn on a wicket which was still very good indeed. And we bowled them out again, for 181. If we could make 179 runs the game would be ours, for the first time in sixteen years.

I think the policy we then adopted was the wrong one. It looked as if our policy was to get the runs in ones and twos, by working hard at it, as it were, discarding the aggressive approach and even the natural way of playing, and concentrating on staying there, and playing safe. There was plenty of time to get the runs, seemed to be the thought, and the great thing was to stay there and get them by small instalments. You have all the time in the world, so don't take any chances, might have been the motto. I have often seen a policy like that fail; so has every cricketer: and it failed this time with a peculiar poignancy, because when we were all out we needed only 28 runs to win. We could easily have done it if we had had a little more nerve and thrown away the handcuffs. But we failed, and it served us right. Next time perhaps we would know better.

The two next times, in the Third and Fourth Tests, did not afford us much opportunity of finding out anything about ourselves, except the rather obvious fact that the Australians were able to defeat us soundly, without leaving the possibility of excuse, or of explanation other than that they could still play cricket a great deal better than we could, when they got down to it, or we failed properly to get down to it. But our day was coming surely and inescapably, fulfilling the expectations of the first two Tests.

The break-through for us came at Melbourne, almost too easily, in a vast stadium which to English senses at least at first seemed to have no real connection with cricket, but to have been raised for soccer, or Rugby football, or American football even. The ground is capable of holding 100,000 and is surrounded on all sides by great stands which, at cricket matches, accommodate 80,000 people, all seated. When you walk out to the lovely strip of turf in the middle you feel, if you are an English cricketer, very far away from everybody, and quite lost. After the casualness and intimacy of, say, the Lord's ground, Melbourne is quite an intimidating experience.

On a hot day it is like an oven. In Melbourne, as in England, the weather is unpredictable, but in a vastly more emphatic way. One day, especially at the time of year when the Test is played, you can have tropical rain; the next the hot winds will blow in off the desert, and you feel choked and stifled in the heat. Even in that great stadium, when the hot wind is blowing, you feel closed in, and long for the green and the cool openness of an English cricket ground.

That key Test Match, the Fifth, was Reg Simpson's game. We lost the toss again, and on another fast green wicket we bowled the Australians out for 217 runs. Then, in our first innings, Reg played his classical knock of 156 runs out of a total of 320. It was a real joy to watch, each stroke beautifully executed, and every stroke in the book played. It was his only great innings of that tour; in fact, the only great innings he played before or since; but it came, uniquely, just when it was needed.

We were in the lead by 103, and the Australians went in again and were bowled out for 197; 95 to win, that's all we needed now—95 to win. Surely we could do it this time. Hutton was at the wicket when I joined him, his score 40, 33 runs only needed to win. Washbrook had got 7 and Simpson 15. As I walked out I said to myself that I was going to stay at the wicket until there were 94 runs on the board, and badly out of form and out of luck as I was, I got down to the task with unaccustomed grimness. Len was in fine form, and he got the runs all right and we won the match, my contribution being a hardly gained 11 runs.

For the England cricketers this was a moment of jubilation. The last time we had done it was away back in 1938 when we made 903 runs and Len had got his record and I had lost my bet with Eddie Paynter. It had been a long and often a dreary time. The smile photographed on Freddie Brown's face epitomises the satisfaction of success long prepared, and achieved at last.

Now the tide was fully on the turn.

CHAPTER VI

LOVELY BLACK EYE

EVERYTHING was far from being all right, either with the team or with me.

On the boat going out to Australia Freddie Brown and I, as captain and vice-captain, had many discussions about the coming tour; the topic which most concerned us was the new players in the side, David Sheppard, Gilbert Parkhouse, John Dewes and Brian Close, and how we might find the best ways of bringing them on. The England team were badly in need of new blood, and as yet we seemed to have had very little success in finding it.

One problem in the handling of players, more perhaps than any other, confronts the captain of a side touring Australia. The circumstances are very different from those of a touring side in this country in which the captain knows that he can rest a player for, say, a week-end, and bring him back in the mid-week game, or vice versa; but in Australia the gaps between matches are so long that a man left out of a State match may not find himself holding a bat for a fortnight: and so the necessity to keep playing the man in form arises, because one absence of two weeks might easily find him out of form at the end of it. A man out of form can have a very difficult time indeed, and may be left for as long as a month without an opportunity to handle a bat or pick up a ball. It is one of the hazards of touring in Australia.

Our concern for these new players was to try to mould them and to give them confidence and encouragement in the early games before the Test, so getting into form and the swing of the tour. As it turned out Brian Close started the tour in excellent shape, with 108 against Western Australia in Perth; but as time went on he proved a disappointment. None of the players I have mentioned really established themselves as a Test player in that series, which was more than a little disheartening, as we could reasonably have expected two and certainly one to have been a success. Of course, David Sheppard has since played a lot of really good cricket; but at that stage his promise had not yet become clear. All of them, it seemed, were suspect to the quick stuff, mainly because they were late in playing their shots, no doubt because they'd never before faced anyone with the pace and venom of Miller and Lindwall.

I found it difficult to understand why Brian Close failed. He seemed to have all the natural ability to become a great cricketer; he was a fine, forceful batsman: a magnificent fielder, a very useful bowler, and in everything that he did, a good mover. He seemed to do everything naturally. And yet he had a most disappointing tour.

I think that his failure arose from his temperament, which did not seem to have the solidity which one usually associates with a Yorkshireman. When he was on top he was very much on top and very much elated; but somehow he seemed easily to lose heart and confidence, and then his play would deteriorate.

But there was profit as well as loss; in fact, a great deal of profit, for on this tour Alec Bedser emerged as a devastatingly effective seam bowler. Season after season, series after series, Alec Bedser seemed rather to have plodded on, without a great deal of success; but suddenly on this tour he became, and was to remain, one of the giants, in every sense, of international cricket.

He bowled beautifully. He moved the ball in the air both ways, swinging it late, and he moved it both ways off the seam. One of his great advantages was the lateness of his swing, when the ball would dip suddenly, at the last moment, as it reached the batsman. By that time he had perfected his leg cutter, the ball that he could bowl consistently, hitting the seam as it struck the pitch, and leaving the batsman. Occasionally, though I doubt if he did it predictably, he could make it move the other way off the seam. And he was deadly accurate. Years and years of practice and thinking were showing their proper results.

Alec never knew when he was beaten. He loved bowling; perhaps it may sound a little odd to say that—but in fact a lot of bowlers don't like to bowl if they find they are not achieving success. That was not so with Alec, and it was one of his great assets. The side on that tour owed a great deal to his persistence and great-heartedness.

Freddie Brown, rather after the fashion of Norman Yardley on the previous Australian tour, also turned out to be a most effective and accurate seam bowler. Going out on the boat we had thought of him as a leg-spinner, and a first-class leg-spinner too; but by the time the tour was over he had established himself as a seamer. The Australians were not very happy against his accuracy or that of Alec; in fact, we were beginning to see what we had for some time strongly suspected, that even if we had not yet produced a really hostile attack with pace bowlers, yet we could go very far against the Australians by relying on consistency and accuracy.

Bill Edrich should have been with us on that tour; his presence might have given the vital extra strength and experience which we needed so badly. The reason that he wasn't with us was because he was "out of favour", that sinister condition which means that a player is excluded from a side on some ground other than that his ability and form does not justify his inclusion. Bill, I believe, was not selected because, by an unhappy coincidence in a previous series, an important selector had become rather closely aware of the fact that Bill had had a late and rather a gay night. Bill would be the last person to say that he had ever acquired the habit of going to bed very early; but his greatness as a cricketer was never in any way affected.

People differ and so do their constitutions. Some players like a quiet dinner, a quiet talk perhaps, or a good book, followed by early bed and rest which I've often suspected has been disturbed by too much anxious thought of how they will play next day. Others like to go out and forget about it, and to replace with beer what they have lost in the day's exertion. They usually sleep better: they certainly don't play any worse: to ask them to sit quietly in an hotel would be to ensure that they would be unsuccessful. Great fast bowlers, incidentally, are often great drinkers of beer: it's again a question of replacement.

On the tour my form of consistency was to fail regularly in Test Matches and frequently to do well in State matches. It was a particularly irritating way to lose form. I started off with a hundred against Western Australia, didn't play at Adelaide, got another century against Victoria, 92 at Sydney, 30-odd against Queensland, and so to the First Test when, in the first innings, I was given out from a catch which came off my wrist, and in the second I was caught at short leg off the first ball. The fact that the umpire later apologised for a bad decision—and I was impressed that he made the apology and was pleased to accept it—was hardly much help or consolation; but bad decisions are a part, even though a small part, of cricket and must be taken with good grace.

In the Third Test I didn't do much better. Miller in the first innings bowled me one quite wide of the wicket; I got an inside edge, on to the wicket. I managed to get 23 in the second innings, but it took me the best part of two hours. I was right out of touch and out of form but, very strangely, only in the Test Matches. In State games I seemed to be quite well able to face up to the same Test attack, and to score runs off it.

In my first innings of the Fourth Test, Lindwall and Tallon had me out by playing on the defect in my batting of which they had long been aware. To a ball on the middle or middle and leg from Ray I moved too far over to the off—as has always been my tendency —played a leg glance from the middle of the bat to fine leg, as I thought, because I was so far over, but in fact straight into Don Tallon's glove. I have always been prone to do this, and it's a defect which I never really succeeded in eliminating; because of it I have been caught at the wicket, or on the leg side, or bowled round my legs, on very many occasions.

By now nearly all my confidence had gone again, but I was holding on with as much sense and serenity as I could find. After my second innings in that Fourth Test, I think, for a while it all went. Bill Johnston bowled me a rank long hop: a quick series of indecisive thoughts ran through my mind—shall I hit it for 4, or for 6, or where shall I hit it, or will I not hit it at all and play safe? In the end, half hesitantly, I made a shot which was no shot at all and lobbed the ball gently into short-leg's hands.

In the first innings of the Fifth Test, Miller dismissed me with a brilliant catch, right-handed, at full stretch, from a shot I made off Lindwall, which to any ordinary mortal would hardly have been a chance. At least I managed 11 runs in the second innings, and to be at the wicket when the game was won. It was of course a great satisfaction to be there when the winning stroke was made, but I didn't feel I had played much part in achieving the victory. I had a wretchedly unsuccessful series, and because I have described it briefly I don't want it to be thought that I seek to make any excuses.

I don't. I was having a bad trot, in the home of that expression, and was doing my best to accept it with what philosophy I could command.

The tour produced another mystery man, Iverson, and I had the small comfort of being able to deal with him fairly adequately so that he never got my wicket. The first time that I faced him, at Victoria, he flummoxed me completely, and I should have been stumped by yards in one of the early overs. Then I began to understand approximately how to deal with him, and I got 100 against bowling which included his in that innings.

I tried all sorts of things against him. When he threw the ball up I used to go up the wicket to get to it and smother the spin before it pitched; in the end I played him mainly off the back foot, watching the ball off the wicket, and then making my stroke.

Iverson didn't resemble the little man Ramadhin, except in mystery; he was a big ungainly man, with a very odd run up and a cumbersome action: at the moment of delivery his body and limbs were screwed into the semblance of a gnarled tree. But he most effectively disguised his off-spinner from his leg-break, and he was most difficult to deal with. He held the ball in two fingers, and gave it the final decisive flick, in a very quick movement, with one. It was all done so quickly that you couldn't be certain what ball he had bowled.

He was not a man with a profound knowledge of cricket. He couldn't really field at all, and some people doubted if he knew the laws of the game. There was one story of his captain telling him to go and field at short leg and his turning round and asking, "Where's that?" I don't suppose it's really true, but it throws some light on a character who was very much out of the ordinary. Our policy was, if possible, to hammer him at an early stage and to knock him out of the Test series: we didn't want him in sight. But we didn't succeed.

As usual, there was a great deal of discussion amongst the players about the new phenomenon, which produced a crop of subtle and ingenious theories, contradictory, and mostly wrong. It's not a good thing to discuss a bowler of this kind too much, for the effect of it is to make him a kind of bogy man, and to give the players an unhelpful complex about his mystery and efficiency.

The Press, both our own and the Australian, were far from kind to us. We didn't have very much constructive criticism, not even from our own people, and we had a great deal that was merely destructive. It seemed to be accepted by the cricket writers that the M.C.C. would be beaten anyway—that was a foregone conclusion, appeared to be their attitude, and was no longer therefore news—so that what was to be done was to look for something sensational, to please or excite or stimulate the cricketing public: for example, if they could find the real hidden reason for Denis Compton's failure in the Test Matches that would do.

Things played right into the hands of the journalists, and for the first time I was beginning to feel that sometimes they could be a good deal less than fair.

It was Christmas-time in Melbourne, and I was at a party at the home of Bill Gluth, an old friend of mine, with Freddie Brown, Godfrey Evans, Cyril Washbrook and Major-General Jim Cassels and others. It was a pleasant, hot southern summer's night, and at about eleven o'clock we were all sitting on the lawn. The drinks were going round hospitably and Bill said to me, "Denis, would you like another drink?"

I gave a Christmas reply and answered, "Yes, please", and as I did so I half turned towards my host. Unhappily, just near where I was sitting, there was a tap of the kind which many a gardener has in his lawn for convenience in watering it and the garden. I struck my right eyebrow on the tap and ripped it open, and very quickly I could feel the warm blood trickling down into my eye.

Christmas-time is not the easiest time to find a doctor, but we eventually did locate one, and he came as quickly as he could and put four stitches into my eyebrow. That was all that happened, no more and no less.

Of course, Freddie Brown and I had enough experience of the Press by then, and in particular of the Australian Press in relation to the England cricketers, to know that if they got hold of the story that Denis Compton had a cut eye, or a damaged eye, or a black eye, they would very quickly draw the most improbable inferences, from his having been mixed up in a brawl to being challenged to a duel by an angry husband. So we had to do something to try and keep it quiet. We discussed it for a while and decided that I should put on a pair of dark glasses, and the next day catch a later plane to Sydney than the rest of the team. It was a simple, even an innocent precaution, and we hoped that perhaps it might work. I am bound to say, knowing the thirst of an Australian journalist for news, that we had our doubts.

They were amply confirmed. I got to Sydney all right, though I think that my absence from the main party had already roused suspicions. In my dark glasses I went unobserved to the hotel and straight to bed. By this time Keith Miller, who was with the *Sydney Sun*, had got wind of what had happened and had organised a little surprise for me.

Next morning I had just woken up and was still unshaved, lying in my bed, when somebody knocked at the door, said "Denis" loudly, and then flung it open, and as I turned took a photograph of me. It was a photographer from the *Sydney Sun*.

The photograph was front page in the *Sydney Sun* and in the Press in this country. It is an interesting photograph. It could correct any over-flattering impressions which certain rather better known pictures in underground stations and other places may have created in people's minds about how I look.

In this one I looked like a gangster, or a murderer at large. It's an adults only picture.

In Australia, and no doubt in England, there was a great wealth of exciting speculation as to the life Denis Compton must lead out of cricketing hours. In the receptive mind no doubt a satisfying explanation had taken root as to why he was so sadly out of form. The Eye had been added to the Knee.

I wasn't much helped by a statement which Brigadier Green, our manager, decided to make; by the time he'd finished seeing the gentlemen from the Press I had lost any chance of making anyone believe that which I said had happened really had happened.

In a moment of aberration he told them, simply, without circumstance, that Denis Compton had caught his eye on a waterspout. Because it was higher, he evidently considered a waterspout more credible.

Either he should have said nothing, or told the whole story in precise detail. Instead, he ruined the pitch.

I could see unbelief in people's eyes: "Waterspout . . . waterspout indeed, you can try getting someone else to believe that . . . we have our own ideas."

I used to get the same question about a hundred times a day: "Denis, how did you really get that black eye?" At first I tried to give some account of what really had happened, but I saw that no one really believed me. "Oh, that's as good a story as any," seemed to be their reaction. In the end I refused to say anything, which gave rise to a fresh set of inferences.

It took a long time for that story to die. No doubt the Press were happy, even if I couldn't say that I was particularly. It made better news than the fact that the M.C.C. were going to get beaten again.

Of course, I laugh about it now.

When I led the M.C.C. team on to the field against Victoria at Melbourne in the early days of November 1950 I was in fact, although I was not in the least conscious of it at the time, creating a little bit of cricketing history, as it was the first time that the M.C.C. had been captained by a professional. My ideas then, and they are the same now, were that the game of cricket should be made more adventurous, with a more deliberate purpose of entertaining the crowd. The dour, negative approach which too often dominates the game today, especially in Australia, could end up by killing the game. In that match, if I got a chance, I proposed to try out some of my ideas, especially as it seemed to me that the selectors knowing my views, had given them some kind of implied approval by making me vice-captain.

The opportunity certainly arose. The game was interrupted by rain, and on the last day of play the situation was that we were 306 for 9 declared and Victoria had made 331 all out. In one day, it seemed fairly obvious to me, there couldn't be a result to the game if ordinary methods were adopted, and the crowd and the players would be bored and probably irritated by a tedious day's batting practice and an ending in a dull draw.

I decided to have a word about it with Lindsay Hassett, who was captaining Victoria. I suggested to him that the M.C.C. should bat for a certain time, and then should make a sporting declaration and let the Australians see if they could get the runs in the time remaining. It would be a good spectacle, I said, even if it did not produce a result, though I considered it possible that it might easily do that too. There didn't seem to be any other way of avoiding a deadly day's cricket.

Keith Miller, if he had been captain, might have listened; but not Lindsay Hassett—his ears were very deaf to the proposal. "No, Denis," he said. "It's a very good idea, but you know we don't really think that that's the way to play cricket."

So out we went to bat again and the weather, as if, I liked to think, to show its disapproval, washed the game out when we were 79 for 4.

I think Lindsay Hassett was wrong to reject my suggestion. Of course, in Test Matches a side must play to win; but outside representative cricket I am sure there is a very strong case, and it probably gets stronger every day, for infusing more life and colour and excitement into the game.

I think this is especially important for Australia, where too many top-class cricketers play for themselves, with an eye on averages and selection for the team going abroad, and too many State games are grim struggles in which in four days each side will have completed only one innings. I am sure the Australian cricket public does not like it, although I have often wondered whether their views on it have been given sufficient consideration by those playing and controlling cricket in Australia. No public, in my experience, would like it. It may be one of the reasons for the very serious loss of ground which cricket in Australia has suffered to lawn tennis.

I captained the side in nine games altogether, including two games against New Zealand, and we had six wins and three draws, quite a reasonable performance in any circumstances; but I was never able to put my own ideas on how a game might be played into practice because I quickly saw that Lindsay Hassett's attitude was shared by other Australian captains.

In one game, that against New South Wales at Sydney, I was very far from happy about the negative attitude which Len Hutton seemed to adopt towards me as a captain. It was a difficult game to start with, though if it hadn't been for the rain we might have gone very near to winning it, as when play ended Washbrook and I were at the wicket, with 143 runs on the board in ninety minutes and only 2 wickets down. We had to get 311 to win at the rate of two runs per minute, and we were ahead of the clock. He was 53 and I was 34, and we were going like bombs. Then the weather came down and that was that.

I had lost the toss, and the New South Wales side, captained by Miller and brimming with Test players, had first use of a beautiful wicket, and they made the best possible use of it. In the result they kept us in the field for two days and made 530 for 3 wickets. There was a good deal of criticism of my captaincy, and no doubt with some justification.

The circumstances were indeed such as would make any captain welcome any assistance he could get from the other players, from those of great experience especially. At one stage I remember going over to Hutton and asking him if he had any ideas. He seemed to shrug my inquiry aside and merely replied: "You'd better send for some more bowlers."

I can laugh at the comment now, but it was not particularly funny then. Len, I felt, was saying that I was the captain and that I had better get on with the job the best way I could. He didn't give at all. I had the feeling that he was being very thankful that I had the job and not him. I'm sure he could have been more helpful than that.

In the end, in that game and in others, I found that I got most assistance from Godfrey Evans who, behind the wicket, knew better than anyone else what the ball was doing, and how effective a bowler or a type of bowler was or might be in the particular circumstances.

I am sure I learnt a great deal from captaining the M.C.C. side on that tour. One of the main things was the importance of having every member of the team one hundred per cent behind you. I wasn't quite sure that I had. Another was that every captain, no matter who he is, does well to seek the advice of the experienced players in the team when he is confronted with a problem: to seek it, not necessarily to take it, for in the last analysis he must make the decision. But the other players can help greatly, as Godfrey certainly helped me.

When I started the return journey to England I had behind me the worst performance in a Test series which I had put up before or since. I was settling down fairly well to accept the fact that from now on my knee would permanently restrict my mobility.

My eye had fully recovered.

Freddie Brown went home by boat, and as vice-captain I took the team back to London by Pan American from New Zealand via Fiji, Honolulu, San Francisco, Chicago and New York. It was the kind of journey which comes the way of the fortunate cricketer.

At Honolulu there was a telegram for Denis Compton.

Not surprisingly, I didn't expect to get telegrams in an island in the middle of the Pacific, nor did I realise that anyone knew that I was in Honolulu. I opened the envelope with some interest. It had been sent by Nigel Bruce, the English actor, famous for his parts in the Sherlock Holmes films. It came from Hollywood.

Would the team come and play cricket in Hollywood, the text seemed to say. I read it again—yes, that was right: would the team come and play cricket in Hollywood? Everything would be arranged and paid for by our hosts; they would even see to the business of getting us on to the different plane route which the broken journey would make necessary. It seemed to me like a wonderful idea. Cricket in Hollywood: I could see myself scoring a century in the Hollywood bowl, at dawn, or under the stars.

I called the team together in the hotel, and with some excitement told them about the invitation—and got one of the biggest surprises of my life. The majority, it seemed, didn't want to go: they'd been from home long enough and wanted to get back—even another eight days would add too much to their absence. I was most disappointed and very puzzled by their decision.

One night at the Palladium in London Danny Kaye had asked me to ring him up if ever I came to America . . . fancy, cricket in the Hollywood bowl with Danny Kaye. It sounded to me like a huge opportunity missed.

CHAPTER VII

A BAD TROT

MOST batsmen have an ambition to get a thousand runs in May, and in that I was like everyone else; but I never got them. Looking back at the records as I write this book I find that I was only 91 runs short in May of 1951, and I regret, now, that at the time I didn't keep a closer check of how things were going for me then. I see that I had four low innings, one of them against Hampshire and another against Lancashire, and it strikes me that if I'd been aware of the necessity I could surely have collected the 91 runs necessary from somewhere.

Not that I have ever thought records or averages should be of any importance to the cricketer. I think the important thing should be the particular performance in the individual and differing circumstances of the particular match. What on the record may look like an innings of no special merit, and an insignificant total, may on the day have been of the utmost importance in the situation of the game —a vital 20 made on a bad wicket against good bowling may not look as well on the record as a double century compiled in an easier context, but there can be no question of its greater importance. What always interested, or intrigued, or satisfied me was how I played on the day I was playing and in the match I was trying to help to win.

I was a bit depressed but not entirely despondent about my batting when I returned from Australia. I knew I must have some ability left because I had been able to score runs in the State matches; but the maddening and frustrating thing was my inability to do any good in the Tests—and Test performances are the true indices of ability.

When the new season started in 1951 I was very determined to get going properly again, partly to put myself right in my own mind: I wanted to achieve success, for my own personal satisfaction, apart from anything else.

Happily things went well with me and in May I got five centuries, one of them against the South Africans in the M.C.C. game when I got 147. Before the season ended, I was right back in form again, and I see from *Wisden* that I had an average of 52 in the Tests and of 54 in the county games.

My knee held out quite well, though it was necessary for me to rest it quite a lot, and I played in all the Tests except the third, when I was out by an odd piece of misfortune because of a poisoned toe. Before a Test, it was necessary for me to miss the immediately preceding county game, and I found that the Middlesex officials and committee were most unselfish about the whole thing, and most considerate to me personally. My whole association with my club, until then and until the end, was pleasant and happy, and I felt very grateful to them particularly at that stage. As one might have expected, the dominant consideration in their minds was not the county interest—though naturally they were anxious to field as strong a side as possible—but a concern to see that if the selectors wanted Compton to play for England, he should go out on to the field in the fittest condition possible.

In the First Test Match against the South Africans at Nottingham I saw a powerful instance of the difference which exceptional gifts of captaincy can make to a side. Dudley Nourse was captain of the South Africans, and Eric Rowan was his vice-captain. In the first innings Nourse played a magnificent innings of 208 and to a large extent put the South Africans in a position where they might be able to win the game; but he had batted with an injured finger and could not take part in the second innings. Eric Rowan took over, with intentions of victory.

He had all the qualities which could have made a great captain. He was, in the proper cricketing sense, a hostile aggressive character in the field; he knew the game inside out; he knew exactly how to control the players, and to inspire them with the determination to win and the confidence that victory could be achieved. He was a positive stimulating personality, who assessed the situation with great penetration, formed a plan to deal with it, and carried it out with great consistency. The players were behind him, and he, in a sense, was behind the players.

In the second innings we needed to make 186 to win, with lots of time, on a wet wicket, the kind of wicket on which we were then considered to be the best batting side in the world. It looked odds on that we were going to win, but Mr. Rowan had very different ideas; he told his players that they could win, and he knew in himself that they could win and he was going to have no respectful awe either for the established form or for established players. In that mood he took the field with his team.

As you batted you could feel they had a sense of victory ahead of them, and a willing co-operative spirit amongst them which seemed to give inspiration and motive to the players. Eric Rowan had been able, as it were, to spread his dominant determined personality through his men. He set a hostile attacking field, switched his bowlers brilliantly, and they responded brilliantly, and we were bowled out for 114, to lose by 71 runs.

Dudley Nourse was a really great player, full of natural and developed ability. He had the necessary gifts: he attacked brilliantly and defended skilfully and tenaciously; he was first class against fast bowling, exceptionally effective against slow; as a batsman there were very few flaws in his make-up. However, a great player does not necessarily make a great captain. For that position I took the view that Nourse was a little too placid, with a tendency to let things drift; I have no doubt that he did have ideas about the particular game or the particular situation—but it sometimes looked as if he did not always formulate them clearly into a definite policy.

Eric Rowan was all flair and brilliance as a captain, and I think it was an unfortunate thing that the officials and selection committee in South Africa didn't give his great gifts the opportunity which they deserved. If they had done I am certain he would have been a great captain and would have done great things for South African cricket.

Of course, not everyone liked Eric Rowan—there are few, if any, of us who are fortunate enough to be universally loved. He was a powerful stimulating outstanding personality who produced strong reactions one way or the other in people. Also he called a spade a spade when he considered that the precise description would be useful. He didn't always please the authorities, or even the manager; but he knew about cricket and he was a great opening batsman. He knew how to give and gave every possible encouragement to the young player: he communicated his knowledge to them; told them what they were doing right and what wrong, and initiated them helpfully into the tense atmosphere of the Test Match. He knew what he wanted from the individual player, and told him, and usually got it. Naturally the young players in the side gravitated towards him.

In the circumstances this was almost bound to happen, the more so because Dudley Nourse and Eric Rowan were not the greatest of friends, and as the tour went on I think there may often have been a hostile and disturbing atmosphere in the dressing-room. Indeed, I formed the impression before the tour was over that the South Africans were split into two factions, one gathered around Nourse, the other, probably the larger one, around Eric Rowan. Indeed, ironically, the victory in the First Test and the way in which it was achieved probably accentuated an already strong tendency. I'm sure it severely diminished their efficiency as a side. None of this was, of course, deliberate on Eric Rowan's part, for he knew as well as anyone that in all circumstances, but more especially on tour, the player's first duty is to give the fullest support to his captain, whether he be good, bad or indifferent.

The pity was all the greater because, potentially, the South Africans were a very good side indeed and should have given a better account of themselves on the tour. Amongst them we saw a nucleus of young players who were later to be part of the formidable South African teams of the future: McLean, Waite (now probably the best batsman-wicket-keeper in the world), McGlew, Van Ryneveld, Athol Rowan, McCarthy, the fast bowler, who was then rather faster than anyone we had. They were names most of which we were to hear very often in the future.

Since the war the England batting had relied mainly upon the old firm. In the six years which had elapsed since 1945, no player had established himself as an England batsman. The selectors had tried hard enough, but without real success up to that stage. To date, their greatest find was an all-rounder, Trevor Bailey, and there seemed some hope that David Sheppard would prove more than useful. All the other youngsters who had been tried had not survived the trial.

Then, in the Fourth Test against South Africa at Leeds, Peter May walked out from the pavilion and scored a century in his first innings in Test cricket, making 138 runs. It was a sound rather than a brilliant innings, and although it contained some beautiful strokes, it didn't quite give the promise of the tremendous stroke play that was to come. Naturally, May played cautiously, hitting the bad ball and concentrating on a sound defence. When he came back from the middle there was no doubt in anyone's mind that at last England had found a new batsman of Test quality and outstanding potential. It was the first find of many that were to come quickly in the next few years, and no doubt the selectors were relieved as well as happy.

In the Fifth Test at the Oval, Peter May got a nought in his second innings—at an early stage in his career, which is the best time to get it, and to get it over with. Not that very many other English batsmen got many runs. It was a very slow scoring match, an exciting battle, with the bowlers dominating the bat. In a way it was Freddie Brown's match, and he played a captain's game. In the first innings South Africa got 202, of which Eric Rowan made 55, a very fine innings and a typical one, a most important contribution to the South African score. We replied with 194. I got 73 of them, though it was a great struggle against accurate top-class bowling from Athol Rowan, Eric's brother, then one of the most effective off-spinners in the world, and Geoff Chubb, a grey-haired man of forty on his first tour of England, a first-class seam bowler who bowled magnificently, bowling his heart out. He was a great friend of mine; I always remember how he used to say, no doubt because of his success here, that he would like to take the English wickets back home to South Africa with him. In the second innings we bowled the South Africans out for 154, leaving us 163 to get.

By the time Freddie Brown came in things were looking very unhealthy indeed for England, with 4 for 90; but Freddie soon changed all that. I think the only cricket he really liked to play, or even perhaps could play, was a forcing attacking cricket; and in a very short time he had made 40 runs and we had as good as won the game. It was a typical Freddie Brown innings.

At all times he was a dangerous batsman. In Australia he had made one or two very useful and vital contributions as a batsman, and, of course, as a bowler he'd been a great success. For him especially the tour had been a near-triumph. Not only had he finished up by leading the side to their first victory in sixteen years, but he had a great personal success, not least with the Australian crowds. They, I think, regarded him as the embodiment of John Bull: a great hunk of a man, with broad shoulders, a nicely developing waistline then, a large florid face and sandy hair. They loved him, and seemed to respond quickly to his personality. There was no doubt that as soon as Freddie Brown walked on to the field you got the feeling that something was going to happen; it might be good or it might be bad: but at least it would happen. There was nothing dull or ordinary about it: he gave liveliness to the game by his mere presence on the field. He was an effective captain, though not, I think, a great one. He could also be quite surprisingly adamant about some things and apparently lacking a little in decision about others.

For me, just as Norman Yardley was my lucky captain, Freddie Brown seemed, in Australia at least, to have been my unlucky one. Try as I might in Australia, I hadn't seemed to be able to do the things that I wanted to do, and I had found it all the more disappointing because as vice-captain I had most particularly wanted to give the fullest support to my captain.

I had had a reasonably good season all round in 1951, both in Test Matches and in the county games, and as the summer of 1952 came nearer I felt that I had probably left behind the lack of form of much of the Australian tour. I was feeling quite fit, and though my knee was still a very disturbing influence, in the last two months before the season opened, and to some extent before, I had been regularly to Bill Tucker's clinic, usually three or four times a week, and the treatment appeared to be very beneficial.

In fact, the way things turned out I think 1952 was the worst season I ever had. Then I think I really did touch bottom. I have looked at the records and find that in the county games I did reasonably well, and I am more than a little surprised to find that I took 79 wickets. I observe too that I made my hundredth century.

Nevertheless I think it was my most unsatisfactory season. When I did get runs I mostly got them in a way which gave me little or no satisfaction; to some extent that had been the case in the previous season too. In four Test Match innings I made 59 runs.

By early July, with the Third Test coming up, I had reached such a stage of self-doubt and lack of confidence that I took steps which became very controversial and caused quite a large number of brick-bats to be pitched in my direction. For some time my mind had been working along these lines: I feel almost sure that I have two or three years' good cricket left in me, if I can only get through this very bad patch; the best way for me to get through is to be left alone to work out my own salvation, otherwise I will never get my form back; in the meantime it would be wrong for the selectors to continue to pick me (as they might do, having regard to past performances) and thereby to exclude someone else who should be given his chance. I thought about it, even worried about it, a good deal. I talked to people and got their views; one of those people I spoke to was my own captain, and always my counsellor, R. W. V. Robins. He agreed with me that I should write the letter.

I did, and I wrote and asked the selectors that I should not be included in the team for the Third Test. Some people understood my motives and said so in print; others did not, and also said so in print, not very flatteringly. Compton, they said in effect, is getting out before he is kicked out. I had a lot of letters from various members of the public. Mainly they were rather kind, saying that I really shouldn't have written the letter, should have played in the Test Matches, and expressed a welcome certainty that I would get my form back. I found such faith in my ability both encouraging and affecting. Others said, quite briefly, that I had acted rightly. A few said: "I see you are getting in first—you were going to get left out anyway."

One newspaper said: "I feel the selectors cannot do less than grant his request, but I do think that Compton might have left the decision to them rather than force the issue." I was grateful for the temperate quality of expression in that article, but I did not and do not think the writer was correct. I had to ensure that I *was* left out, and the only way to do it was by writing and asking that I should be.

I still think I was right to do what I did. I certainly felt more carefree afterwards, and in the next game, against Essex at Colchester, I scored 90 runs out of 113, before lunch, and I got them in a way which gave me some pleasure and satisfaction.

I didn't have a good press during that summer. I don't complain about that: I didn't deserve a good press. I must say, however, that one or two articles did annoy me, because they were unfair, and because they were so plainly written by people who knew nothing about cricket, and seemed to regard the game as just an occasional source of sensation. I have never minded informed criticism, but I have sometimes been made angry and resentful by the random blows struck by those ignorant of the game and innocent of love for it. Previously, perhaps because of my particular kind of play, I was fairly good news: now I was often bad news: it had become almost usual to say that Compton had failed—again.

I had set a standard for myself, and for the time being I was not able to keep up to it, and if I didn't score runs but got a useful 35 or 40 it was regarded as a failure, or if I got a century in a manner not closely resembling my most entertaining centuries, there was something wrong with me, so it was said. It was fair comment, and mostly I agreed with it. I was beginning to experience that most orthodox of phenomena, the descent from the pinnacle of fame and success. It happens to everyone in the public eye, some time or another. Once I had given people a fair amount of entertainment, and I think they tended to expect it from me every time I walked out on to the pitch. I simply couldn't keep it up. After all, I wasn't a machine.

I got a lot of letters throughout that summer, a considerable proportion of them from parents. The fact that I thought they were justified didn't make their reading any more enjoyable. The kind of letter I frequently had would be one from a father or an uncle saying that his young son or nephew had been brought to Lord's especially to see me play, a distance maybe of fifty or sixty miles, and that I had disappointed them by batting so badly. The ending might be the simple question: "What *has* happened to you?" What indeed?

In an odd sort of way I could feel their disappointment because my memories of my own schooldays were sufficiently vivid to know how disappointed I would have been if Sir Jack Hobbs had failed me;

if he'd been dismissed making a stupid shot, my face would have fallen and I would have left the ground in bitter disappointment.

I felt that my failures were a personal thing between me and the crowd, more particularly at Lord's, where it seemed to me that over and over again I was disappointing a friend. From quite an early stage in my career I had that sense of personal relationship with those who were watching me. Happily I felt that my friends were still on my side.

The Indians were in England for the second time since the war in the summer of 1952. They lost the series rather badly, mainly, I think, because of the way that Freddie Trueman bowled at them. Fred made hay, especially at Manchester, where he had 8 wickets for 31 in the first innings. The Indians didn't like him a bit, and I think he was greatly aided by the tendency some of their batsmen had to take guard about middle and umpire. You sometimes gained the impression that one or two of them had made the most careful preparation to get out of the way of the balls he sent down. As a whole, the team were very suspect to genuine pace.

Watching Trueman one could have had no doubts that at last we had found a genuine fast bowler. It was all the more gratifying that season because Peter May continued to play first-class cricket. And David Sheppard now at last found the form of which he had previously been seen to be capable. The flow of new blood into the English side was becoming agreeably strong.

Trueman had a fine action, control, and real pace; but the time hadn't come then for a final opinion of his ability or his prospects. The Indian batting was not sufficiently good to provide any kind of criterion as to his real merit. Naturally, the papers shouted for joy. At last, they said, we've found a real fast bowler, with pace, hostility, accuracy and success. Fiery Fred, they called him, and almost overnight Trueman was a national character, the hero of small boys, the object of critics' praise.

Publicity and the glamour of sudden success make heady wine. Some can stand it, others cannot; at that time I don't think Fred Trueman could. It went a bit to his head, and I'm sure it didn't do his cricket any good. It was very understandable, because he had a sudden ascent from obscurity to the glaring heights of success, and for a time it was rather more than he could take into his system. The best thing to do about enormous publicity such as he was getting is to ignore it. Later, Trueman was to learn that very important lesson, but the time was not yet.

For a time the effect was most unhappy. I had the impression that Trueman began to think the whole business of fast bowling was rather simple—see, after all, how easy and how complete his success had been—you just went up to the wicket and turned your arm over: there was nothing more to learn. At cricket there is always something more to learn, all the time, right up to the last game you play. If you have any other attitude, especially when you're beginning, you will deprive yourself of any chance of improving; in fact, in my experience you will tend to go back.

The Press would have been fairer to him if they had toned down their praise, and made it more balanced and more restrained, but in an imperfect world that's probably too much to ask or expect of the Press. As it was, Fred Trueman tended to disregard the advice of the old hands who could have coached and advised him to greater and more stable proficiency, and it wasn't long before he ran into a very bad patch indeed. Now, of course, he has adjusted himself to success and he is a very fine fast bowler.

Against India the selectors took the opportunity of blooding the first professional to captain an English side since the early days of representative cricket in the second part of the nineteenth century, and Len Hutton was the man chosen. It was, I am quite sure, the right choice. There was no amateur in cricket at that time who had the ability or the necessary cricketing experience to take the job; and Len after all had had nearly twenty years of cricket by then, and, what's more, was at the peak of form.

I am bound to say that although I agreed with the choice I had the feeling that Len's way of playing cricket would not be mine, that some of the attractiveness would go out of the representative game which now stood a chance of being played grimly and dourly, the hard way, for a win no matter what the circumstances.

There never had been any real danger of losing a game against India, and most problems solved themselves, as usually happens with a successful side; so that Len, you could say, was hardly tested as captain. It was, as I have said, the ideal time to make a new departure.

One thing, however, I thought was a little ominous. By the Fourth Test at the Oval we'd won the series, so that nothing terribly important hung on the issue. It was, I would have considered, a time to give the public some of the active, vigorous cricket which they need and want. Len didn't seem to take that view. We batted first, and before lunch he and Sheppard between them made 45 runs for no wickets.

It was the lowest scoring rate of the whole tour.

CHAPTER VIII

FLYING CHAMPAGNE

FORTUNES swung back and forth in the summer of 1953, when we played the Australians again over here. The story of the First Test at Nottingham is simply told. The Australians batted first and got 249, which included a beautiful hundred from Lindsay Hassett. We went in and were bowled out for 144 by great bowling aided by magnificent fielding. Then Bedser had a moment of greatness and took 7 wickets for 44 runs, and we got the Australians out a second time, for 123. We wanted 229 runs to win; but the weather didn't give us time to get them. The weather was dismal, dreary and rainy, and we were 120 for 1 wicket when the rain came down to stay. Morally, if such a test is applicable, the game was ours. On a wet wicket Alec Bedser had bowled beautifully, using his leg-cutter, which whipped and left the batsman off the wicket. In the first innings he bowled 38 overs and got 7 for 55; in the second 17 only, with 7 for 44.

Bedser now began to assume the command over the Australian players which later became almost dominant. He was to be overwhelmingly successful. Somehow the Australians couldn't really deal with him: in particular, Arthur Morris—Bedser got him out every time he went in to bat.

The Second Test sent our morale right up; indeed I think it gave the cricketing public back the faith in England cricketers which they had lost utterly since the war. When it was over, the players and the public felt that sooner rather than later we were going to get the whip-hand of the Australians.

The game was played at Lord's. In the first innings Australia made 346, Lindsay Hassett opening the batting, and himself getting another hundred; then we got 372, to lead by 26 runs. In the second innings, not long before six o'clock on the fourth day, we had bowled the Australians out for 368, so that we wanted only 343 runs to win, and had a little over a day in which to make them, a perfectly possible target. Keith Miller had made a lovely hundred; Arthur Morris had made 89, and Freddie Brown and Alec Bedser had done some very good bowling indeed.

Disaster followed: by 6.30 we had lost Hutton, Graveney and Kenyon for 12 runs, and the Australians had their tails up and were thirsty as only they can be for the kill. I had gone in at about 6.20 and managed to survive until the close of play. It looked as if the game was going the way of all games that you played against the Australians, down to defeat. People were thinking that we'd started down the same old slope again, leaving victory lonely behind on the top.

Next morning I resumed with Willie Watson, and was as determined as I have ever been to stay at the wicket. About ninety minutes later I left, out l.b.w. to a ball from Bill Johnston, which kept right along the ground, with 43 on the board to my credit, out of 73 for 4 wickets. As I started back to the pavilion I remembered wondering if we could save the game now. It didn't seem likely. The usual pattern of Australian success seemed to be knitting together again. It was about an hour after noon, with the rest of the day to play.

Bailey, who followed me in, and Watson, however, were quite unperturbed. They stayed together at the wicket and batted on and on and on, with heartbreaking defiance. Bailey was showing the full face of the bat to the ball, and I have heard it said that after a while the Australians began to think that his bat was about a yard wide. He played forward defensively, and back defensively, very, very correctly. There didn't seem to be anything the Australians could do about him or about the equally magnificent Watson. It was after this that the sleep of Miller and Lindwall, it is said, began to be disturbed by nightmares of bowling endless overs with a large ball to an immovable Bailey holding a monstrous bat very straight.

At six o'clock when Bailey was out the game had been saved. At close of play we were 282 for 7, only 61 runs short of victory—or at least that was how we were seeing it. Bailey and Watson had lifted the spirit of English cricket on to a new level of confidence and hope. Previously people had been saying: we can't beat these Australians; now they said that we were as good as they were, if not better, and that we had the beating of them.

The game at Lord's had been one of the key games of my life.

I was at the crossroads, and fortunately now, at last, I took the right turning. In the First Test I made nought in the first innings and hadn't batted in the second. Now I felt that I had to prove myself again, quickly, or give up.

In the first innings Graveney had been 70 overnight and was out in the first over after the resumption the next morning. I joined Len Hutton at the wicket. The new ball was due, and as I walked out I saw Lindwall ask Hassett if he could take it; with some justification he seemed to be saying to himself that he would dispose of me pretty quickly, as soon as he got the new red cherry into his hand: on my current form it was a very reasonable assumption indeed. He and Miller were fresh, and hostile, and raring to go, and they went. Quite fairly, knowing that my confidence was still somewhere down near my boots, they were going to try and get rid of me by the sharp, sudden methods of which they were the unrivalled masters.

They let loose a series of overs at us as quick as anything they've ever bowled. They sent down bumpers, fast yorkers, in-swingers, out-swingers, balls that came in to you and balls that left you from the pitch, everything they had in their magnificent armoury. It was a desperate spell; for me it was a vital period; but I was still there at lunch-time, though Len was out shortly before, having made a century. I stayed until I had 57, and then in the second innings I got my 43 runs in ninety minutes.

Looked at now on the page the scores are not very impressive, and together add up to only 100 runs; but they were runs made at a time vital to the England side. They also were runs which restored my confidence again as a top-class player, after a long period of unavoidably depressing doubt.

In the Third Test at Manchester we continued our series of near-misses. In the first innings on a wet and difficult wicket I played one of my best knocks of the series, at the wicket with Len Hutton, making 45 runs, with all my old confidence back again. I spoiled the innings perhaps only by restraining my natural play towards the close, because then we still needed 40 to avoid the follow-on, and I wanted to be there next morning: in consequence, as so often happens, I made a stupid unlikely shot and was caught behind the wicket. But I had found my touch and all my strokes again, and Len and I gave Hassett a pretty hard time trying to keep our rate of scoring down.

In this game rain took a prominent part: by two o'clock on the fifth day England were resuming play in their first innings, and, with not much more than an hour left to play, were all out for 276 in reply to Australia's 318. At that point most people would no doubt have said that as a result to the game was now obviously impossible, it wasn't really worth while sending the Australians in to bat. As it turned out it was very much more than worth while, and from the next hour at least one most important point emerged.

It was a turning wicket, and Hutton put Wardle and Laker on to bowl. Before stumps were drawn the Australians had lost 8 wickets for 35 runs, and their confidence had for the moment at least taken a steep dive. It proved once and for all—given a wicket where the ball turned—that England were the better side. It was the advent of the spinner, the destroyer on his day of the Australian batsman. Wardle had taken 4 for 7, and Laker 2 for 11.

But Australians never know when they are beaten, and in the Fourth Test at Leeds they almost ensured that they would retain the Ashes. If it hadn't been for Trevor Bailey, Hutton's tactics as captain would have thrown the game away. Not that I can agree with what Trevor Bailey did: I think it was unfair and should never have been done, though I can fully understand why he did it. He saved the game, and made it possible for England to win the Ashes.

I watched the vital period of play from the pavilion, as I couldn't field because of a finger injured in the first innings. The situation was this: it was the last day and we were all out with a lead of 177 runs, leaving the Australians an hour and fifty-five minutes in which to get them.

Hutton opened the bowling with Bedser and Lock, with the new ball, hoping, I think, that the ball would turn and that he might be able to get the Australians out quickly. There wasn't much time to lose, and it had to be done very quickly indeed. It had not apparently been considered what should be done if the Australians had other and more effective ideas. In conditions such as these it is always a fairly safe bet that the Australians would have very aggressive intentions indeed.

They went for the runs and in an unbelievably short space of time seemed to get sufficient to put victory well within their competence. Lock was getting no help from the wicket; he is primarily an attacking bowler, not of a very consistent length, or accustomed to bowling tight and keeping the runs down. Now he was giving the batsmen a lot of loose balls, and they were scoring runs off him fast. Alec Bedser wasn't being very effective either, and after about twenty minutes it looked to me as if the Australians were going to get the runs.

Hutton's judgment seemed to desert him. Watching with almost unbearable anxiety from the pavilion, I had the impression that momentarily he had lost his head, and that if something didn't happen soon we were going to lose the match. The Australians are sufficiently adept in any circumstances at snatching victory at the unlikely moment, and it was maddening to see the path being made easy for them. I kept saying to myself: "For heaven's sake, Len, why don't you do something to slow down this rate of scoring. . . . Take Lock off . . . try Bailey and see how you get on . . . do something, do something."

For the time being Hutton appeared to have lost his flexibility of decision; he didn't seem to be able to change from his policy of bowling to get the Australians out in the time left to the only feasible or practical one of saving the game at all costs. He kept on bowling Lock, and the Australian batsmen kept driving the score along. Suddenly, it seemed, the situation was that there was forty-five minutes left for play and only 66 runs needed for another Australian victory; and the Australians could see it close ahead of them. If something wasn't done quickly we had once more lost our opportunity of regaining the Ashes.

It was Bailey who took action. He and Bill Edrich went across in the field to Hutton, and told him in effect that he'd got to do something to save the game; at least he must take off the spinners, and try something else: something else must be tried. For instance, Bailey himself could be put on to bowl. Eventually Hutton made a decision, and Bailey took the ball.

All Australian hopes of winning the game faded at once. Bowling mostly outside the leg stump where the Australians couldn't reach the ball, Bailey closed the game right down. It was virtually impossible to make runs off him. He didn't hasten back to his mark either in order to bowl the next ball. The policy was not to get anyone out, but to save the game by making it impossible to score the runs in the time.

It worked, and at the close of play the Australians still needed 30 runs to win.

If you like, it wasn't cricket.

The Australians were furious about it. I don't think at that stage they were particularly fond of Hutton; now for a time at least they could find no affection in their hearts for Trevor Bailey. I consider that their anger was justified.

Of course, Len should never have allowed the game to reach the dangerous stage where only the most drastic methods could save it. He should have taken the spinners off immediately it appeared that they weren't being successful and should have bowled tight and accurately, hoping to get wickets in that way, if only from the kind of bad strokes which the Australians, tied down for any length of time, were prone to make, and which, needing runs quickly, they would have been all the more likely to play at that stage.

We all make mistakes, and this one was Len's. In the result the atmosphere between the two teams was not improved; indeed at this stage you could finally say the series really was a turbulent one.

There had been an incident earlier in the match, involving Frank Chester, standing in the game as one of the umpires with Frank Lee. Frank Chester was a very great umpire; for a long time, I think, the world's No. 1. He was a dominating character, too dominating sometimes perhaps, and he was a man firm in decision and pronounced in his views. In his way, he was a perfectionist and he liked everything done properly, or as he considered proper.

For example, he always took the view that only the bowler and the wicket-keeper should appeal for an l.b.w. decision, as they were the only people in a position to see what had actually happened. This, of course, cut right across the Australian practice: every Australian in the field, from square-leg to cover to the chaps out on the boundary, liked to appeal, loudly, with hands flung high, jumping like kangaroos as if to leap forward down the throats of umpire and batsman. Frank Chester disapproved strongly and often expressedly of the practice, and his were the kinds of expression, of words, tone and face, which made Australians feel very unhappy.

I agree with the view that he held. The loud appeal in concert by many players is really a form of intimidation; it may leave the experienced player or a hard-bitten umpire quite unmoved, but I have no doubt that it can have and has had an unsettling effect on young umpires, and even more so perhaps on young batsmen. The louder the roar, the more immediate the impression of justification. A great yell from six or seven Australians can be in its own way a hidden persuader. Frank didn't like it, and more or less said so. On the other hand, the Australians could say, relying more on letter than on spirit, that there is nothing against it in the rules. And they're right: there isn't.

Things were already tense between Frank Chester and the Australians when we went to Leeds, and they were to become more so. I was batting in the second innings when I edged a ball from Lindwall in the direction of Graeme Hole fielding at slip. It kept very, very low indeed, but finished up in Hole's hand. I was far from certain that it had carried to him without touching the ground, so I stayed at the wicket, and looked expectantly at Hole.

He didn't utter. If he'd said that he'd caught it I would have walked away from the wicket back to the pavilion, but he said nothing, and I kept looking at him. In a moment he went into a huddle with the players near him, seemed to have a discussion, after which he told me in very plain terms that I was out: he, it appeared, had caught me out.

"I am not very convinced about that, Graeme," I said, "it took you rather a long time to make up your mind. . . ." To my way of thinking, it had taken far too long for anyone to be quite certain about it. "Perhaps we'd better ask the umpire?" I suggested.

There was an appeal to Frank Lee, umpiring at the other end. He said that Ray Lindwall, running down the wicket after delivery, had obstructed his view so that he couldn't tell what had happened one way or the other. He consulted the square-leg umpire. Frank Chester was at square-leg, and had seen the whole thing quite clearly.

"Frank," Lee called over, "I didn't see what happened. . . . Was it out or not?"

Frank Chester braced himself in typical style.

"No," he answered, "it was bloody well not out."

There was something of hostility in his tone and in the look on his face and the way he squeezed out the words, which implied a heavy criticism of the appeal. Not surprisingly, the Australians didn't like it.

Frank perhaps was getting a bit old and crotchety, and I think he more than once gave the Australians the impression that he was far from well disposed towards them. In any event, I am bound to say that I sometimes had the feeling from Frank Chester that he almost hated the Australians. It was not surprising, perhaps, that when his name was put forward as one of the suggested umpires for the Fifth Test at the Oval that the Australians should turn it down and ask for someone else to be appointed to do the job.

The final turning-point was at the Oval. By then we'd had four draws and no one wanted a definite result more than the players themselves. Apart from the Leeds Test perhaps, it was the most crucial of the post-war Test Matches.

Despite our victory in the Fifth Test Match in the 1950–1 tour, I'm sure the Australians had come over in that summer full of confidence that they would win the series. The Australians play the game harder, I think, than anyone else, and a part of their hardness is their confidence. It is an important element in their cricketing strength. However the game may look—favourable for us, unfavourable for the Australians—you can be quite sure that you will always find them an extremely tough proposition. They don't like losing—I don't suppose anyone does really; and that year they almost gave the impression, certainly in the early stages, that it was impossible that they could do anything but win, even that it would be contrary to the proper order of things for them to lose.

They started well and went through the counties like fire among thorns. In the M.C.C. game at Lord's they were checked for the first time, and the stand that Bailey and I had in the second innings helped a good deal towards that end. I got 45 and he got 64, not out, after four and a half hours at the wicket. Towards the end of the tour I think that many Australians had a feeling of despair when they saw Bailey walk out from the pavilion to the middle; as time went on, they almost felt they couldn't bowl at him. They had a feeling about him as we, in a different way, had had about Iverson.

Trevor Bailey is a supremely intelligent player, in all the arts of the game. I had the impression that he had worked out a very effective little piece of gamesmanship for Miller and Lindwall. He certainly affected to be completely at ease when facing their attack. He had an almost exaggerated calm and confidence which looked as if it might have been disrespectful to their acknowledged ability, or was designed to appear so, as if he were, with just a trace of arrogance, asking what all the fuss was about. These bowlers are easy, he seemed to say. Watch this! And in a way he made it seem easy, because he was at times apparently impossible to dislodge. I'm sure, by a little deftness, he gained the upper hand psychologically of the Australians.

In the end the Australians both admired and respected him, and perhaps saw that his pretended arrogance was only a pretence, adopted for their benefit; but there was no doubt that at times he annoyed them a great deal. At Lord's, for example, when he was struck on the fingers, he took his gloves slowly off, with an expression of considerable pain on his face, dropped his glove, examined his finger carefully, and walked round the wicket, trying as it were to get better. He took quite a few minutes. For England they were very valuable minutes indeed.

He had his fingers rubbed for three or four minutes at a time, I think; and then he appeared to be ready to resume again, and Miller walked back, turned and was half-way through his run-up; Trevor stood away from the wicket, apparently still in trouble with his hand. He was very cool about it all. I doubt if Miller or Lindwall or very many of the Australians were quite so cool as he was. I remember at one stage that Keith Miller bowled him a fast full toss which missed his head by a whisker.

Miller and Lindwall were still, I thought, at their peak. They were a wonderful combination: Lindwall had a lovely rhythmical action out of which he bowled artistically with fine accuracy and swing, with perfect length and direction and deliberate disguise. It was only rarely that he bowled a really bad ball. From him you got and expected perfection.

Miller specialised in the unexpected. He was a man of moods and of inspiration, temperamental, unpredictable and delightful, a player who gave life to every game he played in. At one moment on the field he might seem a rather depressed-looking character; at another he'd be full of the joys of spring. When he was bowling you never quite knew what was coming. You might get a slow leg-break, or a bouncer, or even a long hop: then suddenly you'd get a fast break back, off a beautiful length, which would pitch outside the off stump, and if you didn't manage to play it, come right across and hit the leg.

I have known days when he'd be bowling down the sort of stuff that would make you say to yourself: there's nothing to this; who is this chap Miller, anyway? This is easy. And perhaps you'd hit him for four. You could see how the stroke would shake him. He seemed to say: "How dare you hit me for four," and for the next twenty minutes maybe, or longer, you wouldn't be able to recognise him as the same bowler. He'd toss his head back and really let go.

I often used to wonder how he got his hair so smooth as he brushed it back with that characteristic gesture of his hand. I don't quite remember when I found out—it may have been that 1953 series—but I discovered that he had a tiny comb, about 3 or 4 inches long, which he could hold in the palm of his hand as he smoothed back his hair, cleverly concealing it from both the spectators and the players. Even close up it was difficult to spot.

With Miller and Lindwall in the side against you, you could never be certain of anything, not of even getting the relatively small number of runs which we needed for victory in the second innings of the last Test at Lord's. In the first innings we got them out for 275 runs, 62 of which were Lindwall's, made in typical forcing and brilliant style. We went in and made 306 and got a lead of 31. By the time the Australians went in again the ball was turning, not much, but turning a little, and Lock and Laker went into action— for the first time. The Australians seemed to have no resistance to them.

The ball wasn't turning very much, but the Australian batsmen played a desperate frenzied sort of cricket, which was most surprising to see, even although we knew by then that they were suspect on a turning wicket. As soon as the ball deviated from the straight course they seemed to be in trouble. Their play was chancy and despairing. Most surprising of all, they didn't seem to be able to fight it out, to say to themselves, well, here is a difficult wicket, let's get down to it, watch the ball on to the bat, and master this turning ball. They appeared to come to the conclusion almost at once that it was a bowler's wicket, and to give up hope. We had them out for 162 and needed only 132 runs to win the Test and the series and to get back the Ashes.

Bill Edrich hadn't come into the side until the Third Test, when he was brought back to add experience and strengthen the team, and very amply he justified his return. We had—to say the least—played a lot of cricket together since 1936 and I was very glad indeed to see him back in a Test side. I remember very clearly before he went out to open the second innings with Len Hutton, his turning to me and saying: "Denis, it would be quite something if we could be at the wicket when these runs are finally hit off." I agreed with him very wholeheartedly—not, of course, that we wanted Len or anyone else out, but perhaps we were both a little sentimental and thought that here would be a glorious climax to our long careers together.

It worked out just the way we hoped it would. When Hutton and May were out I joined Bill at the wicket, and we needed 44 runs for victory. Bill had been batting magnificently, and it seemed plain that as long as I could stay there with him we could easily get the runs together. It didn't matter who got them so long as we were still there at the wicket when they came. Before very long I settled down and we went on quietly and nicely, giving no chances, just as if we were playing at Lord's for Middlesex.

As we pushed the score along, the crowd got quieter and tenser. The applause from scoring strokes seemed to come in shorter bursts, with a curious tautness in it, as if in its expectancy and hope the crowd was unwilling to postpone the moment of anticipated victory even for a few unnecessary seconds.

Australians never consider that a game is lost until it really is lost, and they didn't let up on us until it was absolutely clear that we must win. Then they accepted defeat, and brought Arthur Morris on to bowl. It was appropriate in a way that it should have been Arthur, because his wicket had been taken so many times by Bedser in the series that he was called Bedser's Bunny, and now perhaps was the time to show how well he could do the other kind of bowling, the harmless, funny kind.

I hit the first ball he bowled hard, and I remember thinking, that's it, it's gone for four: the game's over and we've won. I could feel the crowd poised before cheering. But the moment was postponed a few minutes longer, for Davidson fielded the ball brilliantly and there was no run. I hit the next ball even harder, just a little bit wider of Davidson where he couldn't reach it, and started to run down towards the other end, passing a jubilant Bill on my way.

There was a short time of expectant silence, and then the crowd rose in a huge roar of applause and delight and relief, and the cheering burst out from pent-up throats, and I knew that at last we'd got the Ashes back. The crowd yelled and applauded and clapped and cheered, throwing away the memories of so many years of failure in great moments of joy. They flooded out over the field, and Bill, still running, ran into their outstretched arms.

I was luckier than he was, for I was going on my run in the direction of the pavilion and I kept going; but I was soon overtaken, surrounded, clapped on the back deliriously, and congratulated by people I'd never seen before and was never to see again. Somewhere in the increasingly dense crowd behind, Bill also was surrounded, hemmed in so completely, in fact, that it looked as if we were never going to see him again. By using his bat, swinging it about him gently, he gradually carved a homeward way back to the pavilion. Instead of his two thousand pats on the back, I got only eight hundred. Both of us would gladly have had twice as many, if our strength would have lasted out.

It was a time for celebration, and the English and the Australians, the turbulence forgotten, celebrated and revelled together. We started in the dressing-rooms with champagne, and soon there were empty bottles, one of which seemed to be a temptation in Keith Miller's way, as he suddenly picked it up and pitched it through the window, out on to where the members sit and watch the game. Other bottles followed. One of them struck the dressing-room clock. No one seemed to mind particularly, not even the officials. It was an occasion of such exuberance that I am not sure that anything would have been said if we had burnt the Surrey pavilion down.

For Bill Edrich and I it was an occasion of happiness, the most desired culmination of two careers which had always run in the same double track, beginning together, likely to end together, but for the first time in a period of seventeen years' cricket seeing the Ashes won for England. And we had been at the wicket. It was our first real taste of victory. We went on the town. So far as I can remember we had quite a few drinks. I know that Maurice Winnick gave us the hospitality of his flat that night.

Others too had special cause for celebration: Bedser, for example, who did not get any wickets in the last Test but who, with the then record of 39 wickets in a Test series, had laid the foundations of victory and was now the finest medium-paced bowler in the world; and Trevor Bailey, for determination, coolness, and gamesmanship; and Lock and Laker, with their 9 wickets between them in the second innings of that triumphant Test—linked alliterating names which were to have no music for Australian ears.

Lindsay Hassett, certainly like his team not feeling depressed, celebrated with us that evening. Ever since I had been playing in Test cricket against the Australians I had been playing against Lindsay, and after the end of this tour we would not play against one another again. Lindsay had a placid even temperament, and a way of saying things deadpan, which were amusing and full of humour, the full extent of which he didn't always appreciate. He didn't look like an athlete because he was small and neat; but he was an artistic batsman who had a way of making runs quietly, with beautiful timing, a tickle here, a little leg-cut there, a gentle push somewhere else, in a way which you hardly noticed, and when you thought he had made 6 runs, or maybe 10, you looked up at the board and saw that he was 40, and not long afterwards very likely he would get his century. He had a magnificent defence, could play as well as Sidney Barnes on a bad wicket, and often produced some very elegant shots. In his time he had played some wonderful innings for Australia.

Lindsay played cricket the hard Australian way, to win at all costs; he didn't give you that impression at first sight, but that was how he played because he had been taught to play it that way. He had learnt a great deal under Don Bradman, and he was never a dull boy himself—in fact, he was a very bright boy indeed. On the field he flickered to and fro, in his neat way, in complete control, issuing his orders, knowing exactly what he was doing, wittily, whimsically and quietly.

He liked beer, but it never put weight on him. He was a witty after-dinner speaker, and he knew how to handle the Press: he never told them anything he thought they shouldn't know, no matter how much they might want to know it, and yet he kept them good-tempered and well disposed towards himself and his side, and satisfied. He was popular with everyone, English and Australians.

He was a capable, efficient captain, skilled in the knowledgeable school of the greatest of all captains, Don Bradman. If his team had lost the series, it wasn't through any fault of his; the tide had turned now and was flowing strongly for England.

I would be sorry to see Lindsay go back to Australia, I decided that celebrant evening. It reminded me that my career too must be coming to an end, before very long.

But I had a few years left yet.

CHAPTER IX

BOTTLES IN THE SUN

IT USED to be said that the men of the Royal Navy were Britain's ambassadors abroad, wherever they went. These days, in the Commonwealth and Empire at least, it looks as if their place has been taken by Test cricketers.

Before we sailed for the West Indies in the autumn of 1953 the players were brought together at Lord's, and Sir Walter Monckton, as he was then, gave us a talk about the kind of difficulties which might lie ahead of us on the tour of the islands. It was pointed out that the political situation was in some places a delicate one, and our attention was directed to that more intangible and more explosive thing, the difference in the colour of men's faces and the sudden sensitivities to which it might give rise. We were asked very courteously not to provoke any incidents. We listened as intelligently and attentively as we could.

We ran right into a heavy storm. By some stroke of genius somewhere it had been agreed that we should spend a fortnight playing cricket in Bermuda. In that place there really is a colour bar, and no mistake. It's most unfortunate, but it exists. When we got there we found that there were two cricketing organisations, one for men with white faces, and another for men with faces of a different colour, and it was the latter who had invited us and were organising the game during our stay. That, of course, meant a total boycott of play by ninety-nine per cent of the Europeans in the place. We were in it, right up to the neck.

Not the least of our difficulties was the fact that we were staying at an hotel where the colour bar operated strictly—and embarrassingly—for it meant that we couldn't even invite our coloured hosts round to meet us there, for discussion about things or just socially, because they wouldn't have been allowed in. As a result we had to go and meet them elsewhere.

The games were played on a concrete wicket in Hamilton, which is over on the other side of the island, three-quarters of an hour away from the centre of the population. It was too far for most of the coloured people to come apparently, because not many did come; the white ones stayed away; so we played cricket before a man and a dog.

If the tour was to have been organised at all, it should, if possible, have been run jointly, under the auspices of both organisations. As it was, it would have been better not to have gone.

To crown it all, the short tour was an utter financial flop.

It was a bad beginning.

The tour which followed was fiery, violent, contentious; and yet of all the tours I've been on this was the one I would least want to have missed. I loved playing cricket in the West Indies. It was my first and last tour there. Part of the reason that I liked it so much was because it was so massively controversial. In the islands we played on a wonderful batting wicket, fast and true, and that of course greatly affected the pace and quality of the game. Out there the batsman finds he can time the ball more predictably than any other place in the world. The wickets are produced in a different way—instead of rolling them lengthways they are rolled shortways, backwards and forwards across the wicket, which has the effect of binding the soil more closely together, so that it will last longer than most of our wickets, longer even than most of the Australian wickets. It will produce a fast as well as true pitch. We did not have the misery of playing on any feather-bed wickets when we were in the West Indies.

Even more important, the West Indians are stroke players, after the manner of Worrell, Walcott and Weekes; basically, they are all attacking batsmen: they are most unhappy people indeed if you try to keep them quiet, and if you do succeed in imposing quietness on them you should get them out soon after. It's very, very seldom that you see dull or uninteresting cricket from a West Indian side. They enjoy hitting the ball, and making spectacular sensational strokes to their adoring crowds' delight. On the tour we were to see Walcott in full cry, scoring hundred after hundred, and it was a glorious sight.

Cricket is not and should not be allowed to become a sedative for tired business men. No doubt it's pleasant for your busy man after a hectic day in the city to be able to say to himself that he's weary now, after the anxiety of negotiations and the fulsome pleasantry of a business lunch and the continuing telephoning, and it would be nice to go for an hour or two to Lord's before the close of play, and relax, glance at the play, read a little, go to sleep. And if he goes to Lord's, sometimes the kind of cricket he will see will help him to sleep, and banish the trials and tribulations of the day; but it's not my idea of cricket. My idea is the West Indian idea of cricket: colourful, attractive and exciting, with spectacle of entertainment for the crowd. Our cricket spectators, if they could have been transported (as the ancestors of some of those who watched had been) to the West Indies to see some of the cricket played in that series, would have said to themselves, I'm sure: "We haven't ever seen anything like this before. What a really wonderful game this cricket is. . . . We hadn't quite realised before what it is we've been missing. . . ."

I used to like fielding to those West Indians, and to watch the exciting drama of their play. Sometimes I have been bored fielding for days of dull grim cricket; but never in the West Indies. There, neither fielder nor spectator is given the opportunity of boredom; all the time something is happening to gain and keep his interest.

Of course, the West Indian crowd has the greatest enthusiasm for the game of any crowd in the world. You get the impression that nearly every West Indian goes to watch the Test—those who can't get into the ground watch it from outside, perched up among the pale green leaves of the palm-trees, like coco-nuts, which if hit might be dislodged in a black and brown shower. Also, I think the West Indian crowd is the most knowledgeable about cricket in the world, far more knowledgeable than the Australians, for instance, and certainly to some extent more so than ours. If you played a good shot in a match watched by them you got your applause, and you knew it was for the right reasons. It was a kind of incentive to bring out your best strokes.

Cricket, it has been said tiringly often, is part of the Englishman's religion, and perhaps it is; but there can be no doubt that it's the whole of many West Indians'. I remember, in the colony match at Georgetown in British Guiana, I was fielding on the boundary, and an old man with a very black face, wearing a white paper hat, left his seat and came down to the barbed wire, almost beside me and looked at me smilingly for a moment. Then he said: "Massa Compton . . ." he paused for a moment, looking at me brightly, and then went on: "Massa Weekes, Massa Worrell and Massa Walcott come first, and the Lord above comes second."

The West Indians are enthusiastic for cricket, and highly educated in it. I shall always remember the first time I went to the nets in Sabina Park, the ground in Kingston, Jamaica, to put in some of the solid practice and experiment to which I have always tried to give a great deal of time. I was greatly surprised that before long I had more people watching me than you find watching a county game in England, thousands and thousands of them, keen knowledgeable people, who considered our strokes with the eyes of connoisseurs. In a way it was an exhilarating experience, certainly a most encouraging one. They had come along, they said, to watch the "white masters". Unconsciously perhaps they were using the word master as the French use "maître" in its application to a great poet or a musician or a painter: that was just about how they regarded cricket.

It was at Sabina Park too that I had my most exciting experience of West Indian enthusiasm. In our first game against Jamaica, the spectators threw a firework on to the field every time a four was scored, and in seconds the outfield was sparkling with hundreds and hundreds of small explosions. It put you in mind of one of those great Chinese festivals, with dragons; perhaps there was a Chinese element in the crowd—later, as I was to find a little to my cost, there was a Chinaman on the field. I was sorry when the authorities stopped the firework pitching because they considered it dangerous. I was intrigued by it: it was rather like throwing pennies on to the stage when the act pleases you.

On a drive through any of the islands you could see plainly the evidence of the spread of the love for the game. Going through thickly wooded country you occasionally came upon a very small clearing, and you would see that it was occupied by tiny little West Indian boys playing cricket with verve and originality. I stopped once or twice to watch, and found that they made their own rules which varied from clearing to clearing. In one, for example, if the ball was hit up into the trees, and stayed up there, you were out, caught.

Of course, it has to be remembered that the West Indians are an excitable, emotional, combustible people, and we were to get the strongest evidence of this as the tour progressed. We saw a good deal of the other side of the medal.

We had begun badly by visiting Bermuda, and we began badly when we arrived in the West Indies, in Kingston, Jamaica. We were greeted by the West Indian officials and representatives of the West Indian Press and were then taken to an hotel where there was no colour bar, and where, not happily as it turned out, we were to have a kind of reception combined with interviewing and general talk about cricket and the tour which we were beginning.

Almost at once, the Press attempted, and successfully, to hall-mark the tour. It was going to be for the championship of the world, they said: when the West Indies were last in England they were victorious; since then the English had beaten the Australians—so this series must be for the great championship of the world. Whoever would win would be champions of the world. Immediately a nervous tension and conflict had been introduced into things, and you could see that there was something grand and expansive about the idea which infused itself into the minds of the Press representatives themselves, with startling exhilaration.

But when the next day and all succeeding days they ran the story in that mood, at high temperature, it had a most stimulating and exciting effect on the minds and hearts of the ordinary West Indian readers and cricket followers, and, before the first game started, the atmosphere had become taut and explosive, one in which anything might, and did, happen, where small incidents, especially if seized on and written up by the Press, would develop into major situations. We shouldn't have started like that—it's quite right and proper of course to have a keen desire for victory—but when grand notions of world championships are tensely introduced at the moment of a visiting team's landing, especially in a place such as the West Indies, an air of excitable ambition tends to rise only too quickly, an air which can very rapidly become one of violence and hostility. The start had an ominous look about it.

Len Hutton's attitude didn't make things any easier; in fact, I think it quickly made them a good deal worse. Almost from the start, even

(*Central Press Photos*)

MY INNINGS BEGINS AS PATSY HENDREN'S DRAWS TO A
CLOSE

1936, against Surrey

BILL GOT 2000 PATS, I GOT 800: VICTORY AFTER 15 YEARS
TOIL

After winning the Ashes, Oval 1953

SIR DONALD: KILLER INSTINCT

SIR LEONARD: JOYLESS CONCENTRATION

NEGOTIATING A RUN

(Sport and General)

NEGOTIATIONS COMPLETED

(Sport and General)

HARVEY, CAUGHT TRUEMAN: LOCK SCALES HEAVEN
WITH JOY
Leeds Test, 1956

GODFREY'S NOT OUT: RAY LINDWALL YELLS IN AGONY
Melbourne Test, 1950

perhaps from that evening of arrival, he seemed determined to meet the West Indian determination to be champions with a harder, grimmer determination of his own to be captain of the new world champions. He seemed to want to be a non-mixer too, to keep away as much as possible from the West Indian players, not to meet them off the field, and as things got worse and worse, as incident after incident built up the pressure of antagonism and hostility, he seemed to retire more into a shell of reserve and aloofness and to become even less accessible. The West Indians, perhaps more sensitive than most about that kind of thing, were very conscious of it, I know, and I am sure it complicated an already difficult task.

In my view we should have accepted wholeheartedly the fact that we were ambassadors from the senior country, as it were—the home country, for it is as such that many West Indians most loyally regard us. I think this attitude particularly necessary in countries where various changes are taking place in political and social organisation. We should have gone out of our way to be friendly to officials, players and pressmen; should have mixed, conversed and given the most favourable impression that we could manage in the circumstances, so that in the end, whatever their initial feelings might have been, the West Indians would have said that we were a pretty good bunch of chaps, and would have adjusted their wider attitude accordingly towards the country which had sent us out. We should have endeavoured to give the impression that we wanted things to go smoothly and were determined to make them go smoothly.

On a tour there is every possible opportunity to create a good impression, or a bad one, as the case may be. The team attends numerous functions, and it is there that a visiting side, especially perhaps a visiting English side, should make a special effort, by the exercise of ordinary friendliness and courtesy, to make themselves pleasant to their hosts, and through them to the country that is entertaining them. Some functions may be dull and dreary, and often after they are over you may say thank heavens that's finished; but while it is on, every attempt should be made to promote friendly relations.

To do that, I think, was part of our job and in the interests of cricket. Indeed to have done it successfully would to my mind have been more important than winning the series. As everyone knows, we were lamentably bad ambassadors, and I don't attempt to acquit myself of blame in the matter.

Fred Trueman by his behaviour on the field had a substantial share in making difficulties for us, right from the start. Len Hutton had told us that here we had rather an unpredictable boy, a fiery character —but we were to leave him to Len, Yorkshireman to Yorkshireman, as Len, apparently, understood Fred and could handle him. I never got the impression that Len had the faintest notion of how to handle him.

Fred Trueman, then, took some handling: now it is different, but then he was quite a problem player. A bowler, particularly a fast bowler, is no doubt entitled to his exclamations of disappointment when the batsman misses and the ball brushes past the wicket, or is edged and the catch not taken: Miller, for example, could be expressive and Lindwall could look very expressive indeed. But Fiery Fred brought exclamation and expression and demonstration on these occasions to a new and extraordinary level.

He would stand poised in the middle of the wicket, hands on hips, a most intimidating expression on his face (it almost frightened me, quite apart from the West Indian batsman), and used language which was both unusual and colourful, and could be heard at least by the batsman. On occasion the wicket-keeper, if he hadn't held what Fred, alone perhaps, had considered to be a chance, would come within the scope of vigorous expletive. Fred seemed to like being the centre of attention on these occasions, even to consider that it was quite an amusing joke.

I think he was the only one who saw a funny side to his behaviour. His fellows of the M.C.C. side by and large did not, and the West Indians used to be incensed, and showed their feelings in jeers and boos and answering demonstrations; this seemed to egg Trueman on to greater expressiveness and colour in his language, and as the tour went on he got worse and worse, rather than better and better. His behaviour had the most unfortunate effect on the game and on the atmosphere in which we played it, and I'm sure Fred Trueman regrets now what happened then.

He wasn't, of course, the only one who had a bad effect on the crowd—Tony Lock's natural enthusiasm and expectancy as he bowled didn't exactly please them; but Trueman roused them and incensed them regularly.

Frankly, I don't think that all the blame for what happened as a result of his behaviour should be allowed to rest on Trueman's shoulders alone. My own view is that if someone had talked to him pretty sternly at an early stage in the tour, giving perhaps an indication that there was a regular service of boats and aeroplanes going back to England, we would not have seen very much more of his offending antics and demonstrations. Len had told us to leave the problem to him as captain, and it didn't appear that he had done any, or any effective, talking. From what we could judge, Len seemed almost incapable of controlling Trueman's behaviour in the field.

I tried to exercise some discipline over him on one occasion, I think with some success. It was at Barbados, in a colony match, at a stage when I was leading the team, Hutton having left the field. Trueman's language on that occasion lacked nothing of its customary vividness, to such an extent that I felt obliged to call him over before the others and to tell him quite plainly that if he didn't behave himself I'd at least try to ensure that he'd be on the next boat for home. It had some effect, I think, and I know that Fred was penitent afterwards. Of course, he was very young, and there was very much in the atmosphere which anyone would find exceedingly provoking. Experienced as I was by then, I found a lot that was most provocative.

The way the West Indies umpires who stood in the game carried out, or didn't carry out, their duties was perhaps the most provoking thing of all. I don't entirely blame them for what they did, because they were very much under pressure from an irresponsible section of the crowd. What happened at Jamaica in the First Test Match will illustrate the point with peculiar vividness.

Holt was at the wicket, his score 94, in the first innings, and Statham was bowling to him. He played at a ball, missed, went right back on his stumps, and was struck on the pad. Statham appealed, and the umpire gave Holt out. It was plainly and obviously the right decision, but the crowd didn't like it and expressed their dislike with multitudinous vociferation. Holt left the wicket and, we thought, the incident was over. It was far from being over: that night a group of West Indians set upon and assaulted the umpire's wife and their small son.

It was not exactly an aid to impartial umpiring.

In the Fourth Test at Trinidad one of the umpires was a gentleman whose name was E. Achong. He and I were involved in a particularly explosive incident which I set down as it happened, without comment.

The opening stand in the West Indians first innings between Holt and Stollmeyer had realised 70 runs, and the regular bowlers didn't look as if they were going to part them in any reasonably near future. So Len threw the ball to me, and I went on to bowl; let's see if you can break the partnership, Len Hutton's expression seemed to say.

By a freak of fortune perhaps, I did break it: I got Stollmeyer caught and bowled for 40 runs. Everton Weekes was next in, with less than ten minutes to go for lunch. Could I, I wondered, get his wicket too, or Holt's? If I got this powerful, aggressive little man out, or if I got Holt out, I really would have contributed something of importance to the game.

The thought or mention of my bowling usually puts a smirk on the face, and very naturally. I was an occasional bowler, who specialised in the unpredictable. It worked like this: as soon as I was put on to bowl, the batsman tended to relax and, slouching in his false sense of security, might lose concentration, and his wicket. The sight of me running up to bowl seemed to have a restful effect on batsmen. They would feel the same kind of relief at seeing me take the ball as I would seeing Miller or Lindwall having it taken from them. I might bowl anything—a full toss, a ball which bounced three times; anything, including the good one which was so unexpected that it often got the wicket of relaxing batsmen. I was occasional in the sense that I occasionally bowled a ball which did everything I wanted it to do.

That morning before lunch was one of my occasional mornings, and I bowled a googly to Holt which did what I intended it to do, and Holt edged it into the slips to Graveney, who caught it. It wasn't a difficult catch, and it unquestionably was a catch. Holt, however, stayed at the wicket, which I thought was more than a little odd.

I looked at him pointedly, but he seemed unembarrassedly fixed in his crease, with no sign of moving away in the direction of the pavilion. Perhaps he hadn't seen what happened. . . . My astonishment grew.

I turned to Mr. Achong, who was umpiring at my end, and I said to him: "It's quite obvious that Mr. Holt isn't going to leave the wicket—but he edged that ball and Tom Graveney caught it: isn't he out?"

"No," Mr. Achong said, "Mr. Holt is not out . . . the ball touched the ground first."

It was one of those very, very surprising replies.

"Dear, dear, me," I said, meaning a great deal more.

Tom Graveney was looking towards me, and I said to him: "No, Tom. . . . He's been given not out."

In a moment of irritation Tom flung the ball to the ground, before the eyes of 40,000 people, who saw it and didn't approve. They didn't hear Tom say: "Well, I'll be damned. . . . How do you get these fellows out?" But Mr. Achong heard him, and duly noted it. It may be that the expression Tom used was a little stronger than the one I've given here.

I bowled the remaining ball of that over and we walked off the field to the sound of jeering and booing. In the pavilion the members stood up and jeered us all the way to our dressing-room. It was an unpleasant experience, but it didn't end there. Mr. Achong made a complaint to the West Indian Board, and they had something to say, and the Press had a very great deal to say. The English, it appeared, were unsportsmanlike in a big way. It is the first and last time that I have ever been jeered by a crowd.

It wasn't the only incident in that Test. Later on, when Everton Weekes was about 40 and Trevor Bailey was bowling, he made a stroke at one outside the off stump and hit it very hard—everyone in the ground must have heard the sound of it—and Godfrey Evans took the catch behind the stump. How was that? we said. "Not out," the umpire said.

I couldn't leave it there. No doubt I was at fault, but the thing seemed so blatant to me (and I'm told that Everton Weekes afterwards admitted that he had hit the ball) that I went up to the umpire. I was in a sarcastic mood.

"Well," I said, "this is a very different game from what I've been used to playing. . . . Perhaps you have different rules. In England, if a batsman hits the ball, and the wicket-keeper or another fielder catches it before it touches the ground, we feel that's out. . . . Obviously, you don't."

The umpire went over to Hutton and complained of the way I'd spoken, not without justification.

But we insisted that he should give us an explanation. "Will you tell us," we asked, "why you gave him not out?"

The reply was roughly this: "I heard the noise of the ball on the bat, but I did not see the deflection."

There was a good deal which not only Fred Trueman but the rest of us could have found provoking, but I don't think we should have allowed ourselves to be provoked.

The Fourth Test was an unhappy, unpleasant game, and it was perhaps just as well that it was drawn. The kindest memory that I have of it is the phrase of a vivid West Indian journalist, who, speaking of the 133 runs that I got in the first innings, said that Compton hit the ball through the covers with the force of a thousand bulls. Once or twice since I've felt that they were all in china shops.

By and large we got on well with the West Indian officials, but there was one whose unhelpful attitude didn't do the game much good, I thought. He was a Mr. Ray, the secretary of the Kingston Cricket Club in Jamaica, or at least he was the secretary then.

Len Hutton and Godfrey Evans and I had brought our wives out, and they were staying at an hotel at Montiga Bay as the guests of the proprietor, who very naturally asked us if we could get some tickets for him and some of his friends for the First Test Match at Sabina Park. We said that of course we could get tickets, and when Len and Godfrey and I drove up to the ground before play on the first day the hotelier and his friends were waiting, as we had arranged, outside the ground. Len, as captain, had many things to do, and I agreed to take our friends into the ground and to get them their tickets.

I brought them upstairs into the stand and asked them to sit down and make themselves comfortable while I went in search of Mr. Ray and the tickets. At that moment Mr. Ray appeared.

"Who are these people?" he said to me, not very politely.

"Oh, Mr. Ray," I said, "these are friends of Mr. Hutton, the M.C.C. captain, you know. . . ."

I explained how they had come to be there and that our wives were staying at Montiga Bay, and that I had just been going in search of him to get tickets when he'd turned up. Could I have the tickets now, please, I asked.

Mr. Ray was very definite in his reply.

"They're not allowed in here without tickets," he said. "Have they got tickets?"

"Obviously not," I answered, "else why should I be asking you for tickets for them?"

"They're not allowed in here," Mr. Ray repeated. "They must get out."

Mr. Ray was very insistent indeed that they should get out, and I was equally insistent that they should not. There was quite a battle of words and wills, and in the end I got the tickets from someone a little more important than Mr. Ray. It seemed an odd way to treat the friends of the M.C.C. captain, and the incident did nothing to help an atmosphere which was already at that early stage tightening up in preparation for incidents of hostility.

Mr. Ray was later, in the Fifth Test Match, involved in another incident. The Governor arrived at the ground with some pomp and ceremony, and when he'd gone in, his chauffeur parked the big car and walked into the ground, leaned up against the post, and began to watch the game.

Before very long, Mr. Ray came over and asked him for his ticket, and the chauffeur said he hadn't got one. An argument of some heat developed, which Mr. Ray ended by hitting the chauffeur on the jaw so that he had to be carried, prone, from the ground.

In that first Test in Sabina Park we seemed to play our cricket in handcuffs. Len, influenced perhaps by the challenge issued, as it were, on that first day of arrival, had frequently insisted, or at least had laid great emphasis, on the desirability of defensive careful play against the West Indians, presumably to make certain, if not of winning, at least of not losing. I think it had a most unhappy effect on our play in the First Test Match, particularly on that of young players such as Peter May and Tom Graveney. I know it certainly had an effect on my own, although I shouldn't have allowed it to have.

It wasn't effective—I think the cautious defensive way seldom is effective; and we lost the game quite handsomely. We were like medieval knights, playing in defensive armour, and we soon were unhorsed and helpless. The sooner we threw the ironmongery away and played our natural game the better.

Perhaps our most lamentable performance was in the first innings of the Second Test Match at Barbados when we made 181 runs all out and had the remarkable distinction of compiling 128 from 114 overs in one whole day's play on a wicket which was full of runs. This was even worse than handcuffed cricket: it was paralysed cricket, and what with failure, the panning we were getting from the Press and spectators, and the dour atmosphere of defence, the morale of the team had just about touched rock-bottom and the mood was almost of despair.

It was time we did something, and some of us went to see Len Hutton about it. It was time, I pointed out, to throw away our chains and to allow the stroke players to play the game their own way. Watson, May, Graveney and myself must be encouraged to attack, otherwise we were, quite obviously, very hopelessly in the cart. Len said then that he wouldn't interfere with such a policy, and so a new plan went into operation. We were to attack, and attack we did.

We needed to get 495 runs to win on a wicket on which a lot of runs had been made and in which a number of enormous cracks had been opened by the heat. In the result at one stage when we were 250 runs for 3, just before I was out to an l.b.w. decision for 93 runs, there seemed to be a strong possibility that we would get the runs; in fact, after a sudden collapse which followed we ended with a total of 313, 182 short of victory; yet we had made runs, and made them well, and quite quickly. We had showed ourselves what we could do, and we, not anyone else, were the ones who needed showing.

By this stage, and perhaps for most of the rest of the tour, I don't think Len was quite his usual self. He was coming in for a great deal of criticism and had been told he should exercise more control over his players, and I think that in any event the responsibility of the job that he had was beginning to weigh him down. I'm not sure that he always felt equal to or able to cope with the many situations which arose with such explosive frequency. It was a heavy task for any man to have to undertake, and Len did everything that he could. For a time he seemed to become even more silent and withdrawn and taciturn.

However, in the Third Test, in many ways, things brightened up for us. There was no reason in the opposition we were meeting why we shouldn't do very well indeed. For instance, Ramadhin was no longer the mysterious menace that he had been in England, when it had been as good as impossible to read him, to distinguish the leg-break from his off-spinner. In the brighter light and against the brighter background of the West Indies, it seemed to be much easier; either that, or the mystifying little man had lost some of his mystery. I found, and a lot of us found, that now we could see his leg-break, and as soon as we could see that a great deal of his menace had gone. He bowled very well indeed, and so did Valentine, but there was nothing in what they bowled that should make it impossible, or even very difficult, for us to score impressive totals.

The Third Test was the turning-point. In the first innings we made a lot of runs, 435 in fact; Len got 169, I got 60, Bailey had 40, and everybody contributed something. Then the West Indians went in and we bowled them out for 251. Statham bowled most effectively, getting 4 wickets for 64. He was bowling fast and very accurately, and was able to get a lot of lift out of a wicket which would not respond in that way to anyone else. He was a far better bowler on that tour than Fred Trueman, who, perhaps because of the circumstances to which I have already referred, seemed to lose a great deal of his control and accuracy. He still had a good deal of pace and hostility, but he was no longer as effective as he might have been.

The West Indians had tried hard to avoid the follow-on. The stage had come when Holt and McWatt were at the wicket and their eighth-wicket stand together was worth 99 runs. In Georgetown, British Guiana, where the game was played, McWatt was the local hero, even if my black-faced friend with the white paper hat had not included him in his pantheon. Then something happened which seems amusing now more than anything else, but was intimidating then, not least to the West Indian players at the wicket who knew their spectators and their potentialities a little more intimately than we did.

To understand what happened it's helpful to know something of the ways of West Indian spectators. They are great gamblers on the game. For example, if a man is 40, they lay bets on whether he'll get 50. One of their own bowlers has taken 4 wickets: they'll bet he'll take 5; or if he's got 5 wickets for 50, they'll gamble on whether the batsmen will score 80 runs off him. It's the sort of crowd where I should have thought a racing man like Keith Miller would find himself very much at home.

When Holt and McWatt were at the wicket, a stage came where there would have been three things on which the local devotees of McWatt could have had a gamble, and, as the game went, it looked as if they were the kind of gambles which would pay off. These things were: would the two at the wicket break the record stand for the eighth wicket; would they get a century stand; and would they save the follow-on? They had already, when the incident occurred, broken the record; the stand was now worth 99, and 1 only was needed for the century; and 47 runs would save the follow-on. It was a nice situation for a man who had doubled up on his betting; he'd already won on the first gamble, the second was as good as a certainty, and the third—well, anything was not only possible but probable now. There must have been quite a number of people in that crowd who stood to win quite a lot of money, and who, if the later evidence of bottles meant anything, may have been celebrating a little in advance, with a natural, and added, exhilaration.

The ground was absolutely packed, the crowd was expectant, excited, ready to burst out into applause and jubilation at a century partnership.

Then McWatt was hopelessly and utterly run out: he was half-way down the wicket when the ball was received and the bails were removed. The umpire gave him out—there was no other possible decision—and McWatt was on his way back to the pavilion. A thousand bets had been lost. A local hero, for the moment, had been dethroned.

Someone yelled disapproval and threw a bottle on to the pitch; then someone else, and someone else and someone else. Packing cases were added to the bottles. Soon it seemed that everyone was throwing bottles, and they came on to the field in thousands. The mood of the crowd developed quickly into a kind of frenzy and it spread like a bush fire round the ground. It spread even to the West Indian Press, some of whom also threw bottles.

The mounted police were called out and tried without much initial success to restore order. From the middle we watched them carrying out an unhappy task. It didn't feel particularly comfortable where we were. Everyone was yelling and shouting and screaming and jeering, and the bottles were still arriving. I remembered the occasion in India when my revolutionary friend had been so charmingly insistent that play should end. That had seemed a relatively peaceful occasion compared with this.

A West Indian official came on to the field and Len Hutton went over to him.

In effect the official said: "Mr. Hutton, this situation looks dangerous, and I think the game should be brought to a halt for the time being. Would you please bring your players off the field and let's wait until the crowd settles down?"

Len never had a greater moment than when he replied. He was cool, nerveless, courageous, quite unconcerned about the demonstrating crowds which surrounded him in angry thousands.

"No," Len answered, "I'm not leaving the field . . . I want another couple of wickets before the close of play tonight."

It was superbly defiant. It was, if you like, the saying of the century. It was characteristic Len.

There was about forty minutes left for play, and when the game was resumed Len did get his couple of wickets, off West Indians who seemed to be more anxiously watching the simmering crowd than the bowler who was bowling to them.

Len was not the man to miss an opportunity of enforcing the follow-on.

At close of play, when stumps were drawn, the umpire who had given the decision against McWatt, who was a very small man, left the middle like lightning, making for the pavilion and the police escort that would protect him. I shall never forget the speed with which his tiny little legs moved as he went flat out across the ground, hoping to get to safety before the crowd got to him. I am glad to be able to say that he did, all the more so because he was only a last-minute choice as umpire. He had police escort to his house, and a police guard on it all night.

Things were difficult for umpires on that West Indian tour.

Next day Len enforced the follow-on, and we finally won by 9 wickets. After that we had the Fourth Test at Trinidad, which was drawn. There we played our only Test on a matting wicket. The wicket is formed from a mixture of clay and sand, which is watered, and then the matting, close-woven and off-white in colour, is pegged down tightly over it, stretched to its utmost. It makes a hard, perfect, predictable wicket, off which the ball comes at the same height whatever the length, and if it turns, it turns always by the same amount. It makes for mechanical predictable batting. For the first half-hour, if you haven't played on matting before, it's a little strange and difficult, but after that it becomes relatively easy.

The amount of lift and liveliness in the pitch can be controlled by the wetness of the ground underneath. It was the practice to lift the matting at a certain time every morning, before play started, to water underneath it, to roll the ground, and then to relay the matting. In the Test Match at Trinidad the time for doing this was 8.30 in the morning. One morning during the Fourth Test, arriving early at the ground, we found that the ground staff had been repairing a hole dug in the ground the previous day by King, the West Indian fast bowler, and had inadvertently failed to water the pitch at the usual time and in fact had not done so until 9.30. If the game had started at the usual time this would probably have meant a livelier and more favourable wicket for the West Indian bowlers, especially King, but we insisted that the resumption of play should be postponed by three-quarters of an hour, to give the wicket time to dry out.

From there we went back to Sabina Park for the Fifth Test, the one which, if they won, would make the West Indians champions of the world, as they liked to term it.

It was late summer in the West Indies when we played this last Test. During the game it was very hot at Sabina Park, a humid heat, of the kind which I like and which agrees with me. It is rather the same kind of heat you get at Durban; more pleasant, for example, than the burning heat of Adelaide or Johannesburg, which seems to dry you out, makes your skin taut, so that you feel burnt up, like a shrunken skull. In the humid heat you perspire freely and need to change all your clothes at least twice a day, and three times if you can. At British Guiana, below sea-level, it was so humid as to be like playing in a Turkish bath.

Some players, of course, people like Tony Lock, for instance, are greatly affected by the heat, and Len Hutton was also to some extent. I usually feel better in that type of weather, provided a few simple precautions are taken, such, for instance, at Sabina Park, as wearing a singlet to provide some protection against the cool breezes which sometimes blow in off the sea, and make your clothes cling uncomfortably and coldly. Sabina Park is on the landward side of Kingston, but as you play you are conscious that the sea is not very far away.

The ground is surrounded by palm-trees which seem to isolate it from the suburban territory in which it is placed. The pale green leaves of these trees curve over loosely from the centre of the tops inwards to the trunks below, leaving a cup in the middle where the enthusiastic spectators seat themselves to watch the game. Sometimes, in their vividly coloured shirts showing up brightly in the sunshine, they made the palm-trees look as if they had burst vividly into flower.

The pavilion is a tropical styled building, and the facilities there are excellent: first-class dressing-rooms, shower-bath, ordinary bath, everything which can make the game of cricket pleasant in the great heat. The building is placed parallel to the wicket so that when you watch the game from there you get the same kind of view of the play as you would from the Tavern at Lord's or from the score-board at the other side of the ground.

The ground at Sabina Park is not a very large one, and they put up temporary stands for the duration of the game to accommodate 25,000 people or so who can watch from inside the ground. I always had the feeling, looking over at them when I was fielding, that these temporary structures might collapse and be consumed by some kind of spontaneous combustion in the enthusiasm and the heat, like those stands which were ceremonially burnt down at Ceylon, according to tradition, after a game against the M.C.C. team on its way to Australia.

The game at Sabina Park was the calm after the storm. By then the goings-on had been the subject of concern and inquiry at Government House level, where a very serious view indeed, I believe, had been taken of what was happening. I think the action and influence from there had had a calming effect. The Press had probably written themselves out, over acres of pages of newsprint, in thousands and thousands of largely pointless sentences. They had pulled out all the organ stops, and done every cliché in the book to death, and there was practically nothing else they could say. The atmosphere in which we played was serene and courteous and good-tempered. It was a good way to end the series. To some slight extent it made up for what had gone before. The boxers had been called together in the centre of the ring and been told to fight cleanly.

We lost the toss—an important thing to win at Sabina Park—and the West Indies went in to bat. Then Trevor Bailey did one of those unexpected things which we have come to expect him to do: in 16 overs he took 7 wickets for 34 runs, in a brilliantly intelligent piece of bowling—and we had the West Indians all out for 139.

It was a perfect wicket, and there didn't seem to be any obvious reason why Trevor should have been so successful. I think he discovered very early in his spell that he could move the ball a little off the seam—I remember he bowled Everton Weekes with one which came back just enough to beat the bat—and bowling over the top, with his arm close to his head before delivery, he was able to make the maximum use of it. It was, I think, an instance where a bowler who is not very fast, like Bailey, can have the advantage of a really fast bowler like Trueman or Statham, because with the wicket helping only slightly his pace gave the ball time to move a little, whereas Trueman was too quick and his delivery skidded through straightly. I am sure, too, that Bailey governed his pace with just this consideration in mind. It was a typical example of how he makes the maximum and most intelligent use of not very exceptional natural ability.

We made 414 in our first innings. Len made 205 in an innings of the most superb concentration; nothing seemed to disturb him, and he carried through in his own distinctive way, completely master of the situation. You couldn't say that he dominated the game, but he went on and on with unrelenting concentration to a most vital total.

I was batting very well when I was out, for the second time in the Tests that I have played, in rather a strange way. King, the West Indian bowler, was bowling me four or five bouncers an over; he was a tall lanky chap, with a short temper, and that day he was bouncer-happy. At one stage I had already hooked two of them for four when he came up with another one, rather faster, which was on me before I could really get into position. I got quickly out of the way, overbalanced, and my trouser leg knocked one of the bails off.

As I got up, I was asked by one of the West Indian players if I was all right, and I said yes I was, and then he said: "Well, I'm afraid you're out." And so I was; the umpire had given me out.

It was a marginal decision and might have gone either way. The rule, which is perhaps a little difficult to interpret, says that if a bail is dislodged by a player in the kind of manner in which I had knocked it off, then the batsman is out if he was attempting a stroke at the time; if he was not, then he is not out. The previous time this had happened to me was in Nottingham in 1948, when I was 184, and Keith Miller in bad light bowled me a bouncer which when I saw it at a late stage was making straight for my head; I hurriedly got out of the way, overbalanced, and fell on my wicket, and was out, just as I was at Sabina Park.

The West Indies did better in the second innings, getting 346, but that left us needing only 72 runs to win and we got them easily. Tom Graveney, who opened, was quickly out, but Watson, the other opener, and May got the runs without difficulty. In that innings I noticed once again the power of Peter May's play, and remembered a particular instance of it which I had seen in the First Test. To begin with, he had been a little tentative and uncertain. He shaped an attacking stroke at a ball from Ramadhin, seemed to hesitate, but found he had committed himself and went on with the stroke, not getting to the pitch of the ball, but going right through it, and lifting it out of the ground with tremendous strength for six, his first scoring stroke in that innings.

And so we evened the series, and it was a drawn contest. The West Indian Press, I think, were disappointed that there was no champion of the world.

Joint champions seemed a pretty dull kind of condition.

CHAPTER X

CRASH LANDING

IN THE West Indies I started off badly and finished up strongly, in really good form, and my knee seemed to be holding out well. I thought I was having a new, if short, lease of life. I had come through the last bad patch I was to have, back almost to my earlier style of cricket, and in a way I felt that I was on the crest of the wave again.

It wasn't so with Len Hutton, who came back, I think, jaded and overtired and strained with the responsibility of captaining the side in the West Indies. He captained the England side against the 1954 Pakistanis in the First Test, missed the next two in which, I thought rather strangely, David Sheppard not Peter May was captain, and came back into the side for the Fourth Test at the Oval. Len looked badly, almost as if things were too much for him, and in a sense I think that they were. He seemed to be very disturbed in himself, and it may be that if he'd been more willing to seek advice he would have found his burden a great deal easier to bear. In those circumstances it was all the more amazing and creditable that his performances with the bat in the West Indies had been so superb. He'd had an average of 78 runs and a total in eight first-class matches of 780 runs.

In the Nottingham Test against the Pakistanis I made 278 and felt that I had become repossessed of all my old form, of that carefree sense that any stroke I tried would succeed; it was an exhilarating, stimulating experience, and I remember feeling that it was almost like being back at Benoni again. The innings gave me tremendous satisfaction, even although made against only moderate bowling on a perfect wicket. I played all the shots that were in the book and some that were not, and enjoyed myself. It was the kind of enjoyment I'd been in need of for a long time.

I was bowled by a young boy of sixteen called Khalid Hassan of whom I am surprised not to have heard since. He had a nice action

131

and a good leg-break. I've often wondered about him, and hoped that he hasn't had his talents strangled with over-coaching or wrong coaching. Of course, he may have lost it, as young bowlers often do.

When I was his age and learning the game, no one did very much to try to perfect my style, as the expression goes. As long as I hit the ball for four, they said, that's fine, that's the object of batting. Of course, good care was taken to see that I had the fundamental qualities: you must bring the bat up straight, get your body over the ball, watch it on to the bat until the last second, and achieve perfect balance for your strokes. Those are the really important things: if you're orthodox about them you can be as unorthodox as you like about the rest. In fact, in my experience, after you've got those things right it's best to let your natural ability have its way. No one is going to be technically perfect. And if you haven't got the natural ability you could be coached for ten years, eight hours a day, and you'd still be no more than competent, even if you were that.

I know of one particularly disastrous instance of over-coaching in the case of Ian Bedford, who in the 1947 season at the age of seventeen played for Middlesex and achieved great success, and, indeed, looked like a world beater; but after a winter's coaching he came back a completely different bowler, with a changed action: he'd lost his accuracy, lost his length, lost his flight, and in fact never really did very much in first-class cricket again. It was in a way a tragedy.

In any event, unorthodoxy so called, which so often results from tapping the vein of natural cricketing ability, is very frequently a more effective type of batting, if only because it presents more problems to the man setting the field against the unorthodox player and to the bowler who is going to bowl to him. The unexpected is likely to happen, and likely therefore to result in a scoring stroke which would not, in the same circumstances, flow from the orthodox bat.

The Pakistanis drew the series with us, and I would be more pleased about it if on their return home they had not sought to rely on that as evidence that they were up to the standard of the England team. Plainly they were not, and the weather was their greatest friend in saving them from defeat in other Tests. The Fourth and final Test at the Oval which the Pakistanis won was pleasing for two reasons. First of all, Fazal Mahmood against top-class opposition, though on a wicket which favoured him, got 12 wickets for 99 runs, and it was a reward for a hard-working season without a great deal of support. He was a bowler rather like Alec Bedser, a glutton for work, and capable of bowling a more than useful leg-cutter.

The other thing was that Godfrey Evans captured (and I have always thought in his case the word is particularly appropriate) his 131st victim in Test cricket, beat Oldfield's record and set up a new one: thinking back on it now, and remembering that I saw Godfrey from the 1946 Test series in Australia onwards, I can see that it was inevitable that the record should fall to him. He is a genius behind the wicket. His reflexes are so quick that he turns perfectly good strokes on the leg side into what he makes to appear as easy catches, and I have seen him by amazing anticipation dismiss the surprised batsman with such brilliance that I have felt it was almost inhuman, and, in a moment of sympathy with the victim, after a manner which was hardly cricket—but only because no one had been able to do the impossible before. Godfrey is a showman, a crowd-drawer, an inspiration to the side, particularly if the mood is gloomy— then in the dressing-room Godfrey will raise morale with his confidence and refusal to be beaten. He is a great help to the bowler and devastatingly effective, the greatest wicket-keeper ever, in my opinion. He works hard, enjoys a party, and lives with great energy and verve.

In the 1954 season I saw Frank Tyson for the first time in the game against Northants at Lord's in the middle of July. I had heard about him, but neither Bill Edrich nor I expected that he would have the pace he turned out to have. In fact, I found that he was quicker than anything that I had ever before played against.

Bill was a beautiful hooker, and there were never many people who could hit him when he was hooking, but Frank Tyson did, on that first occasion. He bowled a short one, and Bill was back there on the line to hook it all right, but sheer pace beat him, and the ball struck him on the jaw and he had to retire for that day. Bill told me afterwards that he'd seen speed then which he'd never experienced before. Next day, of course, being Bill, he was back at the wicket trying to hook Tyson again.

Tyson was really fast, and also an intelligent person, and although you could see that he had a lot to learn then about control and accuracy, it was plain that he was quite exceptional, and a very hopeful prospect for England—just the thing, Bill and I considered, for the forthcoming tour in Australia. Some said then, in quite legitimate criticism, that although he was full of pace he didn't always know where the ball was going—to which I felt the reply was that in that case the batsman wouldn't either. He was strongly built, with powerful shoulders—just the man we wanted. I heaved a sigh of relief when the selectors finally decided after some hesitation, I think, to send him to Australia.

I didn't go with the rest of the team to Australia, but followed them out by plane a month later. After some discussion with the M.C.C. it was decided that, though my knee had been serving me quite well up till then, yet as I could feel it beginning to trouble me once more, it would be better to give Bill Tucker a month or so to work on it and get me into the best possible shape for Australia. I used to go to the Charing Cross Hospital three or four times a week for brief five-minute sessions of deep X-ray, and then to Bill Tucker's clinic for special exercises designed to build up the strength of the quadriceps muscles in my right thigh. The stronger they were, the less strain would be placed on my right knee. In any event, particular care had to be taken to keep those muscles at full development, as they could get out of condition very easily and very quickly, if, for example, I was failing to walk correctly or was limping.

At the end of a month Bill Tucker had my knee in good condition and it was time to take off by plane for Australia. I suppose a personal legend has grown up about my being late for various appointments, founded to some extent on fact, as when I arrived at London Airport to board a Comet for South Africa, and the girl at one of the desks pointed out of the window and said to me: "Mr. Compton, your Comet. . . . If you look out of the window you'll see it. . . . It waited for ten minutes, you know, which was rather generous, for a Comet." I looked out of the window and saw it fading into the horizon. I had thought I had plenty of time and had stopped for tea on the way to the airport.

This time I was punctual, but either I hadn't had, or my records showed I hadn't had, the correct number of inoculations, and the airport doctor quickly jabbed the relevant needle into my arm. I think in fact I had had the full number, but had lost the record. Anyway, now I was doubly immune.

My travelling companion was a friend who was very keen on cricket, and who had broken down in health and was coming to Australia to relax in the sun and to watch cricket. We flew by Constellation to Beirut and Karachi. We arrived over Karachi Aerodrome about midnight; we didn't land but kept circling and circling and circling until we began to feel that it was more than a little odd. Then there was a sudden tension among the passengers in the plane as we realised that something had gone wrong. First of all we were told that there was another plane in the circuit and after a while someone said pointedly that he'd never known a plane so long in the circuit. Then the navigator came out from the cockpit and said that the trouble was that they couldn't get the nose wheel down. They'd have to throw the plane about a bit, he said, to see if they could loosen it out.

For what seemed a long time they threw the plane about, sickeningly, diving, climbing, gliding, jerking, after which the navigator came out again and told us it was no good, the nose wheel still wouldn't come down, they'd have to make a crash landing. Meanwhile they'd circle a bit longer until they'd used up some more petrol. We circled, I think, for another three-quarters of an hour. It must have been getting on for two in the morning by then. I glanced at my friend. It wasn't much of a rest cure, but he seemed to be supporting it remarkably well.

We fastened our belts, took the children on our laps, and braced our feet on a firm base to counteract the jolt that was coming, and heard the emergency doors open. The main wheels were lifted and the pilot put the nose down and we started to glide in. On my lap the young boy I was holding gripped on to me tightly. We could feel the cool night air coming into the plane.

There was a tearing, grinding, scraping noise, a fair amount of bumping, and we were down: a perfect landing by a pilot who had formerly been in flying-boats and knew what he was doing; and then the cabin was filled with sand as if we were in a storm in the desert.

I heard the Cockney voice of the steward, speaking coolly: "Right, ladies and gentlemen: I want you to unfasten your seat belts, and proceed to leave the plane." Then his control left him and through the sand we heard: "And for Christ's sake hurry up." We made for the bar. I had a whisky, which I needed, and my friend had a ginger ale. He had come through it well. Next day the plane's engineer was killed when the plane collapsed on him because of a faulty jack with which he had raised the fuselage in order to examine it. It was a gloomy ending.

My friend and I flew on by Calcutta, Singapore and Darwin to Sydney, and I got a plane to Adelaide, where I was met just after lunch-time by Godfrey Evans and Bill Edrich. I had been flying for seven days and I was desperately tired. All I wanted was sleep, and I went to bed and slept right through almost without a break until the next morning, when Len came into my room and asked me if I'd like to play in the match that day. He seemed a little doubtful, wondering if I should put in some practice first. "I'll get practice in the game," I said, and told him that I'd play.

I played, and helped the M.C.C. to win against South Australia by scoring 113 runs in the first innings. It was perhaps the most unusual hundred I ever scored, made in, or perhaps after, the most unusual circumstances.

For the First Test Match at Brisbane we made all the wrong decisions, and the result for the M.C.C. side, and for me for different reasons, was disaster. Up to that point I had been doing well: I felt I was at the peak of my form. I had two hundreds and a score of over sixty in the matches in which I had played, the last game before the Test being at Brisbane, against Queensland, on a strip of turf only a few yards from the one on which we were to play the Test. It was, we noted carefully, a fast green wicket, and we predicted the Test wicket close by would be exactly the same.

We then took a bold decision, and decided to play four seam bowlers: Statham, Bailey, Tyson and Bedser, and to leave out the spinners. We also, having won the toss, remembering the Queensland game and the fast green wicket, decided to put the Australians in first. With a side stuffed with seam bowlers we hoped to make an early break-through and to get them out for a moderate total or less.

The Australians went in. In a very short time it was apparent that the wicket was completely different from the Queensland wicket: it was docile, placid and easy paced, and the Australians made an endless 601 runs on it for 8 wickets, Morris, Bedser's old bunny, getting 153, Harvey 162, and Lindwall thrashing a typical 64 off despondent and exhausted bowlers. Frank Tyson bowled 29 overs, and got 1 wicket for 160 runs: he couldn't have had a worse beginning against the Australians. We lost the game catastrophically, and were a gloomy and despondent side. All the decisions we had made had been the wrong decisions. Len had made them after discussion with his vice-captain and committee, but they were hopelessly ill-judged. It was, I think, a very clear lesson, showing the intolerable risk of going into a match with an unbalanced side. If seamers were going to be effective, two would have been sufficient, and the two spinners would have given us the essential variety. I was a party to the decision: it was a very misguided one.

I went in last in both innings because fielding at fine leg and chasing a ball towards the boundary I had attempted to steady myself by catching hold of the fence while moving at full tilt, and I caught my finger in the paling, broke it, and was out of the game for a month. It was a maddening thing to have happened at that early stage, a product of ill-luck and carelessness. It was all the more frustrating because then I felt at the peak of form. However, I batted because even though the situation seemed hopeless I considered that there was a possibility, even if only a remote possibility, that a Brisbane storm might come down and end the game. If I managed to stay a short while at the wicket I thought that I might ensure that we'd still be in the game if and when it happened: but it didn't happen. We were trounced.

At least, however, we had achieved this: that nowadays if anyone should suggest going into a game with one type of bowler only, the idea can be scotched sharply by referring to that great disaster at Brisbane. It was a lesson for posterity.

I played squash and did a lot of running, and tried to keep fit while the broken bone knitted together in the plaster which surrounded it. I kept with the team and attended the game because, particularly at that early stage of the series, I considered it to be of importance that I should do so. I was fresh, and there was therefore no reason for me to be away from cricket. Furthermore, it is a good thing to stay in the developing community of a side, to help to form and to share their mood and spirit and, in addition, to note how the bowlers, ours and theirs, were performing. It was galling to be out of the game, but the next best thing to playing was to be with the players.

The Second Test at Sydney was a wonderful game for many reasons; so too for that matter were the Third and Fourth at Melbourne and at Adelaide. For England they meant excitement, joy, achievement.

At Sydney we didn't pack the side with seamers. Alec Bedser was in fact omitted: he had suffered a depressing and lowering attack of shingles at the start of the tour and it seemed reasonable not to include him. None of us had any inkling of what was to result from his being left out. Alec and I watched the game from the pavilion. We saw something which for many years we never thought our eyes would have the good fortune to see.

When we started badly and were bowled out for 154 runs it looked very much as if the Australians were going to resume, perhaps with an even added permanence, their old ruthless ascendancy. When we got them out for 228, so that we were only 74 runs behind, things looked a little better, however, the more so because not only had Bailey, as usual, pulled something out of the bag when it was really needed and taken 4 wickets, but Frank Tyson with his new run had also taken 4 with some beautiful bowling. In the pavilion Alec and I began to feel a bit better.

But not for very long. Soon, in the second innings, Graveney, Bailey and Hutton were out, and with 55 for 3 we still hadn't wiped off the deficit. The Australians had their tails right up again, and watching them out in the field you could see that their confidence was chin high. As we watched Cowdrey walk out to join May at the wicket, I was nagged by the old familiar misgivings. Another wicket—and why not Cowdrey's, the new boy of the side, the baby, young, inexperienced, untried—and the game was as good as in the Australian bag, or pouch. The old, old story.

I hope I may be forgiven such thoughts: in view of what soon started to happen they now seem inexcusable. Almost at once you were conscious that a new Test batsman had arrived. Colin Cowdrey ("Kipper" to his fellow cricketers because of his sensible fondness for resting on his bed whenever possible) was serene and unhurried right from the start. He had the clear hall-mark of a great player: he always looked as if he had plenty of time to play the ball. Miller wasn't playing in that Test, but Lindwall, Archer and Bill Johnston were; and Cowdrey, large, almost portly looking, but quick-moving at the wicket, played them as if he had all the time in the world. As you watched him you even began to think that the bowlers were bowling rather slowly.

Peter May and Cowdrey put on 116 runs together, Cowdrey being out when he was 54, after having as good as saved the game for us with May. Then Bill Edrich and May had a stand of 51, and before we were out we had 296 on the board, which included a bowler's stand between Statham and Appleyard of 46 runs for the last wicket. Peter May had made a masterly, quick and essential hundred. We were 222 ahead. It was better than 122, of course, or than 150, but as I watched the Australian opening batsmen go out to the middle it seemed to me that for a side of their strength 223 wasn't a lot of runs to get, on a lovely batting wicket too where they were now about to take strike.

Frank Tyson had no such depressing thoughts in his head. In oppressive heat he bowled fast and accurately and with sustained power, and he took 6 wickets for 85 runs in 18·4 overs, and the Australians were out for 184 runs, and the game was ours. We had evened up matters. Between Brisbane and Sydney, Frank had accepted advice. Your run up, we had told him after the First Test, is far too long, especially in this tiring heat: by the time you get to the wicket you're on your knees and you can't do yourself justice. Try and shorten your run, we counselled, and Frank, our advice taken, went off to the nets and with intelligence and humility worked the thing out for himself. He came into the Test with an economical run, and with all his devastating power and fire intact. He had acted boldly and courageously and at a critical point in the series it paid off handsomely.

As the Third Test was due to start at Melbourne, Len Hutton's nerves began to give. For a long time you could observe the signs of strain on his face and in his behaviour. It was not surprising when you remembered the size of the load he was carrying.

On the morning of the match some of us went to his room in

the hotel at 10.30. Len was still in bed. He seemed to be in a very disturbed state indeed as if suddenly things had got too much for him, and he couldn't or wouldn't go on. Bill Edrich, Godfrey Evans and myself stood and sat around his bed in some bewilderment and dismay.

"I am not feeling too well," Len was saying. "I'm not feeling too well . . . I don't think I can play today." He said that and similar things a number of times. His confidence and some of his control seemed to have left him.

If he wasn't going to play, the result could be disastrous. We were one-all in the series now, and every game was vital. If Len didn't play, it would give a tremendous lift to Australian morale and confidence, because though out of form up to that stage, they still regarded him as a most formidable obstacle to their designs and ambitions. If only for that reason he must, if possible, be persuaded to play.

There was a very long discussion between the four of us, and the time for the start of play at noon got appallingly nearer and nearer. Finally we persuaded Len at least not to make a decision at that moment, but to leave his bed, have a bath and come down to the ground with us. Then perhaps he might be in a better position to come to a more reliable decision.

Not long afterwards we were sitting dejectedly in a corner of our dressing-room at the ground waiting anxiously to see what Len was going to decide. He looked a troubled, exhausted person, and I had a slight feeling of unreality and weirdness as I sat there watching and waiting and wondering what was going to happen. I had the impression that Len would have liked to get away from it all, from the atmosphere and the strain and the burden of responsibility.

In the end he said quite suddenly, in answer to our continuing attempts at persuasion: "Yes, all right . . . I'll play."

We sighed, partly with relief.

But the time for relief was not quite yet. There was still the question of who was going to play in the side in less than an hour's time. Alec Bedser was in the twelve players named, but, plainly, in view of the success of Tyson in the Second Test, and the way Statham had been bowling since the series commenced, there was the gravest doubt as to whether he could properly be included for this Third Test. Godfrey Evans was against including him, so was Bill Edrich, and so was I. The ultimate decision, of course, was Len's, but he had yet to make it. He had about forty-five minutes left in which to do so. It was to be a terminal moment in big Alec's career.

Len called me over and asked me to take Alec out to have a look at the wicket and then to tell him what Alec's reactions were. Alec and I walked out to the wicket, both of us, I suppose, a bit mystified, myself a little concerned about the whole thing as I had played so long with Alec and had seen him develop so tremendously as a bowler that I couldn't help feeling a little melancholy about the fact that this might be the last time he would walk out to a Test wicket against Australia. Every career in Test cricket, I could say, must end some time, but that doesn't make it any easier for any of us.

Out in the middle we stood and looked down at the wicket, and tested it with our thumbs. I asked Alec if he thought he could bowl well on it, and he said yes, he thought he could: it seemed much the same as all the other wickets he'd bowled on in Australia—he was used to them. "I'd like to play," he told me, "if I do, I'd be trying," he added, "I'd be trying." It was always a certainty that Alec would be trying, whatever the odds.

We went back to the pavilion, and I told Len what had happened, and repeated my view that Alec should be left out, and Godfrey and Bill said the same. Eventually Len decided he would not include him in the side—and that was that. It was a most difficult decision to advise upon or to make, and I couldn't help feeling sorry about it, especially as the trip to the wicket must inevitably have raised Alec's hopes. But the team had to come first, and I'm sure the decision was right.

Everything might have been tolerably pleasant, even at that late stage, if Len had gone to Alec and given him the decision himself, and told him the obvious reasons. But it didn't happen that way. The first Alec knew about it was from the little sheet of paper with the team list on it which he saw pinned on the door of the dressing-room. That was how he became aware of the decision; so far as I know that was all he was ever told about it, to this day.

It was almost a bitter ending to the Test career against Australia of a great bowler and a valiant man. As the Australians took the field and the game began you couldn't help feeling a kind of gloom about things, with Len apparently exhausted and without all his usual nerve, and Alec so tactlessly, even woundingly, omitted from the side.

But nothing save exhilarating success was ahead of us in that game. We got 191 in the first innings, with a lovely 102 runs from Cowdrey's bat. He played beautifully, and as he played I watched one of the really great innings I have seen in my career, and there haven't been all that many. Colin was a new and brilliant star.

Then, as if to underline the correctness of Len's decision, Statham came through with a fine piece of bowling, taking 5 wickets for 60 runs, and achieving the kind of result which his accuracy and pace and lift deserved to have more consistently but which in a strange way seemed unjustly to elude him so frequently. Some Australians went so far as to say he was Tyson's equal, if not in some ways a better bowler. He wasn't so fast, but he was consistent and accurate, and always made the batsman play especially with the new ball, but also with the old. Certainly, one at either end, they were a havoc-making combination. We had the Australians out for 231 and they were 40 ahead, still a hopeful position for us. Peter May got 91 in our second innings, and everyone in the middle order getting some runs, we made 279. The Australians needed 240 runs to win—for most Australian sides a very possible task.

They started batting in the morning, and we settled down for what we thought would be a hard struggle; but it was all over by lunch-time and they were out for 111. Frank Tyson, incredibly powerful and accurate, consistent, ascendant, had taken 7 wickets for 27 runs in 12 overs. In 79 minutes the Australian innings was over. Not long after one o'clock we were drinking champagne in celebration in the dressing-room.

That day Frank Tyson completely demoralised the Australians. I had never thought I'd see an Australian cricket team demoralised, but Frank had done it before my wondering eyes. For some time he had been gaining an ascendancy over them, and now, in this game he mastered and dominated them completely, at the age of twenty-three. For particular batsmen he really slipped himself. I remember in that second innings when Keith Miller, tossing his hair back, was leaving the pavilion and coming out towards the middle, I turned to Frank and said: "Frank, here's Keith. . . . He can be a dangerous batsman if he gets set. . . . It's always nice to see the back of him. . . . If you were really to give him one, the first ball . . . you know. . . ."

Frank nodded, knowingly. "I think maybe you're right," he said, "let's see what we can do." He turned and with characteristic flinging-outwards of his feet walked back to take his run. Keith took guard, looked around at the field and waited for what was to come.

What did come was perhaps the fastest ball I've ever seen bowled; it wasn't a bouncer, but it was pitched a little short of a good length, and it went past Keith's cap like a rocket. Fielding where I was at mid-off, I found the pace of it disturbing, and I rather fancy Keith did too. Not long afterwards, after a nervy unhappy-looking innings, he edged a ball from Tyson to Hutton at slip, who couldn't hold it; but it hit his hand, went up in the air, and Bill Edrich caught it. Next, Tyson had Neil Harvey caught by the impenetrable Evans behind the stumps, and the Australians were on the way out, fast. By the end of the game we had made up for our disastrous start and we were two-one up. If we could win the next game at Adelaide the champagne would go down with an even greater propriety.

Before we went to Adelaide we crossed the sea to the green tidy little island of Tasmania, which is such a homely change from the brown soil of Australia. It's a cool island, attractive to look at, and puts the bronzed and parched Englander strongly in mind of home. The cricket we played there was friendly and not too strenuous, and everybody entertained us. On Sunday we could have a day's fishing, even if all of us were not great fishermen, in the wide harbour of Hobart. I enjoyed myself, and was in good form, and kept my eye in with scores of around 50. When we left I was refreshed and so were most of the others, as if we'd had a week's holiday.

At Adelaide, always my lucky ground, I hit 182 runs in my innings against South Australia in the game before the Fourth Test, and found that I was almost back in my best form. The long lay-off because of my finger hadn't helped me much, and I had only had a few innings since I'd returned to the team. Now everything seemed all right again, and I was eager to get going on that Fourth Test.

We lost the toss and Australia got 323 in their first innings; Maddocks, in his second Test against us, made 69 runs. He played extremely well and held us up for a long time and for that we found him a most irritating boy indeed. He was deputising for the injured Langley and did it most effectively, though it's doubtful if as a wicket-keeper he had quite Langley's quiet efficiency: on figures Langley was one of the great wicket-keepers of the game. Then we batted and got a lead of 18 runs—negligible in the circumstances. The game, and the series, was still finely in the balance, and it could go either way. The series would be squared or won.

In Australia's second innings we seemed suddenly and devastatingly to put the issue beyond doubt in our favour. On the fifth day Australia started batting with 69 runs on the board for 3 wickets; then Statham bowled Miller for 14, and the Australian innings disintegrated, leaving 111 runs in a scanty pile neatly on the top. We needed 94 runs to win, I calculated, as we walked off the field. Len was walking near me; despite the victory in the Third Test he didn't yet seem to be fully himself again. He still had his troubled and anxious look as he spoke to me in what I found quite surprising terms: "Denis," he said, "I don't feel like going in again. . . . Would you mind going in first?" It looked to me as if Len had almost had enough, as if the mental strain of the whole thing was becoming almost unbearable. As our second innings went on, he seemed to have got worse and worse.

I answered that, of course, I would go in first if he wanted me to, even though I was without experience in that position. We went into the dressing-room and I started to get padded up. After a few moments I looked up and with a good deal of amazement saw that Len too was getting padded up. I went across to him and asked him if he still wanted me to go in first. He replied: "Oh, no, no . . . I'll be going in first . . . I'll be going in first." In a moment of irritation I felt he might have communicated his change of mind to me; but Len seemed so exhausted and so much under pressure that it was understandable that he should overlook things. It was a startling example of the strain which modern cricket imposes.

Then everything seemed to go wrong for us, and it looked as if we might after all lose the game. Len was out for 5, and I can always remember his look almost of anguish as he said to me as I sat there padded up, soon to go in: "The so-and-so's have done it again. . . . This fellow Miller. . . . We're going to be beaten . . . I can see it

. . . we're going to lose. . . ." I tried to tell him that we still had a good chance, but he wouldn't be persuaded and left the little room from which the M.C.C. watch the game, disappeared into the dressing-room, and didn't see another ball bowled. He emerged only when the game was over.

When I got to the wicket there were 18 runs on the board for 3 wickets, all of them Miller's, and Miller was really letting go. He was plainly saying to himself that if they should get two more wickets they'd have us, and the game. He was hostile, very quick, accurate. Off a docile, placid wicket he was moving the ball both ways. It was a typical piece of Miller's inspired aggression: the unpredictable match-winner was in full cry. Peter May and I managed to stay there until we got Miller off—he'd more or less blown himself out by then; but as if to show us he was still there he dismissed Peter May with a brilliant catch off Johnston. Then Bailey came in and we took the score to 90, before he was out. Godfrey, striding out with brisk jaunty short steps, joined me at the wicket and bet me five bob he'd make the winning hit. He did, and the match was ours. I had 34 of the most satisfying runs I have ever made. It was a very close thing; afterwards Bill Johnston told me that when we were 3 for 18 he was quite confident of victory, and those hard-fighting relentless Australians never let up until we'd taken the score past 70.

It had been 1932 when we'd last won a series in Australia, so that it was time to uncork the champagne bottles once more. We did, in large numbers, sharing about sixty bottles with the guests in the hotel twelve miles or so out from the centre of Adelaide where we were staying. It was a triumphant, hilarious party, enlivened with song. At some time, I can't quite remember when, some of us left the hotel and went to the house of friends who had been most generous and hospitable to us each time we had been in Adelaide. There, in a sudden disconcerting moment, we discovered that we'd lost our star, our match-winner, our typhoon: he'd come with us, we did know that, but he was no longer with us, we could see that. Someone suggested, awesomely, that perhaps he had gone out and lost himself in the endless bush near by; we searched. Before long we found him.

He was stretched out under a sofa, breathing gently, peacefully asleep. How he got under there we never could quite make out, but he had. And after what he'd done towards victory we reckoned that Frank Tyson was entitled to his sleep, under a sofa if that was what he wanted.

After that to some extent it was anticlimax, and the weather deteriorated in a ghastly manner. We were beaten at Victoria by a New South Wales side captained by Keith Miller. The result set the Australian Press going again with an even greater energy. As soon as their team had begun to be defeated the journalists had attacked their own cricketers with a force and lack of restraint which made me, for once, very glad that this time I was not the victim. Sometimes, I thought, the edge of criticism was so sharp that it was almost vicious, and I couldn't help feeling that what Australians wrote and printed in their newspapers was not helpful either to cricket or cricketers. They really gave their own side the full treatment. Now they took up the Miller-for-captain-Johnson-for-captain controversy once again, with renewed conviction and venom. Miller should have been captain of the Australian side, it was said loudly by some—then things would have been different.

I think they might easily have been different, though not so different as to have turned defeat into victory. Miller was a bold, shrewd and aggressive captain and, of course, had exceptional cricketing ability to contribute to the resources of the side. I doubt if much can be said in support of Ian Johnson's captaincy, on the field at least. Miller, in my opinion, should have had the position, and both experience and ability qualified him for it. It is regrettable, if true, that Don Bradman, implacable spirit of Australian cricket, should have turned his thumb down at the mention of Miller's name for the captaincy of the Australian side. It is equally regrettable and certainly true that the controversy should have been run publicly in the newspapers. It was bound to have and did have an unsettling effect on the Australian side and undoubtedly reduced their efficiency.

The Fifth and last Test, which was the only one drawn, remains in my memory for three things: the weather, Graveney's innings of 111, and the collapse of the Australian side. We didn't get started until two o'clock on the fourth day, and then we went in and made 371 runs; Graveney, previously tense and subdued, now in an elegant confident innings made his first Test century of the tour, and

I remember wishing as I compiled a rather laboured 84 that I could have borrowed some of his ease and fluency.

Then we had the Australians out for 221 in their first innings: they followed on, and then we got 6 of them for 118. If we'd had another hour I think we would have beaten them—in a little more than a day and a half. Johnny Wardle got in amongst them with his chinamen and googlies, and no Australian seemed to have any confidence or to give any appearance that he was going to make any runs.

It was the full incoming of the tide for England, the completion of their victory. If it hadn't been for the rain and floods we'd have won the series by four Tests to one.

The M.C.C. team crossed over to New Zealand and had a successful tour; but I didn't go with them. My month's treatment in England before coming out had justified itself, as my knee had lasted out; but now it was giving me the signals I had learnt only too well to interpret, and I knew it needed a rest, otherwise something very unpleasant might happen. My wife was in South Africa, and, after a short stay with friends in Melbourne, I caught the plane for Perth, and from there I flew to the Cocos Islands in the Indian Ocean on my way to meet her.

When we arrived we were told that there was a storm over Mauritius, our next stop, 2,000 miles away, and that our flight would be delayed for twenty-four hours or so. They were taking no chances with that very, very long hop over the wide ocean.

There wasn't much on the island—an airstrip, huts, palm-trees—but someone organised a game of cricket, perhaps so that I could take part. In the middle of the Indian Ocean, under the fierce sun, on a concrete runway, we played cricket at three o'clock in the afternoon. By then I was bronzed and blackened by the heat of Australia, so I played in plimsolls and shorts—nothing else. In an hour my insteps and back were raw, and in that state I took off late at night for Mauritius and then South Africa. I was hobbling, in a good deal more than discomfort. I couldn't help wondering what my wife would think when I limped from the plane at Johannesburg and she came out to greet me.

As we taxied in to the airport at Johannesburg, which is an enormous place, I could see that it was packed with thousands and thousands of people. No doubt, I thought, as I stared at them, they are here to give greetings to their Prime Minister, or someone like that. Perhaps he was on the plane, though I wasn't aware of it; perhaps he was flying in from somewhere else, at about the same time as our plane was arriving.

But no—the greeting was apparently for my arrival.

I was interviewed by broadcasting officials. Then with my raw back and my raw insteps and my face burnt nearly black by the Australian sun, I hobbled forward to a tremendous reception of clapping and cheering and welcoming shouts. Partly, I suppose, the reception *was* for me personally, all the more so because my wife was South African; but mainly I think it was an expression of joy at the success at last of the M.C.C. team in Australia. In any event, I found it very moving.

CHAPTER XI

UPHILL

IN THE cooling evening, in the summer of 1955, the tall man stamped, leaped and danced, almost in a frenzy, denting the Buckinghamshire turf with his feet. The guests stood and sat around on the grass with drinks in their hands, judging the dance, some of them with practised eyes. A good rendering, someone said, almost good enough to have been done by a Zulu—all the more surprising perhaps because the dancer, fair-haired, 6 ft. 4 in. in height, didn't look in the least like a Zulu. In fact, it was Peter Heine, dancing his favourite Zulu war dance on the lawn of my home on the Saturday evening of the Second Test Match at Lord's, at a party which my wife and I had given for the South Africans at Gerrard's Cross. Afterwards, jokingly, they said the party was the reason they'd lost the Test.

It wasn't the reason—but Brian Statham, in the main, was. In the second innings he took 7 wickets for 39 runs in 29 overs, and bowled unchanged right through the innings in one of the best fast-bowling spells I have ever seen. In fact, I think he took too much out of himself on that sustained occasion and was never quite the same bowler again during the rest of the season. He had used up too much of his resources in one magnificent effort. In the result, we won by 75 runs, and we were two up on the South Africans, after an exciting game. At Trent Bridge, in the First Test, we had won easily, and dully. The South Africans, true to form, were building slowly up to full potential in their 1955 tour.

In the Lord's game in two innings I got 89 runs. I've often had more, but these runs were of particular value to me as they completed my 5,000 runs in Test cricket, and I joined the exclusive company of Hammond, Hutton, Hobbs and Bradman. I played well in that season, and felt myself back on my old form, until the last Test at the Oval, after which I was as good as sure that I was finished as a cricketer.

At Lord's, Godfrey Evans, on occasions with an incredible agility, took six catches off the fast bowlers, and had one stumping to Wardle's bowling. He seemed to be better than ever, if that was possible, standing back and taking catches off the fast stuff which flashed back like lightning from the edge of the bat.

The really exciting Test was the third at Manchester in July. For one thing we saw an innings of 108, in a South African first innings total (8 wickets) of 521, from Paul Winslow, lithe, slim, tall, inevitably dubbed "The Winslow Boy" by the Press, and a beautiful hitter. He hit the most magnificent six I think I've ever seen. He had reached 94, slamming a six here, a four there, and we expected the usual period of subdued tension which comes down on a man as he nears his first century in Test cricket. Tony Lock was bowling to him, and bowling well. Then to one delivery he walked up the wicket, let the full stretch of his arm go in a beautiful swing, timed and middled the ball, and sent it soaring over the television cameras into the practice ground. Now he was a century exactly. I've never seen a hundred so precisely, boldly and beautifully completed.

Batting first, we had made 284 runs, of which I made 158, and had two stands, one with May and one with Bailey. Mine was an innings which moved from the aggressive, sometimes almost carefree, to the very cautious and subdued. It was, I think, a good example of the kind of discipline and control which playing in big cricket must sooner or later impose, when you have to judge the needs of the situation and adjust your play accordingly. And yet, in the second innings, when I joined May out in the middle with our score at 23 runs for 2 wickets, both of us seemed to do the exact opposite of what the circumstances might have been held to require. We both went for the bowling right away, and added 124 runs in 105 minutes, when I was out for 71, Peter going on to make 117.

It was my best innings of the series, and yet might have seemed to be incautiously played, in a critical situation. In the actual circumstances I don't think it was, because both of us seemed on such good form that the bold decision seemed the right one at that particular moment. In cricket there is no rule of thumb: it is too subtle and challenging a game to allow that.

On the last day South Africa needed 145 runs to win in two and a quarter hours, and for a time didn't seem like getting them, although they were going for the runs, until McLean came to the wicket. Frank Tyson was bowling, and no doubt, remembering the terror and success which his bouncers had achieved in Australia, he now sent down three of them in succession to McLean. McLean hit two in front of the wicket and one square, and suddenly had added 12 much-needed runs. He saw these tremendously quick balls early, and wasn't in consequence late on the stroke. Until that moment I don't think that Frank had quite appreciated that anyone could hook with such power and speed.

McLean hit 50 runs in his entertaining, attacking style and was effectively supported by McGlew, a fine judge of a run and an expert runner between the wickets, so that he can take runs off his defensive strokes.

First of all McLean was out, and then McGlew, with 48. Winslow came in and made a fast 16. With Waite and Tayfield at the wicket South Africa needed 10 more runs, with 3 wickets and very little time left. It was a taut climax to a brilliant five days' cricket, and the crowd stood and sat around the ground in a silence stretched and reacting like the membrane of a drum. Then with three minutes to go, and perhaps one over left, Waite drove Tyson through the covers for 4, and South Africa had made the break-through by winning their first Test. The only closer finish I have been in was in Durban in 1948, when we hit the winning run off the last ball of the game.

It was Alec Bedser's last Test against any country, and the end of a powerful and wonderful career. Peter May, in his first season as captain of England, Len Hutton having retired after his return from Australia, was doing the job intelligently, feeling his way through his difficulties and responsibilities, and making his full contribution with the bat and in the field. You could see that he was someone who knew what he wanted, and usually would get it, and he was sensibly expressing his views to the players.

At Leeds in the Fourth Test the South Africans, bearing out fully the promise they had shown in 1951, showed that they were not only a strong batting side, with capable and efficient bowlers, but also that they had a stiffening of real fighting spirit.

They won the toss and went in first. Before very long half the side were out for 38 runs on a placid wicket, on which batsmen should make runs; but then McLean, Endean, Tayfield and even

Heine, the fast bowler, not a batsman, got their backs to the wall and managed to scrape 171 runs together. It was a most unimpressive total, whichever way you looked at it.

But then ours, in our following innings, wasn't a great deal better, and they had us out for 191, by keen and aggressive fielding which once or twice burst out in rare brilliance, and by means of Peter Heine's top-class bowling. There was nothing for him in the wicket; it was docile and without pace; but he put everything he had into that wicket and he got something out, as often happens—4 wickets for 70 runs in fact. The knowledge of his side's vulnerable situation seemed to spur and urge him on, and he bowled with hostile accuracy and all the pace that was in the wicket, and apparently a little more.

In their second innings the South Africans made no mistakes. This time they got 500 runs, with a great fighting innings of 133 from little McGlew and a century from Endean, going in at No. 8.

We needed 481 runs to win, and if we made a run a minute we could do it. It could be done and I'd seen others do it in less time— like Bradman and his men at Leeds in 1948. We started quite correctly and went for the runs, but didn't get them. By the time we'd lost 5 wickets we had only 210 on the board, and the moment had come to settle down to cautious play and the saving of the game. Plainly we couldn't win it; instead we made quite certain of losing it, by continuing to attack the bowling and by almost, it appeared, throwing our wickets away. In the second innings Peter Heine, because of the footholds worn by him and other bowlers in the wicket, was unable to bowl as he couldn't get a foot down anywhere, so that the wickets were taken by Tayfield and Goddard. In my view the fact that the rules don't allow the holes to be repaired operated very unfairly in the circumstances against the South Africans. The rule is stupid and should be changed to allow the groundsmen to repair the holes at the end of each day's play.

By the afternoon of the fifth day the South Africans had won and had squared the series two-all. The final, as usual, would be played at the Oval. If enthusiasm, keenness, a refusal to consider themselves beaten, and a cohesive team spirit could win, the game would be the South Africans'.

At this point the South Africans faced a nasty problem. Cheetham, the captain, had been injured but was now fit to play again. He had missed the two Tests which his team had won under McGlew's substitute captaincy: he had led it in defeat in the two other games. Should he now return to captain the side? Whether he should have done so or not, he did; and when the game was over the repercussions in South Africa were severe, and Cheetham was on a licking to nothing.

At the Oval, as seems to happen so often in recent Test Matches, the wicket favoured Laker and Lock, the England spinners. We won the toss, made 151 in our first innings, had the South Africans out for a meagre 112 in theirs, went back in and made 204, and left the South Africans to get 244 to win on a wicket which was turning.

I didn't field in the South African second innings, and it was a long time before I was to field again. I had been at the wicket in our second innings with Peter May when I felt my knee give way, finally; I'd had some fairly clear warnings from it previously, but I hadn't chosen to pay a great deal of heed to them, and in any case Bill Tucker's deep therapy and heat treatment and massage had kept me going so remarkably well during the season that I had almost come to believe that it would last out until the end; but it didn't, and when I was out in the middle with May it swelled up very considerably.

I was determined to stay at the wicket and make what runs I could, and in fact Peter and I added 62 runs for our wicket; it may be, as things turned out, almost the vital runs for the winning of the game. The problem, of course, arose as to whether I should have a runner, but I decided not to. I was so bad a runner myself between the wickets that to have someone running for me might worsen confusion and turn it into catastrophe. So I hobbled from end to end, no doubt losing many runs, but staying out there nevertheless. It wasn't particularly easy or particularly comfortable.

I was glad not to have to field afterwards, and grateful to Cheetham for not raising any difficulties, as he might properly have done in the circumstances, about the twelfth man fielding in my place. He might easily have said: "Here is a man who has helped his captain to add runs which may be vital runs indeed in this game. . . . We think that he should field." But he didn't say it, or anything like it, or even hint it. I was more than appreciative.

The South Africans began disastrously on that wicket so helpful to Lock and Laker. Four of their wickets were down for 33 runs, all four going in fact while 5 runs were being added, Endean and McLean being given out l.b.w. making desperate sweeps at Laker, although it could reasonably be argued that both decisions were very doubtful ones indeed. But after that they fought back, and Waite in an imperturbable innings made 60 runs before Laker finally bowled him. Not long afterwards they were all out for 151, and once more at the Oval we had won game and series.

Lock and Laker between them took 6 wickets in the first innings and all 9 in the second, Fuller being run out. They had finally established themselves as the best two bowlers in the world on this type of wicket. In the early stages of the second innings the South Africans seemed to panic a little against them, rather as the Australians had done, and were to do; but they fought back, and showed themselves a more determined and a better fighting side against the turning ball than the Australians.

I had had a good season, playing cricket that satisfied me, after the manner of my play in 1947 and 1948. It seemed a pity that it all had to end so suddenly, and so finally as it then appeared to me.

What followed in the next eight months was a difficult time in my life.

First of all, Bill Tucker told me, we'd have to wait until the swelling round my knee had gone down; then there were X-rays; after that Bill called Mr. Osmond Clarke into consultation. Together they looked at me, thought about me, went away and thought some more, and came back and gave me their conclusions, frankly and squarely.

The only possible chance—and it was a thin one—of my ever playing cricket again, or even of being free of pain, was to have my kneecap, my patella they called it, removed. If that was done, there was a slight possibility that I might play again.

I thought a lot about what they said, and I discussed it with my wife Valerie, and thought about it again. In the end I decided to have the operation: even if I never played cricket again at least I'd probably be able to move around reasonably well for other things, and I wouldn't have any more pain or much more pain. So I went on to the operating table and they removed my kneecap.

The operation was performed in University College Hospital, and by what was a strange and rather affecting coincidence Tom Whittaker was ill there when I went in. He left hospital shortly after my operation was over, but returned again after I had left, to die.

At about this time I had a letter which reminded me of that winter's afternoon before the war when I had collided with the Charlton goalkeeper as I was playing for the Arsenal, and I had been carried off and laid on a table in the dressing-room. About five minutes later young Carr, our centre-forward, was carried in and laid on the table beside me. He also, in collision with the goal-keeper, had injured his knee, indeed his injury more or less finished his career in football. We were strapped up, taken home, and then sent to hospital, me for the first of my operations.

I haven't got the letter now, but it went in something like these terms: "Dear Mr. Compton, I am terribly sorry for the trouble that I must have caused you over these years. It must have started with the injury in 1938, and now see all the trouble you are having. I am very sorry indeed." It was signed, "Sincerely, Sid Hobbins."

Sid Hobbins was the Charlton goalkeeper in 1938. It had been a long time.

That was in November. By Christmas I was able to move around a little, awkwardly, with an almost stiff leg. I felt low, and sometimes rather miserable. I had visions of having a stiff leg for the rest of my life, and I didn't like it one little bit. At home I was bad-tempered, a wretched person to live with; I felt frustrated and hemmed in and without much hope. Valerie was patient with me, and tolerant and helped me to an extent beyond the reach of the greatest gratitude.

The trouble was that my knee would not bend properly; I could bend it so far and no further, and not nearly far enough to enable me to move around with anything like ease. I had weeks and weeks of treatment, but it didn't seem to do any good. The knee simply would not bend. It got a certain distance and then it felt as if it had come up against an immovable obstacle, such as a brick wall. It was harassing and depressing. If it remained like that I would never be able to walk properly, not to speak of playing cricket again.

Then in April I had a first glimpse of hope. The Australians had arrived for their 1956 tour, and I had been invited to the dinner which the cricket writers gave to welcome them. Mr. Osmond

Clarke was also there; and during the evening he came over to me and said that he'd just had a new idea about my knee and that he was going to discuss it with Bill Tucker. I wanted very keenly to know what it was, but he wouldn't tell me: he thought it better to talk it over with Bill Tucker first—and I have no doubt that he was right. But there was something about the way he spoke to me, an optimism, I thought, which gave me hope again, and I enjoyed the latter part of that dinner more than the earlier.

Mr. Clarke and Bill Tucker had their discussion and decided to try a different treatment, a rather more drastic treatment. I went to the operating table again, and while under a general anaesthetic they manipulated my knee, forcing it to bend a little more each time, breaking down the adhesions and strapping it for a while in the position of maximum flexion. Until they took the strapping off, it used to be more than a little painful; but I didn't mind pain if I thought I was going to get the use, or some use, of my knee again.

In fact, after the third manipulation, they got a seventy-five per cent flexion, and that, it was considered, was the best that could be achieved; and it turned out to be and remained quite good enough. I remember how glad I was when Bill Tucker told me that if I could retain that degree of flexion I would be able to play cricket again. I was thankful and more than thankful to my two advisers who had taken a bold and imaginative decision.

At first my knee was weak, still weak; but at least it would bend, and I began to have real hopes again. Gradually some little strength came back into it, and I was able to get down to the nets, at first for short spells and then for longer ones, until finally I was strong enough to play in some one-day matches, as, for example, for the M.C.C. against Eton College. I made 60 runs against them, but I was hopeless in the field. I couldn't touch anything a bit wide of me. After that game I was reasonably happy: but I still felt I was no good for first-class cricket.

However, the day came when I felt I could try myself out in a county game, and I did, in July, against Lancashire at Lord's. It was worth it, even if only for the wonderful and very moving reception I had from the crowd, who clapped me and cheered me as I came out on to the field with the Middlesex team. I even bowled a few overs and got a couple of wickets. But after a day in the field in the

hot sun I was just about all in and was limping badly as we went to
the pavilion at 6.30. I was a bit better on Monday, but not much.
I didn't make any runs and I wasn't any good in the field—yet I had
got through the game, which was something. Most people, I know,
wanted to encourage me—in fact, during all that time I was made to
realise how many kind friends I had—but in their hearts I think they
were saying: "No, he won't make it"; and I didn't think I'd make
it myself.

Then I got two centuries: one against Kent at Lord's with Godfrey
Evans behind the wicket encouraging me and having a laugh with
me and talking to me, in his usual welcome style, even as the bowler
was running up; and another against Somerset at Glastonbury,
where I was tickled to death to be able to hold two catches jumping
to my left and where I bowled a few overs. At last, after a bleak
ten months, I began to feel that I was beginning to get somewhere
again.

That apparently was the selectors' feeling too. Before the Fifth Test
at the Oval in August, with the 1956 series against the Australians
already won, Gubby Allen came to me and asked if I thought I was
fit enough to play in the Test. It was a most difficult question to
answer. Deep down, I didn't feel that I was sufficiently fit; and yet
I thought, at another level, perhaps I am—after all, look at those
two centuries recently made—and, further, the Ashes have been
won. Yes, I answered Gubby eventually, yes, I think I'm fit enough
to play.

Before I went in to bat in the first innings, and even as I walked
out to the middle, there was a crowd of thoughts in my mind. I felt
that if I failed, people would say that I should never have played;
that I should have recognised my weakness and that my career
was over, and should have stood aside to let some younger player
have his chance—I'd had long enough at the game and success
enough, and now it was someone else's turn. And then Peter May
was comparatively new to captaincy, and a very young captain, and
must have had his doubts about the advisability of my playing. He
might reasonably have considered that I might be a liability. I was
very anxious indeed not to let him down by proving to be a liability.
Again, some members of the team to tour South Africa in the
following winter had been chosen, but there were still some vacant

places. Would I fill one of them? It depended on what I did when I reached the wicket and began to play the bowling. I very much wanted to be in that side.

Above all, I didn't want to fail. If I did, I would never play again and would retire, leaving the game in the unhappiest manner possible, on a note of failure, with very likely a bitter taste in my mouth. I should have hated to leave the scene in that way. Furthermore, I hadn't been encouraged to make the decision to play; substantially it was my own decision. I must try and justify it.

As I took guard, glanced round the field, and turned to face the bowling, I felt that I was at one of the most crucial moments of my life, and that I was entering on perhaps my most uphill battle.

Wisden for 1957, I see, describes my innings of 94 on that day as a classical Compton innings, and Don Bradman was kind enough to say that it was the best innings of the whole series. For me it was in some senses a cruel and painful innings, though I know my timing was good and I was playing my strokes well. Thank God I've scored those runs, I said: I have faced and overcome the challenge. I'm not sure that any other score I've made quite equals that one in satisfaction and a sense of achievement.

Not long afterwards it was announced that I was in the team for South Africa.

Almost as soon as that innings was over—I was out at about six o'clock—I jumped into a bath, put on a dinner-jacket, and got a taxi to the Savoy, where I was to be one of the guests at a private dinner being given by Sir Arthur Sims, a great lover of the game who played it many years ago. Sir Jack Hobbs, my old hero, was there, and Sir Don Bradman, Sir Pelham Warner and Sir Leonard Hutton, retired since the end of the M.C.C. tour in Australia and the recipient of the great honour of a knighthood.

Len was writing a cricket column in the *Evening News*. He had said, a little oddly, I remember thinking, that I shouldn't be selected to play in the game at the Oval, but that I should be chosen as twelfth man, for what purpose I have never been able to imagine or discover: he could hardly have thought that I would be the ideal substitute fielder if someone were injured or required a rest.

Everyone enveloped me in congratulations, except Len. He wasn't being unkind or ungenerous—I'm sure of that; but as he came over to me he gave me the impression that he hadn't retired at all but was still playing the game, and was still, as I'd last seen him in Australia, getting no enjoyment whatsoever out of it.

"Well, Denis," he said to me, in effect, "what enjoyment did you really get out of that innings?"

For a moment I felt like reeling back in amazement.

"Len," I answered unbelievingly, "Len, you can't really mean that question. . . ."

But Len, apparently, did. "Aye," he said, "didn't you find it ruddy hard work?"

Perhaps in a way I did, but in my elation I had already forgotten it.

After dinner one of the other guests, Mr. Menzies, the Prime Minister of Australia, spoke to us off the cuff, brilliantly, spontaneously, with a subtle understated humour. He was, he told us—and we already knew very well—a great lover of the game. Somehow, he said, since he'd been Prime Minister, it had often occurred that whenever he travelled a great distance, even 12,000 miles, to a conference or a political meeting, when he arrived a Test Match between England and Australia would be in progress. It was, he made us feel, the happiest and most unorganised of coincidences.

Of course, I had met him several times before, and knew his great, almost fanatical, love of the game, and the relaxation and refreshment it gave him to watch it. The last time I'd been in Australia, as on other occasions, we'd played against the Prime Minister's team, and Mr. Menzies had presented each of us with a special tie: a bright green tie, with a yellow stripe. I cherish it, but have found it difficult to discover a suit to go with it.

I enjoyed that dinner as perhaps I have never enjoyed another.

It is both facile and complacent to talk about the superiority of English cricket over Australian at the end of the 1956 series. To be accurate it should be said that on a turning wicket, especially on one that turned from the first ball bowled, England's batsmen and England's bowlers were superior. I don't think the 1956 series justifies any wider self-praise than that.

Of course, Laker's performances with the ball were great performances, and his 19 wickets in one game at Old Trafford in the

Fourth Test is an indelible part of cricket history. It was a great and outstanding performance, and one unlikely ever to be equalled. But it was done on a wicket which turned from the start and of which, in my view, the Australians were fully justified in making complaint and even in feeling anger. I remember watching the game at Manchester on television and seeing the first ball that Keith Miller bowled bounce twice before it reached the wicket-keeper. After that Keith kept his sweater on, and I didn't blame him.

The fair way to look at the whole matter of the English and Australian performances is to consider what happened in the Second Test at Lord's. In that game there was a good wicket to start with, and it remained reasonably good while the game lasted, and the weather held out. It was a very fine Test indeed and Australia won it. Miller took 5 wickets in each innings and, in the second innings, Richie Benaud, going in No. 8 for Australia, made a defiant and unstoppable 97 in the sudden rugged style so typical of his country-men. The result was the right one; the Australians deserved to win; in that game they were the better team. It was the only game in which there was really a reasonable wicket.

I don't say the Australians would have won if all the wickets had been as the Lord's wicket: I don't think they would have done—but the issue would have remained longer and more closely in the balance. Some of the wickets that were played on were not worthy of a Test Match; there was a plush green outfield and in the middle a desert spurting clouds of dust. They were wickets which happened to favour our particular brand of spin bowling and not the Australian brand of Johnson and Benaud. That, perhaps, was just our luck.

Nevertheless, having said all that, I must add that the Australians played hopeless, despairing cricket against the turning ball and their performances were often pathetic. I am quite sure that the English side faced by Lock and Laker on similar wickets would have put up a much more competent show. It could, of course, be said by way of excuse for the Australians that in their country they ordinarily have no experience of the kind of wicket on which they played over here; and yet a number of their players had been here before and had had a good look at our wickets, and should have known what to expect.

Their 84 in the first innings in the Fourth Test Match at Manchester was the worst exhibition of batting that you could ever wish not to see from anyone. From the beginning their attitude seemed to be: well, we haven't got a hope—and they went out to the wicket and just made desperate shots. What they needed, but never acquired or began to acquire, was the ability to play the forward defensive shot, holding the bat with a dropped and loosened wrist, the shot which Len Hutton used to play so effectively. Consequently, because of their inability to play the turning ball not only Laker but also his short-legs had a field day.

For us, of course, it was more than pleasing to see that England had certainly found an opening batsman in Peter Richardson. In that season he confirmed all his previous promise, and I'm sure he will maintain his high standard of performance for many years to come. He is a keen, calm player, with the most serene and matter-of-fact temperament. For him to go to the wicket in a key situation in a Test Match is, it would appear as you watch, merely to take, and enjoy, an afternoon's stroll. And he continued to look like that when he was playing, with nerveless competence and skill. He had a steadying effect on the side, especially on the man at the wicket with him, who could see him treating even the most crucial of Test Matches as if it were just another game of cricket. He is not one of your players who can be seen pounding up and down the dressing-room before going out to bat or hiding himself away in a book. He plays sound cricket and has some very good shots indeed. Nothing ruffles him: if he plays a bad shot and is out he comes quite serenely back from the wicket and may allow himself the comment that the shot was not really a very good one. Other people, myself included, are accustomed to express themselves a little more colourfully on such occasions.

The year 1956 was the last in England of the explosive Lindwall-Miller combination. We shall be lucky if we see their like again.

They were a wonderful pair, and Australia were lucky and should be proud that they came up together, as it were, and lasted for ten brilliant, devastating years. They were also a great contrast—Ray, of medium height, broad and powerful in the shoulders, wiry, tough and hostile-looking, and a very concentrated and craftsmanlike person indeed; Keith, all sparkle, flash, temperament and inspiration, with his lean face and the lock of hair falling down over it, and his tall, agile and powerful build. Both were fast bowlers, both great all-rounders. On the field they bowled together and wrought their joint havoc. Off the field they were friends and buddies.

Ray Lindwall was the greatest controlled fast bowler I have ever seen, as well as one of the greatest all-rounders. He was also the quickest bowler I have ever played against. He had rhythm, grace, elegance, variety, change of pace, swing and the capacity for complete or almost complete concealment of what he intended to do next. I remember when he appeared in England for the first time in 1948 the excited and appreciative conversation of the old-timers in the pavilion at Lord's, who had seen everyone, including McDonald and Larwood; Lindwall, the majority said, was the most graceful, the greatest fast bowler they had ever seen.

What so often impressed me about him was the way he seemed to be able to conserve his energy. He'd come up to the wicket and bowl a seemingly ordinary ball that took nothing out of him and produced nothing in the way of pace, and immediately afterwards with the same elegant, one could almost say gentle, run up he would send one down which was faster than you'd ever seen before and put you in mind of the old advertisement for Shell. He disguised everything he did so completely and so intelligently that it gave his bowling an extra force and difficulty.

His temperament was right too. In his loathing of batsmen he reminded me of O'Reilly—and I think to be effective as a bowler, especially as a fast bowler, you must loathe all batsmen as a man would loathe a natural or traditional enemy. Ray certainly loathed them intensely. Not that he ever expressed it in any way except in the efficiency and brilliance of his bowling. Indeed, for an Australian, he was remarkably taciturn in the presence of disappointment, and would roar only briefly with disappointment or anger at a narrowly missed wicket or a dropped catch.

He didn't have a high action, and he got all his pace from his shoulders and from his body, rather as Larwood did, although certainly at times in 1948 he was considered to be as fast, if not faster, than Larwood ever was. He was a controlled and intelligent bowler who bowled differently to each batsman and knew precisely how to send him down what he least wanted to receive. He could bowl two kinds of out-swinger: one which started early and which you might be able to see, and another which moved away very late and which I thought was his most dangerous ball. By 1950, after taking thought—because he was a player who thought a great deal about his bowling—he had acquired a magnificent in-swinger, one which dipped in late and made you play hurriedly and often so that you were snapped up by one of his short-legs.

His bouncers were most effective, and I found them more disturbing than any bowled by any other fast bowler. Because of his low action they used to skid through head high and were never really pitched short; as a result you had little time to play them, obviously less time to get out of the way—but you had to do something definite, either to duck low or to try a hook. If you didn't, you very likely got hit. It was quite a terrifying experience sometimes.

Not content with all that, Ray could bowl a wonderful slow ball, perfectly disguised. In fact, as I have said already, all his changes were most effectively concealed, and in all the hectic ten years that I faced him I could never tell with any real certainty what he was going to send down to me next.

Like Brian Statham, Ray used and conserved the new ball without waste. He probably did it better than any other bowler of any kind that I ever knew. Each ball he bowled to you, you had to play, because he made you play it, bowling it straight at the wicket. There was never any question of one or two pitched outside the off-stump so that you could pad up and let them go through to the wicket-keeper: not with the economical Ray Lindwall.

In addition he was a forcing batsman, with a full range of strokes, and the kind of dangerous player who could change the course of a game in half an hour at the wicket. I remember him in the Fifth Test Match at the Oval in 1953 when he made 62 runs magnificently, with great hitting, and he seemed all set to do something of the same kind in the second innings when I caught him in front of the pavilion, leaning out over the rails with my feet inside in order to reach the ball. Otherwise it would have been six off Laker. In 1946 he scored a century against us in Australia.

I know that it has been said that in the 1956 series Lindwall wasn't the effective Test bowler he had previously been. I don't think that's true. Admittedly, perhaps, he had passed his peak, and was, it may be, a little reluctant to acknowledge a sad fact which must come at some time to every player. But he was still in my view a most dangerous bowler, and I doubt if Ian Johnson made enough use of him, especially in that Fifth Test at the Oval.

He came on with the new ball and bowled beautifully, and got Cowdrey caught off a flashing out-swinger. After four overs, with the batsmen looking extremely uncomfortable against him, he was taken off and not brought back until the middle of the afternoon. The English players were very pleased and rather puzzled that he wasn't used more. He wasn't fit for the Second Test, fortunately for England, I think; had he been he would have given proof that he was still a very great bowler. The wickets in the other Tests were not suitable for his type of bowling.

Ray was a very good close-to-the-wicket fielder too. In fact, a fully equipped cricketer, a great player and a magnificent craftsman of the game.

Keith, on the other hand, was as moody and temperamental as any artist from Chelsea. Perhaps that was one of the reasons for his being such a fine cricketer.

Like Learie Constantine, he was always in the game, one way or another, either with the bat—and at times he could make runs with consummate skill—or bowling in one of his fiery and devastating spells, or taking some impossible catch at an eight- or ten-feet stretch. When you were playing against him you could never forget that he was there. If you did, he'd quickly remind you of his presence.

He and I, no doubt, were different in many ways, but there was, I think, sufficient similarity between us to make us good friends almost immediately on meeting. As soon as I would walk out on the field with the bat I would see him moving slowly towards me, and as I passed there would be some comment from him, most frequently the immortal phrase which the Indian revolutionary had used. When he was bowling to me, and I hit him for four, he would pause and look at me and say, a little ominously: "Good shot, Denis." Then the next ball would come down, fiery and awkward and hostile, and I would call back: "Well bowled, Keith." With us that sort of thing was a continuous performance.

He was a player of soaring and plunging moods and needed to be provoked or challenged, by a good shot made off him, for example, or by a really difficult situation, before he would really dig down and bring the best out of himself. He might be bowling with his sweater on, as he often did, and he'd send down a bad one which you'd hit for four. The reaction would be instantaneous. Off would come the sweater; it would be pitched to the umpire, and the head would be shot aggressively back. Then Keith would come ambling up with his easy economical run, and the next ball would almost certainly be an incredible delivery in speed and behaviour. He could get the ball up, get it to lift, on even the most docile of wickets, and when he wanted he seemed to be able to make the bat shake in your hand as you played the ball.

His run was a characteristic oddity, and yet a lovely run up in its way, perhaps because of Keith's wonderful build. He never organised it by marking it out or pacing it or anything like that. He just seemed to have a vague idea of the spot to which he would return, and when he thought he was there he'd turn and start on his easy economical way.

He was a man of diverse and inconsistent interests. He liked and was a judge of classical music; after a concert he'd find equal enjoyment in one of the less well-known night clubs. And, of course, he was interested in horses, and expert and knowledgeable about horses; at least about Australian horses, if not so much so about ours. He backed his fancy, whatever it was, with regularity. Often we used to go to the races together when the game allowed. Sometimes, I have suspected, Keith went whether it allowed or not.

He was a diligent student of form, and in the Australian dressing-room he could be seen giving an almost academic concentration and attention to the Racing Bible, mugging up on English bloodstock. Also he had friends who were trainers or jockeys, and they gave him information which they thought might be useful.

When Keith was playing, the Australian twelfth man had a very definite additional function to perform. At Lord's, say, one of his duties would be to go down to the tape and get the results as they came in of the 2.30, the three o'clock, the 3.30, and so on, and then to go on the Australian balcony. Keith would be looking up expectantly and from the tic-tac of the twelfth man would get to know whether what he'd backed had won or been placed or hadn't been heard of. If he had, say, two or three losers in a row, his mood might become despondent, and he might retire to a remote corner of the out-field to think it out.

But I am quite certain that these other interests, various and individual as they were, had the effect of improving Keith's cricket, because they kept him more lively and more interested, and satisfied the varied aspects of a complicated and gifted temperament. He was the better player for them.

Keith, in my opinion, should have been made captain of the 1956 Australian side. He contributed vastly to their effectiveness in every respect, and I am sure if he'd been captain these performances alone, quite apart from anything else, would have given inspiration to the Australian players and would have got even better cricket out of them. Keith could be inspired and could himself inspire. Ian Johnson was a most charming and intelligent person, and, I thought, behaved with great tact in what he must have realised, as everybody else certainly realised, was a difficult situation. I never felt that he made even that minimum contribution which a captain must make to the side's resources of ability. Off the field, of course, he was most diplomatic, an excellent ambassador, friendly, and made excellently witty and humorous speeches; but that, I think, was not enough to have justified his choice as captain. For Keith it would have been the happiest way to end a great career in cricket which had lasted for more than ten years, and I feel it was something which should not have been denied him.

I saw him set off for Australia and a career in television, and retirement, with mixed feelings. My own retirement couldn't be far off now, even if my knee lasted out a little longer for cricket.

CHAPTER XII

BOUGAINVILLAEA AND JACARANDA

IF SOMEONE had said to me: "Well, now, Denis, you've got one more tour to do and it's going to be your last because of old age and what have you. . . . Where would you like it to be?" my reply, unhesitatingly, would have been "South Africa". I have always liked South Africa and South Africans, even before I married into them, and the more so now. Something in my temperament and theirs seems to have a meeting-point, and we get on very well together.

So my luck still held, and my last tour, in the winter of 1956–7, was in South Africa. It was going to be a hard tour, we knew, because by now, in my opinion, South Africa had the second strongest team in the world, second, that is, to us. By the time the tour was over, I wasn't quite so certain about the placing.

One of the things I shall always remember happened on that tour at Salisbury, at the Mayor's reception for the visiting M.C.C. side. I had attended many receptions like it, and so has every cricketer who has gone on tour, and it wouldn't be true if I said that I found each one of them full of entertainment. Many have been a little tedious, and this one went on for too long, to begin with.

The Mayor read a longish speech from a pile of notes which we watched eagerly as it diminished slowly. The Mayor was making a thorough speech, covering all the points, and wasn't going to be hurried. Towards the end he came on to the topic of Peter May's wonderful performances: up to that point he'd had four centuries in four innings.

Then the Mayor paused and looked up from his notes at us. "I," he said, with a touch of drama, "I consider this an opportune moment for me to make my contribution to South African cricket . . . I have a presentation which I would like to make to Peter May."

He reached behind a curtain and something was put into his hand, and Peter came on to the stage to receive it.

It was a live duck. The Mayor presented it with elegant formality, amid laughter, and Peter, all smiles, took it on our behalf. It turned out to be a very evil duck.

We left Salisbury and went to Johannesburg for our first game against the Transvaal. There were 40,000 people at the ground, and as Peter May walked out to the wicket their clapping and cheering seemed to indicate that most of them had come to see him. The South Africans are an eager, expectant crowd, always anxious to see a great player, whether their own or of the opposition. And here was Peter May going out into the middle, the English captain, twenty-six years old, with four centuries in his last four innings.

Almost immediately they were watching him walk back in a surprised, cheated silence. Peter, unhappily, was caught behind the wicket, first ball, off Peter Heine. Already the duck was at its destructive work. "That so-and-so man," Peter said, "and his ruddy duck!"

From then onwards nothing much seemed to go right for Peter. He didn't make very many runs after that, but, strangely, he never seemed to be out of form. The trouble was that if there was any bad luck it seemed to go his way, and he would find himself dismissed in a startling manner. One instance was at Johannesburg in the Fourth Test when, off Heine, Peter played a lovely shot, about a foot off the ground, just in front of square-leg. Endean was a little behind square, about twenty yards from the wicket; he dived powerfully, and body, legs and arms off the ground, at full stretch, grabbed the ball and held it, and Peter was out. It was a magnificent piece of cricket.

For a moment Peter stood there at the wicket, in surprise and amazement, wondering whether what he had seen had been dream or nightmare. Then he realised it had really happened, and he left the wicket and walked back to the pavilion.

The South Africans were superb in the field, and their brilliance gave verve and confidence to their bowlers. Under Van Ryneveld and their manager, Viljoen, they set out to organise to the maximum the admittedly fairly limited ability at their disposal. They were very fit. They practised hard: before Test Matches, and even before provincial matches, they would turn up at the ground an hour and a half or an hour and three-quarters before the start of the game, and when we arrived later we would find that they would all be changed, every one of them, and out in the field, hitting the ball to one another, throwing it, practising catches and so on, going through the whole routine. About half an hour before play started they would come back to the pavilion, thoroughly loosened up, keen and full of enthusiasm, and change again for the day's play.

I think this keenness, and the good performance which resulted from it, produced a very marked increase in the interest in cricket in South Africa and has been very good for the game there. Out there, of course, Rugby is one of the main religions, especially with the Afrikaans. On this tour, however, in great contrast to the previous one I had been on, I found a quite considerable interest in cricket among the Afrikaans, and discovered that they were even teaching it in their schools.

The South Africans were an efficient side with a great deal of confidence among their players: a great fielding side, efficient in their batting, very good in their bowling. Heine and Adcock were a first-class pair of fast bowlers, Tayfield was an accurate and consistent off-spinner, and Goddard as well as being a brilliant slip fielder and an opening bat could bowl tight for long periods. His bowling could quite justly be called negative bowling, and some have tended to dismiss it as being something which any bowler could do, if he set his mind to it. But I don't think so: Goddard would go on and bowl and bowl on the leg stump with the ball coming into you accurately in a way almost impossible to score off; before long you would be in a frustrated state of mind, pinned down, with never a loose ball; then he bowled the one which went the other way, and quite often you'd be out. Occasionally he does bowl this type of ball, in fact, although I don't think he himself always knows when he is going to do so: in those circumstances the batsman is unlikely to know either.

I mention the bowlers in particular because in a way this series was a bowler's series and it should be acknowledged as such. They kept the scores down on what were mostly good batting wickets. It will no doubt sound strange when I say that batsman as I have been, I have often felt sorry for bowlers, not because I may have hammered them, but because they often don't get the credit properly theirs. I have always said that I am glad I was born a batsman, not a bowler.

Suppose a batsman gets a brilliant hundred; then he receives lavish praise and flashing publicity. However, think of a game where the bowlers have been on top of the bat—on, say, a good batting wicket. In that case it is howled that the batsmen have failed; never, oddly enough, thought that the bowlers on form and ability have dominated the bat by their skill. Neither way do the bowlers seem to have it. On that 1956-7 tour of South Africa it was the bowlers mainly who earned and should be given praise.

It was a drawn series and it splits easily into two phases. In the earlier we dominated all the games leading up to the First Test and then that Test and the Second. We seemed to be completely superior to the South Africans. At Johannesburg in the first game we won very easily, and bowled our opponents out for 72 runs in their second innings with Bailey bowling with great success and taking 5 wickets for 20 on a wicket which didn't give him much help. It was yet another instance of the kind of performance we had seen already in the West Indies, of Bailey's capacity for a sudden and surprising success.

The Second Test, at Cape Town, we won, if anything more easily; this time on a turning wicket Johnny Wardle, with 5 for 53 and 7 for 36, baffled and defeated the South Africans with his left-arm chinaman bowled over the wicket. At that stage we looked like the unbeatable champions of the world, and for a time the South Africans suffered a lack of confidence and may even have felt a little demoralised.

But those of us with experience of the South Africans should have remembered that the South Africans nearly always start slowly and badly, and finish with a strong punch.

Cape Town in fact was the end of the first phase; and Durban saw the start of the second. In the Third Test we had the worst of the drawn game, and we saw the South Africans regaining their confidence. We went back to Johannesburg for a beating in the Fourth Test. At one stage we all thought quite reasonably that it would be an easy win for us in that game—and then the series would be ours, three-one at the worst; but it turned out very differently.

In our second innings we needed 85 runs with 6 wickets in hand, and plenty of time. Tayfield and Goddard, however, with their tight and accurate bowling, supported by splendid fielding, soon had us all out for 214 after a complete collapse, to defeat us by 17 runs, before a crowd almost hysterical with excitement and joy. Now it was two–one and the South Africans could save the series. At Port Elizabeth for the Fifth Test we found ourselves playing on the oddest of wickets. The ground staff had worked very hard to make a good wicket, but were completely defeated by some trouble in the soil which they could not cure. In the result large cracks opened in the ground, and the ball played peculiar tricks, such as keeping very low or shooting along the ground or jumping this way and that where it hit the cracks. As the match went on, it got worse and worse, and at no time was it possible to play strokes on it. It was a good game, however, and we lost by 58 runs. The South Africans had ended the second phase, against all the odds, by squaring the series two-all.

By the end of the series I think that Peter May was feeling the strain of captaincy quite severely. He had had a long spell, beginning with the South Africa tour of England in 1955, and now things were weighing heavily on him. He is a serious-minded person, but with a good sense of humour. I thought he took his responsibilities more closely to heart than a more carefree person who was more accustomed not to let things bother him would have done.

The strain showed at Johannesburg when he said to me that there was only one more Test to go, and he thought he could just about last out that long. You had the feeling that for the time being he had had enough.

My knee stood up well to the tour and I didn't have to miss many matches, but I never fielded close to the wicket but was placed right out on the boundary where I could have more time to move from point to point. Bill Tucker and his colleague had done their tricky job well on me.

Batting, my form was good, bad and indifferent, but not because of my knee. I found it very hard to score off the South African bowlers in the Tests, but so did most of our batsmen, and nobody really got very many runs. Peter Richardson made a century in the First Test, but it took him more than eight hours to do so in a masterpiece of concentration. It was different, of course, in the provincial games, where we scored much more freely. In the Tests the

South Africans seemed eventually to find both the will and the ability first to contain and then to defeat us.

South Africa is an exciting, colourful, manifold land.

The M.C.C. team had good opportunities of visiting the famous and the beautiful and the unusual places in it, as indeed they have in every country in which they tour. In my time as a cricketer I have been paid for seeing half the countries of the world. South Africa, perhaps, best exemplifies the kind of place it was possible to visit.

The Western Provinces' ground at Newlands outside Cape Town is the most beautiful I have ever played on. You're between the oceans: not very far away to the west is Seapoint on the Atlantic with the cold invigorating water in which the South Africans take pleasure in bracing themselves; a similar distance away on the east coast is Muizenberg on the Indian Ocean where the water is balmy and relaxing and where I went when I wanted to swim.

It's not a big ground; it holds about 16,000 people. At the back Table Mountain stands up massively, with the sun gleaming and glinting on the white rock and on the green of the trees. The air is clear and sparkling. There are oak-trees on two sides of the ground and under them the kind of old-fashioned wooden seats which you'd find on the village green in the English counties. The setting is English and tropical at the same time: it is Lord's set out abroad, tropical issue as it were. And the members at Newlands, I felt, were at least as English as the English themselves.

The ground is entirely devoted to cricket. There is no question of Rugby being played on it in the Rugby season as happens elsewhere, as at the old ground at Johannesburg and at Port Elizabeth. Newlands is sacred to bat, ball and wicket. Custom and tradition lurk in its trees and buildings and grounds with a slightly self-conscious pride.

From Newlands the M.C.C. go on a two-day journey by the Garden Route to Port Elizabeth, with a stop in a rondavaal in the grounds of the honeymoon hotel called the Wilderness. The road runs along the coast about two or three miles inland from the sea. On either side, for hundreds of miles, the trees because of the heavy rainfall are lush and green and flourishing. There are oaks and weeping willows and shrubs and flowers and flowering trees in profusion. In the sun and the rain they grow richly. Amongst them are the great yellow blossoms of the Bougainvillaea and the violet-blues and the soft purples of the Jacaranda. The Garden Route burns and glows with colour. Often you see waterfalls coming down whitely over the rocks, and you have glimpses of the blue sea and the white and yellow sands of the beaches.

In 1949 I had travelled that route and the memory of it was still very vividly in my mind in 1957. I told the other members of the team about it with enthusiasm: "Bring your ciné cameras and your ordinary cameras," I said, "you're going to enjoy this, I can tell you, and you'll get some wonderful pictures." By the time they got into the coach to leave Newlands I had induced high hopes in them.

For the first day of the journey it rained without stopping, heavily and obscuringly, and we saw nothing. When we reached the Wilderness I avoided much conversation and went quickly to my rondavaal, one of the little white-painted African-style huts where you sleep and wash but leave to go to the main hotel building for meals. Next morning we had news of the Suez crisis, and that day it rained as solidly as the day before, all the rest of the way to Port Elizabeth. We still saw nothing.

I had many questions from the team: "What did you say the Garden Route was like, Denis?" I was asked by someone, fingering a camera significantly. "We haven't seen it yet, you know, Denis." And they never did see it, and unhappily missed sights of great beauty.

After the game at Bulawayo we flew up to Victoria Falls and spent two days there, about as far from the atmosphere of cricket as you could get, and restful therefore, lolling and lazing around in the humid steamy air, wearing shorts, old shirts and plimsolls. We went up the Zambezi to Monkey Island, where we fed the monkeys, much as children feed the pigeons in Trafalgar Square. To me the monkeys, more apt, seemed also more commercialised than the pigeons. We didn't swim in the Zambezi, because the crocodiles were already doing that.

We walked round the Falls and looked over the top, down the dizzying heights to the bottom, over the tumbling weight of the millions of gallons of water which crashed downwards in mist and spray every second. There was a constant roar of sound. In the shape roughly of a figure 6 a rainbow hooped out from the top, curved round the Falls and inwards at the bottom where the water was piling and crashing on the glistening rocks, the colours shining dazzlingly in the falling and drifting mist and spray. In the grip of fascination we stood and watched one of the greatest sights in the world.

Near by is the rain forest, green trees and green shrubs and not much else, soaked with the water that blows over it and on to it from the Falls, as if it were raining continually, so that it gives you the impression of a tropical bogland or marshland. As you walk through it you get soaked, but you linger there, because it is a green constantly dripping place, refreshing in its coolness, like being in a desultory showerbath.

The members of the team went on differing outings from the Falls, according to taste, and there were many to choose from. Among others, Colin Cowdrey, Peter Richardson and I decided to spend £5 a head on a trip in an aeroplane, a single-engined aeroplane owned by an intrepid character who for that money would fly you up and down the Zambezi and up and over the Falls. He was a very experienced pilot, so I knew, and so I constantly told myself, more particularly as we made for the white waters of the Falls, and then saw them terrifyingly a little below us, so that it seemed we must go plunging down too with the waters. Along the river we flew very low and on either side could see giraffe and elephants and, in the river itself, the crocodiles, basking and enjoying the swimming against which the notice-boards warned so insistently. That air trip was the best way of spending £5 that I know.

The majority of the team preferred to stay on the ground that day. They left the hotel at about five o'clock in the morning in cars, bound for the great Wanki game reserve. The rain had been coming down in African torrents, which was one of the reasons that I had decided on my one-engined aircraft, as I thought that the ground would be bogland and when they got to the reserve they might sink into it. In a way I wasn't far wrong.

Freddie Brown, who managed the side on that tour, Brian Statham, Peter Loader and Trevor Bailey were in one car and hadn't been long in the game reserve when they decided to go down what appeared to be an interesting track, even although it was one of the tracks which the keeper had told them not to take. They didn't travel far before their car bogged down deeply in the soaked ground, and they couldn't move it no matter how they tried. It was still comparatively early in the day and to begin with they felt that someone would soon notice their absence and go in search of them, and, with expert knowledge of the reserve, find them pretty quickly. With any luck they wouldn't have to wait long before someone came and pulled them out.

Search parties were out for them but without success, the day advanced, got hotter and hotter, and in the intense heat of the noon-day and the early afternoon the team manager and his men sat in the car uncomfortably, with hopes fading, drinking occasionally from the few bottles of Coca-Cola which they had brought with them. The fact that they had no food didn't make things any easier.

Dusk came down and the team manager, considering the situation carefully, decided, even although there was danger from the wild animals such as lions that roamed the reserve, and again in contravention of the orders he had received, that he and his little team of men would get out of the car and light a fire. That would be the most certain method of keeping man-eating beasts at bay. In any event it would keep them warm during the dark tropical night that was ahead of them.

Before very long, when they had got together a good pile of branches for the fire, they began to have the feeling that they were being watched. The team manager glanced behind him, and a surprised and rather anxious look came on to his face. About fifty yards away a lioness, sitting on her haunches, was studying every move they made with an intent interest.

Quite quickly they lit that fire.

Shortly afterwards they were found by one of the keepers, and their car was pulled out of the bog. It had been a long, hot and immobile day for the team manager and his men on their first safari.

Their experience reminded me of a little safari of my own, and others, on my previous tour of South Africa. Billy Griffiths, George Mann and I had had a week off and we were on our way by car from Durban to the Test at Johannesburg, driving in turns, along the great lonely stretches of the 400-mile route. The car had been provided for us by our hosts, and it was a good car, but like all cars liable to break down at an inconvenient moment. It did break down, when we were apparently a hundred miles from the nearest house. Not one of the three of us had any mechanical skill, so, in the hot dusty sun, out in the *bundu*, we sat and stood around and waited for help to come.

Before very long, far away in the distance, coming towards us down the sloping road in a little cloud of dust, we saw what we could soon recognise as an Austin Seven, 1937 vintage perhaps. When it arrived at where we were waiting it stopped, and a great bald-headed Afrikaans giant got out and asked us if we were in trouble. We replied that we were, and he told us that there was a garage (we hadn't noticed it) some fifteen miles away and he'd go and get us help.

He climbed hugely back into the little car and drove off. Happier now, we got out our golf clubs from the back of the car and started to practise chip shots across the road into the *bundu*.

Almost immediately it seemed to us, the little car and the bald giant were back again. He got out and came over to us, with a smile of dawning recognition on his face.

"Man," he said to me, "you're members of the M.C.C., aren't you, man?"

Puzzled still, we nodded our heads.

Smiling more broadly, the big man pulled out an autograph book and got all our signatures.

"Man," he said, "I'm pleased. . . . When I was about seven miles down the road I said to myself, man, those fellows are members of the M.C.C. . . . So I turned round, man, and came back to get your autographs." He put his autograph book in his pocket. "Now I'll go and get help for you," he added. "Man, I'm pleased to find you."

He squeezed into the car and drove away and some time later help came. Eventually we got to Johannesburg.

The giant's name was Dinklemann, Doctor Dinklemann. He was, as I have said, bald; he weighed more than sixteen stone, was more than six feet high, and could do the hundred yards in evens. The last time the Springboks were over here, Doctor Dinklemann was their most devastating forward, as many a Rugby player knows who has been in the way of his great figure as he surged and crashed down the field. On that sunny day, out in the *bundu*, if we'd known who he was we would have demanded his autograph in return.

In South Africa a touring team in my experience is looked after more expertly and more attentively than anywhere else. Unless you want to be bored and want to stay in your hotel, there is never any need to be bored. Apart from official functions, dances, parties, braaivleis and the like are specially laid on, to taste. I particularly enjoyed the braaivleis, of which we had quite a number. Little fires were built out in the open air, and the meat was brought along and cooked on a spit. There were barrels of beer, bottles of other things, and music in the background and excellent company, and bowlers and batsmen could forget averages or wickets and the captain his situation or his problems.

In each place that we visited, the Transvaal, Natal, Western Provinces, special committees were formed to deal with our requirements. One person, a stockbroker or a lawyer or a business man, would be put in charge of one aspect of matters. For example, someone, perhaps a banker, would deal with everything we required in the dressing-room; another, an architect maybe, would look after the entertainment side and would organise partners for the dances which were given for us. Transport was always available for wherever we might want to go, and tickets for the cinemas, or for a play, or a concert. It was all expertly done, with the finest courtesy and generosity, and by the time the tour was over I felt we had been thoroughly spoiled.

Perhaps I am biased about South Africa, but I enjoyed myself on tours there more than anywhere else, not least because the cricket, though hard-fought with nothing given away, lacked some of that hard intensity which it seems to acquire so easily elsewhere. I enjoyed that tour in 1956-7 very much, all the more, perhaps, because it was to be my last. I was bidding an extended farewell to international cricket.

When the tour was over I went to stay with Valerie and her family at Issipingo, a little place on the coast about fourteen miles south of Durban, where Valerie's family have lived for the past one hundred and fifty years, since her great-grandfather, Lawrence Platt, emigrated from on the borders of Lancashire and Yorkshire, where, even today, there are still dozens of families of the same name. I bathed and lay on the beach, and continued as I swam in the water or dried myself out in the hot sun to think about something which had never been far from my mind at any time during the tour.

It was of course the question of retirement. I hadn't wanted to think about it because it was a decision that I didn't really want to face, and would have liked to put off for as long as possible, for ever, if that could have been possible. Sometimes, too, I couldn't help feeling that if I'd had a sound right leg I would have been able to postpone the decision for another two or three years maybe. I had occasional and unasked-for twinges of regret. Since the age of fifteen, apart from the war years, my life had mainly been in cricket, and it was hard to think about leaving any part of it behind me.

And yet, I told myself, really the only thing I had cause for was thankfulness that I had had so many years of colourful, exciting and varied life, and that it would be mean-spirited to entertain regrets of any kind. Besides, I would be retiring from international cricket only—I would make the announcement when Valerie and I and the two children got back by ship to England: I would still have another full season as a professional with Middlesex. I had started with them and would end with them.

I still had something to look forward to: I wasn't really retiring yet.

CHAPTER XIII

FALL OF AN INNINGS

THE moment had now come for me as it comes for every man who has lived his life in cricket.

It was a Saturday, the last day of August 1957, and we were playing Worcestershire at Lord's before a big crowd. Walton had been at the wicket, and I was watching, padded up. I had already batted in the first innings and I was waiting to go in in the second, for the last time ever as a regular player for Middlesex. Then Walton was out, caught and bowled Chesterton, and it was my turn. I picked up my bat for the last time, with a slight feeling of unreality, walked through the dressing-room and then down the wide stairs with their broad treads, past the prints and the photographs on the walls of cricketers of other years, down to the bottom where just before I went out into the sunshine I glanced sideways at the elderly men in the high chairs in the Long Room, who were watching the game through the window, the same people it seemed to me who'd been there when I first walked out on to the pitch twenty seasons before.

Outside it was bright in the sunshine. In the enclosure the members seemed to be awaiting me, because as soon as I emerged they stood up and began to clap, and I could hear one or two very friendly words spoken as I went down the steps and through the familiar white gate on to the green turf. The crowd, it seemed, had spotted me too, and they were clapping and applauding and I, in a curious way, could sense their friendliness and warmth as I walked out towards the middle. They kept it up all the time as I travelled that well-loved route to the middle and didn't stop until I had taken guard and was looking round to see how Peter Richardson had placed the field for me. For the last time I turned then to see what the bowling was like, and felt that slight familiar tension as I waited for the first delivery to be sent down.

I was glad that this farewell should be at Lord's. I could say, and in melancholy moments during the season past I had frequently said to myself, that it wasn't really my last season—after it was over I would still be playing the odd game as an amateur for Middlesex, if they asked me to do so. But I knew that that was only a way of trying to coat what was inevitably a slightly bitter pill. Now was the real farewell without doubt, and the best thing I could do was to accept it fully without any comfortable retreat. And Lord's on a day of sunshine was the only place I'd want it to happen.

I'd grown up there almost as much as I'd grown up anywhere else. Ever since the age of fifteen I'd been turning up daily for many months of the year at the gate behind the Nursery End and later on at the Grace gate. It was full of homely memories for me, of people and incidents and situations. I had been happy there and always would be in that friendly informal atmosphere laden with tradition.

When I had first gone to Lord's, Harry White was the groundsman. He looked like a farmer with a Johnny Walker complexion, and he loved cricket. His cap was tiny, perched over a red face and a little moustache, on a bald head; he was short and squat and wore tight trousers and heavy boots with turned-up toes. He called everyone his boys, including the players, but particularly the ground staff of which I was then becoming a member. "Will you get my boys along with the heavy roller?" he used to say, and we'd struggle with the five-ton monster, hauling and tugging and dragging on the rope to get it into motion. He seemed to me to have been there for ever and to be a part of the place. It was hard to think he'd ever die, but the fact that he was no longer to be seen at Lord's must mean that even he did. He was old, I had thought, and ageless and permanent, like the figure with the scythe on the weather-vane.

Dickie Owen had been there too when I first arrived. We always thought of him as Dickie Owen from Biggleswade, just like that: Dickie Owen from Biggleswade. We knew that he came from there because he used to return every Sunday of his life for the fifty or more years that he worked at Lord's. His job had been a special one: on a declaration or on the fall of an innings he used to walk out to the wicket, white-haired, aged over seventy, with his little basket and besom broom, and sweep up at each end. It wasn't a hard job, but he did it lovingly and well. He was himself lovable, and he had grown old gracefully with a kind of dignity.

Every day, provided there didn't seem to be any chance that an innings was going to come to an end, he'd leave the ground and get the midday paper and go round to the little room near the nursery where the groundsmen had their tea and sandwiches and pinned their heroes or their pin-ups on the wall, and where I had often sat in my early days and listened to them talk. There he'd sit down and study the form of the dogs and the horses, on both of which, but especially on dogs, he was a foremost authority. Even Keith Miller, always keen to get useful information from anyone, used to consult him. "What do you know, Dickie?" Keith had often said to him. "What do you know?" And Dickie Owen from Biggleswade would tell him, to his advantage, with that humorous twinkle that you so often saw in his eyes.

At Lord's, daily, I had always seen the same people and said good morning or good afternoon to the same people, and no doubt they grew older, but yet they had never seemed to change. Ted Swannell, who'd prepared the wicket I was playing on that last day in my last game, had been one of Harry White's assistants when I had gone first to Lord's. He had started as a boy, as I did, and wouldn't leave or go elsewhere. I had said to him that summer: "Ted, how long have you been here now?" And he told me he had been there forty years. "And I could never leave," he went on, "because it's part of me now." The same could be said quite truthfully of me.

Charlie Wray had been in the ticket office in my early days, and he was still there now; with Bill Mavins I used to operate the top score-box, and Bill was now Ted Swannell's assistant. In the bottom score-box old Dick Gaby would be changing the numbers, while his two sons, Dick and Joe, worked in the pavilion, as they still did. During that season as I walked into Lord's I used to say good morning to George Thompson, the gardener. One morning he had been working among the beds, and he looked up at me as I greeted him. "Denis," he said, "do you remember when you used to work with me on the beds?" Of course I remembered because he'd always been the gardener as long as I'd been at Lord's.

I remembered too, when I was on the ground staff, how with the other youngsters I used to go out of the ground for our tea-break and walk down to the café, where they gave us tea in pint mugs. After a while we had begun to notice that every time we went in there an oldish man was sitting down at a table drinking his tea and anxious apparently to talk to us. After a while he did talk to us, copiously, giving us his personal reminiscences about Sir Jack Hobbs and the cricket he'd seen in his days. We had found out that he was the man who swept the section of the road near Lord's.

Once during that season I had seen him on the road as I walked to the ground on a route that I didn't often take. I went over to him. He leaned on his brush and shook my hand. "Haven't seen you for years," he had said, smiling at me.

"And are you still here, still sweeping?" I had asked jokingly.

"The same roads," he had answered, "and I know every ruddy brick on 'em."

At Lord's there is glitter and glamour and success, and no doubt I've experienced all three of them there; but my first thoughts had been for those homely and friendly people because of their character and humanity, and in a way because they give the place permanence, never seeming to age or to grow old.

At Lord's, too, I had seen the Marylebone Cricket Club reign gloriously, with a slight bias against change. The world over, in Fiji, in Australia, Pakistan, in Hollywood, wherever cricket is played, their words and their decisions are heard with attention and respect and often with obedience. International cricket is a lame and impossible conception without adding in the M.C.C. It's an autocratic, charming institution, not over-flexible, but content and secure in the knowledge that the basic requirements for the running of the game never change, and they know the basic requirements, from long years of experience.

Somehow the club's local habitation at Lord's gives the place a greater dignity and awe and influence. When you are there you feel yourself at the very heart and centre of cricket and immersed in its essential moods. I had always been conscious of the presence there of the M.C.C., less remotely and distantly as the years had gone on, and it had always been an added link tying me to Lord's. I'm glad I was born in Middlesex, and played all my days at Lord's, as I was playing on that day of farewell.

The M.C.C. are not quick to do new things. In the 1956 season the sight-screens experimentally were painted a duck-egg blue, to see if the colour would be more effective than white, as, in my view, it in fact turned out to be. Nigel Haig, captain of Middlesex thirty years previously, and a famous captain, who lives in Wales now and occasionally comes up to Lord's, one day had said to me about the experiment: "Denis, more than thirty years ago I suggested those duck-egg blue sight-screens and now they've taken my advice. It just shows you what fast workers the M.C.C. are."

The changelessness is part of Lord's attraction. It may have been that which had brought Len Braund there year after year until he died at the age of eighty-two. In his day he played for Somerset and England and he had been a smart dresser, the best-dressed cricketer of his day, they used to say. Even when he had both his legs amputated when he was in his middle seventies, he had still been turned out smartly as he sat in his invalid chair, and he still came to Lord's, parking at the end of the passageway that leads down to the ground between the pavilion and the members' stand. He'd sit there in the sunshine of some lovely day, and watch the game that plainly meant so much to him. Often he had sent up a message to me asking if I'd come and have a chat with him, and I'd go, and be well entertained by him, in his last sunny days.

On the pitch where I was now facing the last overs that would be bowled to me in my professional career many great Middlesex players had played before me. Many competent and humorous and great ones had played with me there, or had played shove-ha'p'ny against me in the dressing-room. There had been an old shove-ha'p'ny board which we all used and continued to play at even after a new one had been provided. In the dressing-room you advanced stage by stage, acquiring better seats as you acquired seniority. My seat for the past years had been a comfortable one on a settee on the right as you came in from the balcony. Beside me was Bill Edrich's, whose career and mine had been joined as those of Patsy Hendren and J. W. Hearne whom we'd replaced as No. 3 and No. 4 for Middlesex had once been joined.

As I played that day Patsy was still with Middlesex, was scoring as usual in the score-box and was coaching for them, travelling round with them, and giving advice to youngsters, still in the environment of the game. In his day he had been an entertaining cricketer, exciting to watch, a man who moved up the wicket to the ball and someone who was always full of humour. I remembered that in his last game he had scored a century. J. W. Hearne that day too, was, as he is, the coach at Lord's and the talent-spotter for Middlesex. Hendren and Hearne had come and gone at Lord's and now Compton and Edrich, who had replaced them, were themselves on their way out.

I would never have wanted to play with any county other than Middlesex. I had been happy there—in particular I could never forget how they had helped and shown understanding over all the times that my knee had troubled and hindered me—and I had thought the county excellently run, even though, as would have been inevitable anywhere, there had been one or two things which had made me uneasy, particularly perhaps the uncertainty which in the few years past had seemed to trouble the committee as to whether Bill Edrich should remain as captain. The side had been absolutely behind Bill and liked and respected him and his captaincy: and I had never been able quite to appreciate or understand why there should have been any hesitations.

Bill and I had had our spell as joint captains, partly, I think, as a gesture by the county to show its appreciation of what we had done on the Lord's and other grounds. We had in our turn appreciated the gesture. But I had doubted afterwards if the arrangement had been a satisfactory one as it meant unsettling switches of the side between different styles of captaincy, and an unhelpful thing in all circumstances and perhaps all the more so when one style, mine, had tended so strongly in the direction of the adventurous, the enter-taining and the let's-have-a-result-if-we-possibly-can.

R. W. V. Robins—"Robbie" we had called him—a great discipli-narian and a great captain, had been, I supposed, the man who had most influenced me in my attitude towards the game and towards captaincy. He had always been a great entertainer, and I had wanted to be that too. On the field he was like a cat on very hot bricks; he always wanted victory, and he inspired and urged and talked so that every player was on the ball. Often it seemed that either he'd get victory or lose the match, and it was fascination and joy for any young player to watch or play under him. Cricket was his great love, and he knew about it encyclopaedically, and he talked about it greatly, on and off the field, and thought and theorised about it, and he had studied every single aspect of it.

He had been captain of England when I first played in a Test against New Zealand in 1937, and I remembered his short, slim, active figure as he moved eagerly about the field, like a little ball of fire. He was a man who had a policy for a game or a situation and he let you know what it was, and you followed it, or else! I could hear him saying that he wanted so many runs by such-and-such a time, and that we were to get them, and no fooling around or shutting up shop—get those runs. If you didn't, and he suspected that you hadn't really tried to carry out the policy laid down, there'd be hell to pay. "What sort of batting do you think that was?" would then be one, but only one, of the questions on his lips.

If things were going slowly in the game I'd heard him say with characteristic certainty: "I'll get the game livened up." In a situation where Middlesex were fielding and the other side playing very slowly and looking as if they'd never get out, he'd take the ball himself and bowl maybe five high full tosses so that the batsman on the other side had to play strokes and to start things moving.

He was a fiery and positive personality, a critical and demanding and helpful judge of play and captaincy, both while playing and after he had retired, and a person who was quick to show generous appreciation if you did well or tried hard. Perhaps, sometimes, he had expected more than some people were able to give—but that was a fault of his virtues. He was a great cricketer and he did great things for cricket. His attitude towards the game, if not all his ideas, could be widely spread through the counties for the benefit of the game today.

What I would always remember most clearly about Gubby Allen was his bowling. He was really quick, playing for and captaining England and Middlesex, and apart from Lindwall's I don't think I have ever seen a lovelier run up to the wicket or a lovelier action. He was a great theorist about cricket and about every game that he played, and a very fine judge of a player. A great deal of his time he gave, and gives, to helping the young or promising players of Middlesex, in particular the bowlers; he would never hesitate to go down to the nets with a player when he thought he showed promise or had possibilities. In the same way, as an England selector, he gave his time and energy and thought to the problems of selecting a side to represent England, travelling from place to place and game to game and watching individual players in order to form the most reliable estimate of their present ability or potential. Indeed, I thought that the success of the English sides in the years before that last year of mine were due in considerable measure to the time and thought that Gubby Allen had given to the processes of elimination and selection.

During that last season in which I was now playing towards the fall of a last innings I had been conscious of them both, Robbie and Gubby, as I think I always had been, as the watchful spirits of the county who always knew what was going on whether they were at the ground or behind the scenes. They had views which they expressed by telephone to the dressing-room, if necessary.

Jack Young had retired two years before that season in which I was retiring. Jack had been on the ground staff with me, and we'd played for Middlesex together for most of our careers. He was our literary man, the genius of the dressing-room, where he imitated Jim Swanton's broadcasting style to applause, the reader and quoter of the poets, a man of moods who in good humour could lift the spirits of the Middlesex side more almost than anyone I knew, and certainly more quickly and effectively. He read Shakespeare and Keats and Rupert Brooke and Francis Thompson, and no doubt a great many others of whom I never knew. His quotations from his favourite poets would vary with the weather, the situation or the environment, always with the greatest aptness. Like any fine bowler he hated batsmen. Literary man though he was, he had seemed to hate Yorkshire batsmen in particular, and after the war he bowled them out with unyielding consistency.

When we'd come in from a tiring day in the field in the hot weather and sit down mopping our faces with handkerchiefs and towels, and the boy would bring in the beer, that would be the time for Keats. Jack would begin, before he touched his pint:

> "Oh, for a draught of vintage, that hath been
>   Cool'd a long age in the deep delvèd earth,
> Tasting of Flora and the country green,
>   Dance, and Provençal song, and sunburnt mirth:
> O for a beaker full of the warm south,
>   Full of the true, the blushful Hippocrene. . . ."

At that moment Jack would pause, and bring his pint closer to him, and say:

> "With beaded bubbles winking at the brim,
> And purple-stainèd mouth."

Then Jack would drink his pint: especially he seemed to like the "beaded bubbles winking at the brim".

In the lovely settings of games in Kent with the trees round the ground, and the coloured marquees set up by the various clubs, Francis Thompson would seem to him more fitting. He'd stand out in the middle, looking at the beautiful surroundings and say:

> "It is little I repair to the matches of the Southron folk,
> Though my own red roses there may blow;
> It is little I repair to the matches of the Southron folk,
> Though the red roses crest the caps, I know.
> For the field is full of shades as I near the shadowy coast,
> And a ghostly batsman plays to the bowling of a ghost,
> And I look through my tears on a soundless clapping host
> As the run stealers flicker to and fro,
> To and fro:
> O my Hornby and my Barlow long ago."

Jack had provided humour, as well as poetry. In the dressing-room at Lord's there were a great many lockers, and in some of them, if you searched, you'd find equipment and clothing which had been there unmoved for maybe forty or fifty years, belonging probably to some Middlesex member of long ago, in the days when the dressing-room was exclusively for amateurs. Once during a county game we had found in one of them a very old Middlesex cap, of an ancient design and cut, with a tiny peak, though in the familiar dark blue with swords. We persuaded Jack to put it on. It sat up oddly on his head, with an antiquated air, the tiny peak sticking out incongruously, and he seemed suddenly to be a nineteenth-century cricketer haunting the scene of his manhood.

At his usual No. 11 Jack had gone in wearing the cap and brought the house down. He had stood at the wicket, the strange hat on his head, and flailed away at the bowling—when they could bowl to him, for the bowlers would start their run-up, catch a glimpse of

Jack and his headgear as they approached the crease, and start laughing, so that they would have to halt and start all over again. It was one of the best innings Jack ever played.

Particularly when things were going well with his bowling Jack would enliven the game with a great variety of facial contortion. He loved the theatre and had a good deal in him that was theatrical. When he'd very narrowly missed the wicket with a ball, or just missed having someone out from a catch, he'd fix the batsman with a fierce and comical expression which was really one more of humour than disappointment.

Dick Coleman used to umpire. He was a gentle and placid Leicestershire man who kept a pub in a small village in winter-time, and he had a distinctively emphatic way of pronouncing his decisions, particularly if there had been an appeal and he was refusing it. "N-O-T O-U-T," he would say emphatically, in his Leicestershire accent. His "N-O-T O-U-T" became famous. One day Jack was bowling and he had hit the batsman on the pad; obviously it was not l.b.w.—but Jack, in a moment of devilment, turned suddenly and appealed to Coleman. Before he could answer, Jack, looking round the field, said "N-O-T O-U-T" in Dick's tone, and with Dick's fierce look and compressed lips. It was so aptly done that I don't think even Dick minded at all the laughter it caused.

Jack Young had dominated the dressing-room and he was a master of sharp and observant comment; but he said things with such humour, or usually with such humour, that they seemed to have no real sting in them, and the target laughed with the rest. In his years there he had given a special character and flavour to Lord's.

He wasn't the only man given to poetry that I had met in my cricketing years. There was Alec Skelding, the umpire, who wrote his own verses and who regularly sent them to me. One morning I opened my post and found this one, which I called Skell's Elegy:

> "How was it! How is it! How's this, how's that?"
> Appeals required to be answered "hand pat";
>   Some frantic and fierce, some pleading,
>   With gestures that could be misleading;
> He *must* decide—laws provide no time for chat.

He can no question make of "ayes or noes",
Deciding whether batsman stays or goes;
   For 'tis ordered his decision
   Must be prompt, and with precision,
For he's s'posed to be the only man who knows.

Each year his Club sends in his nomination,
Accompanied by M.O.'s examination
   As to eyesight, health and hearing,
   And it must at least be cheering,
To have a chance at all for application.

Beginneth then his winter's discontent,
With eight months o'er his errors to lament;
   And he may be re-elected,
   When his record is inspected,
Or he may not—so he tries to be content.

So now, you willow-wielders,
And you volley-catching fielders;
   You who stand there at the wicket,
   Injured innocent—"Didn't snick it";
Bowlers who are apt to squeal
At a negative appeal;
   Think of Umpire Jack, or Jim;
   Think kindly, please—and pity him!

Alec seemed to have a special fondness for me. One day at Lord's the ball hit my pads, and there was a very loud and a very confident appeal, which I rather think was more than justified; but Alec had other views. "No, no," he said, with a humorous look, "no . . . he's not out, the crowd want to see him. . . . The crowd want to see him." And I batted on.

I had had many years at Lord's with Jack Robertson, and in the first innings of that last game I was now playing we had had a final stand of 225 together. He was a wonderful servant of Middlesex, and I am very doubtful whether he received the national recognition that his ability really deserved. He could have helped England a great deal at various times had he been given the opportunity. He scored a glorious century in his second innings against New Zealand in 1949 at Lord's in the Second Test, but he was never, inexplicably, selected to play for England again. At best, he had played in the odd representative game, and it was hardly fair to have made a final judgment on such disconnected appearances. If the selectors had persevered with him he would have been a great success in international cricket.

He was a great player and he had quite literally every stroke in the book: he was as near technical perfection as any player I have ever watched. All his shots were elegantly and perfectly played. He was a fine stylist and very, very good indeed against the new ball. As you watched him you found yourself saying continually: "What a lovely stroke", or when he was out: "What a lovely innings." I had often felt that his unfortunate experience on his first playing against Lindwall in 1948 at Lord's told heavily against him afterwards, although it was difficult to see why it should. He ducked into a fast one from Ray and was injured; but it was the kind of misfortune which might have happened to anyone.

I had enjoyed my last season as a professional cricketer, playing for Middlesex, if not any longer for England, and had great joy in it. I had played in a lot of matches and played quite well too and my knee held out with remarkable stamina. I did have matches off to have treatment, yet the limb was quite reliable. Indeed it wouldn't be possible to express enough gratitude to Bill Tucker for what he had done. I could even play 36 holes of golf on it, which with my sort of golf means walking ten or twelve miles, because too many of my drives with the club are bent-elbow drives, through the covers for 4 or 6, rather than drives down the centre of the green fairway.

Elder statesman-like perhaps, I had watched the younger players in the side with a more than fatherly eye wondering about the future when Bill and I had flickered off the field for the last time: for years, of course, I had taken a great interest in the youngsters, but that year the interest was keener and more avuncular. I had concluded that if the junior members of the side worked a bit harder and more ambitiously, in two or three years from then Middlesex would be a very strong side indeed.

I refer to ambition—or call it keenness perhaps—because I think it is a necessary quality for a player to have, an urge to drive him on to proficiency and success. On one occasion I had been surprised to find a dull lack of it among some of the Middlesex players. As it was my last season and Bill's last season, I had suggested to Bill, who was captain, that he and I shouldn't go in at No. 3 and 4 as we always had done since Patsy and J.W. had retired, not for all the matches anyway, but should let the players lower down the list occupy these positions and get the kind of experience which would help them in the following year when they would have to take over from us in any case. We could go in lower down in the order.

Bill had thought the idea a good one, and the suggestion was put to some of the younger chaps; but it was not received well, or at all. They were quite happy it seemed to continue where they were, not doing very brilliantly but not doing badly, getting along comfortably, suited very well, thank you. I had been appalled at their attitude. At their age that certainly wouldn't have been my attitude: I'd have grabbed the opportunity, thank you. People, evidently, are differently built.

John Murray, it seemed to me as I had watched him during that season, would have a brilliant future as a wicket-keeper-batsman, in the tradition of Leslie Ames. His batting had intrigued me, with its fine stroke play and elegant, graceful, powerful hitting of the ball, particularly on the off side. He is a frail-looking chap in a way, but very impressive indeed when he goes out to the wicket. I don't know a great deal about wicket-keeping, but it had seemed to me that Murray had the kind of natural ability which could perhaps enable Godfrey Evans to train him up as his successor. Anyone succeeding Godfrey would have a formidable task, but I thought and think that John Murray could do it.

Don Bennett started his career excellently, when very young, but had not perhaps developed by the 1957 season as much as might have been hoped, although he was still in his early twenties, and I remember thinking that with more application he could develop a great deal more. The same, I was sure, was the case with Fred Titmus, especially in relation to his bowling. He was bowling his off-spinners too fast and needed to study himself more and discover and remedy his weaknesses, which could easily be remedied. Jim Laker no doubt would be able to help him. Moss bowled reasonably well during the season, and I was sure would continue to do so for many seasons more, and I had thought I saw in Bick, very young as an opening batsman, a great deal of potentiality. But of nearly all of them I had felt that harder and keener work was necessary if they were going to achieve their full capacity as cricketers.

The season had seemed to be a season of farewells, as the crowds had assumed, and in most cases rightly, that whenever I appeared at a ground other than Lord's it would be my last appearance. It was the case on the Kent grounds, which I loved as much as Jack Young ever loved them, and at Nottingham, a ground where I always made a century, except on one occasion when I played there in a Test Match. I had been sorry to have to say good-bye and the crowds warm-heartedly seemed to be sorry too. At Old Trafford, my lucky ground, in a game very typically almost washed out by rain, I had been able to content the crowd and myself by getting a century in my last game there. Getting a century was about as good a way as I knew of taking my leave of them.

On that last journey out to the wicket, and as I faced the Worcester-shire bowlers, I thought more than once about Patsy Hendren. He had loved his career in cricket and so had I. I had played in the same side with him in his last season for Middlesex; I, very young and relatively inexperienced, going in No. 5 or No. 6, and Patsy, senior and genial and distinguished, going in at No. 4. I could remember how he used to walk down the wicket to me when we were out in the middle together, and give me information—he never gave me advice on how to play the ball, wisely of course—but just gave me useful information: this bowler was bowling or might bowl out-swingers, and that one could spin it quite a lot from the leg, if he wanted to, so I had better look out, and so on. He was a great help, and it was a great experience to be at the wicket with him. Then he retired and I had taken his place in the Middlesex team at No. 4. In his last game Patsy got a century in his first innings.

Now I too had made a century in the first innings of my last game. I had been lucky, because when I was six I hooked a ball from Flavell in the direction of Peter Richardson's young brother Dick, who managed to get his hands to it, but then juggled and finally it fell to the ground—and I was still there. I was never happier to see a shot dropped, because I wanted desperately to make a century—for sentimental reasons, I suppose—but I wanted desperately to do it. Then the runs came freely and easily and, to applause, I hit my hundredth run.

Now I was in my second innings, and Bill Edrich and I were at the wicket together. Horton was bowling to me, and I had nearly reached my half-century. Then Horton sent down one which I thought should be hit, and I opened my shoulders and hit the ball, and watched it climb towards the boundary. It looked like being a six. Then I saw Outschoorn going back for it. The ball began to drop from the top of its arc, and it seemed to be coming down unbearably slowly . . . and just across the boundary . . . but no, Outschoorn was there, leaning across the boundary, and first juggling, then taking and holding the catch. I was out, for the last time. It was as nice a way as any to be dismissed.

I started the walk back from the wicket, over the familiar turf, in the friendly surroundings. The clock beyond the Nursery End showed just a quarter to one—not long to go for lunch; on the scoreboard they were altering the details: I had scored 48 runs and I was caught Outschoorn bowled Horton. The weather-vane over the grandstand balcony was swinging almost imperceptibly. Out of the corner of my eye I noticed that someone near the Tavern was holding up a glass of beer towards me as I walked in.

The Worcestershire players were all looking at me and clapping, and so was Bill. Applause from the crowd was ringing the ground with noise; many people were standing, some, I think, were cheering, and there was what I thought was a sympathetic buzz of talk and comment. As I approached the pavilion, I could see that the members too were standing and clapping and smiling. Once or twice I raised my bat in acknowledgment, though I wanted to keep my head well down.

Then I opened the white gate, ascended the steps between the standing members as some of them patted me on the shoulders, and went back into the pavilion.

CHAPTER XIV

THE SHOULDERED SCYTHE

I HAVE loved and had joy all my life from the game of cricket. In twenty years I saw some changes in the game, but nothing of its compelling charm has altered.

Some changes have been for the better, more not: change, good or bad, is no doubt inevitable. When I began to play there was quite a marked distinction between the amateur and the professional: a sort of gulf or distance between them, placed there by a tradition which may have tended to be snobbish, but so far as I could judge, it never really affected the relationship person to person of the amateur and the professional players concerned. It has gone now, because it had become pointless. The sides who play cricket are now just eleven human beings, and probably it is all for the better.

Yet I never minded or felt the distinction, though it was there quite precisely in my early days, and I don't remember any of the other professionals minding either. Certainly it had the effect of making the young professional show respect for the amateur; for instance, by calling him "Sir", and it thus inculcated in his mind, I thought, a respect for people generally, particularly for those senior to him, such as the senior professional and older people. I am sure that that was an excellent thing and its rather obvious absence is felt today. I am equally sure that it had a good effect upon the formation of character.

But the distinction has gone now and had to go in the changing circumstances of social and economic life, and I think the amateur is as happy as the professional, if not more so, that it has disappeared. The barriers were really seen to be falling when shortly before the war at Lord's it was decided that for all games, Tests and county games, the amateurs and the professionals should share the same dressing-room. It was then that I moved from the little place on the grandstand side of the pavilion with its special gate near by, from which the professionals used to emerge, to the amateurs' dressing-room as it was then but now is no longer called.

In one way at least the old idea that an amateur was a man of private means who didn't need to work and played his cricket just for his pleasure, has persisted as a kind of pretence in the fact that on tour these days an amateur is only given a relatively meagre allowance to cover his expenses, which will always be considerable—anything over and above that he must find in his own pocket. Today most amateurs in big cricket are not wealthy men, and the inadequate allowance has often told hardly on them before a tour is over. It is plain, in my view, that they should be given an allowance equal to the professional, if not indeed greater, because, again in the persistence of the pretence, an amateur has frequently to do more entertaining than a professional.

Amateurs can, of course, lend their names to advertisements, and write and talk and broadcast and telecast about the game, and so can professionals; and I think it must be obvious, provided standards are kept up, that it is appropriate that they should be allowed to supplement their earnings in this way. I feel, and I think it is the general feeling, that the cricketer who so often provides entertainment for the crowd should be allowed, indeed encouraged, during the relatively short span of his effective earning life, to supplement his income as largely as he can from commercial sources outside the game.

There are of course dangers in entering the commercial field in that way, at least on your own. In whatever profession a man may find himself he is usually so taken up with the doing of it and adding to and perfecting his skill that he has little time or energy left to wonder what his work is worth. Barristers have clerks, writers agents, boxers and actors have managers: they in fact go into a kind of partnership with the people who know what they are worth, and their worth, less percentage, they usually obtain. If a cricketer, or any other sportsman for that matter, tries to sell an aspect of himself, say, to an advertiser, he is in danger, acting on his own, of finding the price very much cut. People quickly take advantage of your comparative ignorance and simplicity in a strange field. I don't complain: that no doubt is business. I had one or two experiences of it which were not very happy.

If you work on your own you might find yourself in some case getting £50 where you are really worth £400—and I can see no reason why the cricketer shouldn't have the proper reward of his labour if he has climbed to the top, the labourer being worthy of his hire. Furthermore, if you get little, you would probably try if it were, say, advertising that you were concerned with, to spread yourself, as it were, around too many products, and in consequence lower your own and the cricketer's prestige and value.

Some years ago Bagenal Harvey and I got together, and I formed myself into a limited company and he acted as my business manager —that left me free to get on with my real career of playing cricket, while he could use his commercial experience and ability to help me to reap the full rewards of my play. After all, anyone else in the public eye who expends even half of the nervous energy and stamina of a cricketer gets paid usually a great deal more and over a much longer period—so why not a sportsman? Bagenal and I have made quite a good fist of it, and we've been pretty lucky. My experience convinces me that any sportsman arriving at the top needs a business manager. In a modern world it's the only effective answer to the sportsman's financial problems. I think we have found that answer and that we have probably helped sportsmen generally quite a lot. It's a change we've made and I have no doubt it is for the better.

Another change has been in the wickets on which the game is played. In my day I have seen a great alteration. On most of the wickets of today I don't think Bradman could play that innings which he regards as his best—the 300 he made at Leeds in 1930, without once lifting the ball off the floor, with 100 before lunch, 100 between lunch and tea, and another 100 before the close of play. At the present time I think his main problem would be one of survival.

There were times, of course, before the war when the bat completely dominated the ball, and the batsman made huge totals and the bowler bowled his heart out without result. It wasn't on those occasions a fair game of cricket.

After the war the M.C.C. suggested that wickets should be made more helpful to the bowler, and a very good suggestion it plainly was until the groundsmen, seeing more in it than was intended, began to prepare wickets so favourable to the bowler that you couldn't hope to see any good cricket on them, the ball turning a foot on the first day, one standing up to you and the next one keeping low. Some of the wickets prepared for recent Test Matches have been disgraceful—a strip of desert out in the middle. If we had been faced with wickets of that kind in Australia or in the West Indies, I'm sure we'd have come away with a nasty and perhaps a slightly bitter taste in our mouths.

Today's groundsmen in my opinion have gone too far. I think perhaps if at every ground the groundsman took his instructions about preparing a wicket from one person, and from one person only, it might be partly the answer. The next part would come if he then went and prepared a hard, fast, very fast wicket, which would help the fast bowler in the first stages of the game, and the slower bowler later on when it begins to turn with a bit of pace; and the batsman would be happy too, because the ball would be coming on to the bat and he'd be able to make his strokes.

When I was on the ground staff at Lord's, there was an enormous roller in use which it took about ten of us to pull, and we used ropes, and groaned and sweated and swore as we moved it up and down the wicket. But it did make a good wicket, a firm wicket with firm foundations. Now it has been abandoned and it is not used any more. It stands in an obscure corner of the ground, like a relic of another more primitive age, like some of the exhibits in the Science Museum in South Kensington. I think it and more like it, even heavier, ropes and all, should be brought back into use. Then we would have better wickets, with a bit of life and pace in them. Winning Test Matches on wickets as dusty as the desert takes a great deal of the proper glamour from victory, however great the performances of the members of the winning side.

The way of bowling has altered too. Sir Don Bradman was probably the greatest batsman ever, but I don't think I'm being disrespectful to his genius if I say that against the type of bowling bowled today he would have been lucky to get 170 runs in a day's cricket, even on a beautiful wicket like that one at Leeds, in the same brightness and sunshine. In earlier days the bowler was always trying to bowl the batsman out—to which you might say: but, of course, that's the object of bowling—and I would reply that it is, but the bowlers were trying so diligently to achieve that principal object that they risked giving runs away, and gave them away. Today things are done a little differently. These are days when there is a tendency to play negative cricket, and in consequence to produce a very dull game indeed.

Cricket is not, and should not be, a dull game: it is a spectacle, an entertainment, disciplined, elegantly white, formal and traditional; but nevertheless an entertainment. But negative cricket does not fit into this pattern and could go far to kill the game. The answer is in the hands of the players and captains themselves. They must, I think, be made to understand and to realise that cricket will no longer hold its charm and attraction for people if it is played negatively and selfishly, as it is too often played at the moment. If county captains would take a leaf from the book R. W. V. Robins used and would allow cricket to be an entertaining game once more, the problem would be solved.

Today there are too many average-chasers, players who always know how many runs they've made or balls they've bowled or wickets they've taken. A good average does not make a good cricketer. A fine 30 made in a difficult situation is a great deal better than a century slowly and cautiously compiled in a way that ensures a dull draw or at the expense of the side's ability to gain victory, and even, as sometimes happens, in a way to make sure of their defeat. A good cricketer is one who plays the innings the team requires at any given moment, not the one which his average may require or which he thinks may make the committee think better of him, especially if his average does not drop below a certain figure.

These are not original thoughts; but I put them forward because they often seem to have been forgotten. I am emboldened to do so by the love and gratitude I have for the game of cricket and by my concern to see it continue in its charm and brilliance and adventure.

Cricket is of England, English.

I realised that with some vividness one day at Lord's in 1948, when we were presented to the Queen. A few days earlier in the Manchester Test I'd received a blow on the head from one of Ray Lindwall's bouncers, and for the time being it hadn't much improved my looks.

The Queen stopped and spoke to me:

"Mr. Compton," she said to me, "how is your poor head? ... My husband and I saw what happened to you, on television. . . . You poor boy. I do hope it's better now."

From the greatest downwards an interest in cricket is shared by and unites the people who live in England. That afternoon it was quite plain that Her Majesty knew a great deal about the individual cricketer and what he'd done and the things that had happened to him.

Cricket is a social game. It takes place in the open air, in the summer, sometimes in the sunshine, always, in the mind's eye, in the sunshine. People are gathered together for a long afternoon, or a whole day, or three or five days, and they sit around and converse, discuss, have a drink at some place like the Tavern, argue about the game being played then or about other games and other situations. It is formal and informal, elegant, but the white clothes may be streaked heavily with green when a player falls. It is a discipline, a formative part of many people's lives, certainly of mine.

It differs from all other games and is therefore unique. For instance, in football you get a benefit, under your contract, at the discretion of the directors. In cricket it's really the crowd that gives you your benefit, according as they think you deserve for the way you have performed before them. When the game of soccer is over, it's completely over—you have your bath or shower, dress and go and that's that. Cricket is leisurely, gregarious and essentially human.

I used to enjoy particularly playing at Maidstone and Canterbury, in the lovely countryside, with the marquees set up around us. After the day's play the mayor's card would come into the dressing-room, asking you to go to his tent for a drink in the warm summer evening. There would be other cards too, from the clubs in the other marquees, and you'd go and drink with them as the light faded and the darkness of a summer night began to come down. People were friendly and welcoming, and you enjoyed yourself, traditional style. It was the same at Bournemouth when Hampshire were having their Cricket Week, and elsewhere. Things like that never seem to change. When it began I don't know, but it always seemed to me that it must have been a very long time ago.

I played in I don't know how many charity games, quite often on a pitch laid out on the fields near a stately home of England. Two years running, I remember, I played in charity games at Tichborne Park for Sir Anthony Tichborne's Eleven against the village team. Terence Rattigan was our captain on the first occasion. Among the spectators were Zsa Zsa Gabor (Cha Cha Gaabore, she told me, was the right way to pronounce it) and Porfirio Rubirosa with whom she was friends then. Zsa Zsa brought the drinks out on to the field, looking elegantly beautiful, and it had been arranged that I should go and welcome her as she walked suavely and gracefully across the traditional turf towards the wicket.

I went and met her and said: "Welcome, Miss Gabor, to Tichborne Park," and kissed her loudly, very loudly, on the cheek.

She smiled gaily, even a little appreciatively, and answered in her continental voice: "Meester Compton, I understand you're . . . you're a good cricketer, no? . . . Tell me, I've never seen this game before. . . . It remind me of croquet, no?"

"Oh, yes," I commented, a bit hesitantly.

"I play a leetle croquet," Zsa Zsa went on.

"I should say you play a good, fast game of croquet, Miss Gabor," I replied.

We laughed, and she took the drinks round to the thirsty players.

Next year in the same game at the same place Tyrone Power, the film actor, was in Sir Anthony's team. He turned up on the gravel in front of the historic house, in an enormous Bentley, with registration No. TP1—Tyrone Power One. In those surroundings it looked particularly impressive.

Later, we found ourselves at the wicket together and he called down to my end: "Say, Denis," he said, "I wonder can you give me some idea about what we do here?"

I walked up the pitch to him.

"Tyrone," I said, "this is how you hold the bat," and I showed him. "Rather as you might hold a baseball bat," I pointed out.

"And then what do you do with it?" he asked.

"The idea, then," I answered, "is to swing the bat as the bowler bowls the thing and to try and make contact—try to hit it, as hard as you can. Then the idea is to get as many runs as you can, running up and down here, from one wicket to another."

"I get the idea," he said, "it's all right so's you hit this ball thing."

"That's the idea," I said.

The bowler came up and bowled, and Tyrone swung as I had told him, made contact, and flailed the ball out of the ground for six.

"How's that, Denis?" he called down the wicket. "Do I run now?"

"No," I answered, "you don't run for that, Tyrone, that's six."

"Was that good or bad?" he asked.

"That was excellent, Tyrone," I said; "if I could do that every time the bowler bowled to me, I would be the greatest player the world had ever known."

"Thanks, Denis," Tyrone said.

"You do it again, and that'll be absolutely marvellous," I replied.

He swung again, with even more vigour, missed, and there was the death-rattle behind him as the ball hit the stumps.

Under my instructions he left the wicket, and went back to the big Bentley, registration No. TP1.

Wherever I played or wherever I was there was always humour. For me the game had excitement and colour, and always humour. If I were to take thought I could probably bring to mind enough of it to make a book all on its own. I remember an incident when we were on our way to Australia by boat in 1950. John Warr, a great humorist of Middlesex and now the county's captain, was a member of the M.C.C. party, being taken out for his fast bowling. One night was fancy-dress night and we were all strangely apparelled—I was W. G. Grace, I remember—by the time the before-dinner cocktail parties started in various parts of the ship. We attended many of them, and they had made us feel very happy.

John Warr was not by any means the unhappiest. As well, he was Gorgeous Gussie; though not with his height and sinewy limbs particularly gorgeous, he was certainly oddly fascinating. His girl friends aboard had provided him with a little pleated skirt, exotic panties and a blouse with the right outline. He was scented and made up, with plenty of mascara. He carried a tennis racket, and swung it as he reckoned Gorgeous had swung.

As we entered the saloon for dinner, Gorgeous Gussie threw a ball up, swung lustily, and revealingly, and produced what looked like an ace. It flashed across the tables and, on its way, took with it a full soup spoon which the kindest of old ladies was at that moment raising to her lips. There was a liberal spray and mist of ship's soup about her as she threw her hands up in surprise.

"Sorry, fault!" Gorgeous cried ecstatically; then, recollecting himself, John gave the amplest apologies, which were most graciously received.

The evening was far from over. Freddie Brown was a Maori chief, having in his hand the chiefly staff called a *Taiaha*, made of leather and wool, with which he quietly belaboured those about him. He looked very Polynesian indeed. Jim Swanton was a stage grander, and was dressed up very convincingly as King Farouk; indeed the similarity was so close that most listeners to or viewers of cricket would have been startled to see him. He was strutting about regally, as a king should, with his chin up and a sophisticated air. This was too much for the less civilised Maori chieftain, who walked up to the Egyptian king, and felled him with a blow of his *Taiaha* on the place where the crown should rest. For a moment the king was not amused, and the assembly of fancy-dressed figures, with Gorgeous Gussie swinging her racket in encouragement, saw the portly chief and the even more portly king scrapping amiably on the dining-room floor in mid-ocean.

For most of the time that I have played cricket, I have also played golf—I got a taste for it when I played it as part of the Arsenal's regular training. Danny Kaye also plays golf, and one winter we were training for a cup-tie at the club's course out at Totteridge, where Dai Rees is professional, and we had a game which consisted of Tom Whittaker, myself, Danny Kaye and someone else. This four-ball was much photographed, and Danny Kaye showed a wonderful talent for flinging his long figure flat on the ground after each stroke. The fun, if not the golf, was good.

Not very long afterwards at the midnight matinée in aid of Sid Fields's wife, Danny Kaye saw me in the audience and called me up on the stage to show him how to hold a cricket bat. Then, with that perfect imitation of a slightly foppish Englishman, killingly dressed as a cricketer, he in turn showed the audience how cricket should be played, prancing and contorting himself in a way which would flatten any bowler before he got half-way through his run-up. The audience loved it. It was one of the most interesting games of cricket I ever played.

When the show was over, Valerie and I went backstage with Danny Kaye and met Orson Welles, Sir Laurence Olivier and many others. Danny introduced us to his manager, who was smoking a cigar about a foot long. He became very interested when he heard that Valerie was from South Africa.

"Well . . ." he said to Valerie, "now tell me all about South Africa. I'm thinking of sending Danny over there for a tour. . . . But have you got any cars or coaches or any kind of aeroplanes? Is there any method of transport there? Have you got any good roads?"

Valerie didn't seem to know whether it was a leg-pull or not. She was bridling just a little.

"As a matter of fact," she said firmly, "we do have aeroplanes and airports and wide roads—and American cars, and you can get from one province to another quite nicely. . . . You don't have to go by horse and cart."

I don't know if Danny ever went to South Africa, but at least we'd made available some preliminary information.

It was on that occasion that he told me to phone him up if ever I was in the United States. Cricket with him in Hollywood would have been at least as good as cricket at the Palladium or golf at South Herts.

In cricket, or in connection with cricket, I have met every sort and kind of person: politicians, Prime Ministers, doctors, writers, painters, actors, other sportsmen, business men, playwrights—the lot, you might say. It has added greatly to the richness and interest of my life, in a way which I could hardly have thought possible, or even conceived, when I was first playing cricket with the little bat my father gave me, near the house in Hendon where I grew up.

I have discussed cricket in the Lord's dressing-room with a Russian. He came, I suppose, from the Embassy and he spoke perfect English and handed round Russian cigarettes, which we all found very interesting to smoke. He said he much enjoyed watching the game, and that he intended to remain for the rest of the day. He told me that he'd be most pleased if we would come and demonstrate the game for them in Moscow. I said, a little hesitantly, that I thought that that would be wonderful. We would show them the fundamentals of the game, I said, and they could take it from there. I never received any kind of official invitation afterwards, which is a pity, because I think that a cricket pitch in the Kremlin might have a very beneficial effect.

As well as the richness and the humour and the excitement of the game and all the other delightful things, there was, of course, the glare and hard glitter and phoney glamour of publicity. All cricketers who get to the top must live in it, in greater measure or less; for me, deservedly or undeservedly, it was constantly the greater: I started with the praise, came in for the kicks, and in the end went back to the praise; but by then, and for a long time previously, I had acquired a kind of protective covering against it, which neither admiration nor denigration could pierce. I had to do that to survive, to keep my own personality for anything that it was, intact.

Out of my own experience it's a course I'd recommend to any cricketer who seems like occupying the headlines, or is occupying them. Get that protective covering—and keep your head, is certainly one of the best bits of advice that I can give. When a youngster does well he quickly catches the public eye, and that of the pressmen, who reach for their superlatived clichés and the dark, heavy type. They spread him over the sports page or even the front page, say the kindest things and really give him a big build-up. The young player can then do one of two things: he can say—that's wonderful, now I'm a recognised player—a great batsman or a great bowler or a great all-rounder: I've learnt it all, there's no need for me to learn any more. That's the fatal thing to do, the one which can make a batsman say to himself as he goes out to face the bowling: this is easy, it doesn't matter who's bowling, it's easy—and he starts playing badly, then with a complementary suddenness he begins to lose confidence, and finally perhaps all ability. Unhappily, I have seen just this kind of thing happen, more than once.

The prudent attitude, when a player reads flattering headlines and comments, is to say, that's kind of them—and then pay no further attention whatever, to put it entirely from the mind and get on with the job of playing cricket; to point out to yourself all the more strongly the inescapable truth that cricket is never a game which is easy, whether you play one year or twenty years. It's still as difficult after twenty years as after one, and there's still something to learn. I have ended a long career with that very firm conviction.

I have made my criticisms, given some advice, expressed, I hope, a little of the joy and delight that I have had in the game. And I come back again to this—that cricket has been my life, my whole life, and that I owe practically everything to it. I am told sometimes that I have made a contribution to the game myself, and no doubt I have; but cricket has given back to me a hundred times more than I have ever given it. It has made me, in every sense; completed an education which was as good as I could be given in the circumstances, but not very extensive, by travel and contact and contest; sharpened and developed my mind by the necessity of constant reflection and thought about the game and its situations; helped me out of the shyness, which was and is very much a part of me, into an easier and more mature ability to meet anyone, whoever he is, on a more or less equal level. It has given me the opportunity to stimulate, broaden and enrich my mind. At Lord's when I was a boy I submitted myself to the discipline of cricket, and it has formed me and given me a lavish return for my labour beyond my most extravagant dreams.

I have no regrets or complaints whatever, and I look back on my career with tremendous satisfaction. There were ups and there were downs and they were inevitable and in different ways equally useful. I don't look back and wish for what might have been, or that I had done this, or that or the other. I did exactly what I had in fact always wanted to do, and I am grateful, and, I think, a happy and contented person. I can't remember ever meeting anyone who'd had a long career in cricket, at Lord's or Maidstone or Old Trafford or anywhere else, ever saying anything other than that he'd loved playing cricket and had loved the people he'd met through it and what it had given him. I am no different.

I leave active participation in the game (I am very careful to put it that way) at a time when England are stronger in every kind of bowling talent than I have ever known, stronger perhaps than they have ever been, when people like Lock and Laker and Tyson and Statham and Trueman are all available to play for their country. It's the same with batting: I think players such as May, Cowdrey, Richardson, Bailey, Sheppard and Graveney are as good with the bat as any batsmen I have known and played against. Godfrey Evans is still the greatest wicket-keeper in the world. So it's a good time to go.

But I'm not going very far. I shall remain in the environment of cricket, and I hope to write about it, broadcast about it, and to appear on television with the commentators during Test Matches. In the meantime I shall be trying to learn and to become proficient at a new career in advertising. And I hope to play a few games as an amateur in the summer, if Middlesex should want me. No doubt when I go up to Lord's, for the first few games anyway, and find myself in the role of an onlooker merely, I shall have twinges of nostalgia and of a desire to be playing again—and I shall have to put up with them as best I can—there in the home of cricket, telling myself that the wrench could have been a much greater one than it in fact will be. At the very least I shall still be very closely connected with the game which I know will continue to exercise all its old pull and fascination.

And I shall still have a club at Lord's, where my club has always been—though in a different way. On the same day, as I wrote this book, I had two pieces of wonderful news: firstly, that Her Majesty had graciously been pleased to signify that she intended to make me a Commander of the Order of the British Empire, and secondly that I had been made a member of the M.C.C. It was almost too much for one day. Later on I was asked to serve on the Middlesex Committee.

When my name appeared in the Honours' List, I had many letters and telegrams of congratulation, and of two, a telegram and a letter, that I in fact opened one after the other, the first from Parliament House, Canberra, was signed R. G. Menzies, and the second, in the failing handwriting (for which the writer movingly apologised) of an eighty-four-year-old man, was from Sir Pelham Warner, expressing with the kindliness and warmth I'd always had from him, his delight in the honour which had come my way. It seemed almost as if my innings was ending as it had begun, with Sir Pelham's encouraging eye upon me.

As an M.C.C. member I shall sit in the pavilion at Lord's. Sometimes, no doubt, I shall be seen with old friends near or outside the Tavern; but mostly, I suppose, I shall be in the pavilion, and find myself able to join in that old and excellent tradition in which members stand for a batsman when he comes from the wicket, not when he has made a century or even a double century, but only, whatever his score, when he's played what they consider to be a great innings, in the home of cricket.

I don't know whether I shall ever occupy one of those high chairs in the Long Room and look out on the green turf of Lord's from there. Perhaps some day I will. But from wherever I watch I shall have before my eyes a place where out of nerve and strength and skill and desire I fulfilled all my ambition.

For me, you could say it's all over; but the game goes on, and the weather-vane with its arrow pointing and the stooped figure and the shouldered scythe will still swing in the wind and sunshine above the Grandstand Balcony.

Lord's: 1957.

All books from the Pavilion Cricket Library are available from your local bookshop, price £12.95 hardback, £6.95 paperback new titles, £5.95 backlist, or they can be ordered direct from Pavilion Books Limited.

New Titles

Farewell to Cricket
Don Bradman

Jack Hobbs
Ronald Mason

Backlist

In Celebration of Cricket
Kenneth Gregory

The Best Loved Game
Geoffrey Moorhouse

Bowler's Turn
Ian Peebles

Lord's 1787–1945
Sir Pelham Warner

Lord's 1946–1970
Diana Rait Kerr and Ian Peebles

P.G.H. Fender
Richard Streeton

Through the Caribbean
Alan Ross

Hirst and Rhodes
A.A. Thomson

Two Summers at the Tests
John Arlott

End of an Innings
Denis Compton

Ranji
Alan Ross

Batter's Castle
Ian Peebles

The Ashes Crown the Year
Jack Fingleton

Life Worth Living
C.B. Fry

Cricket Crisis
Jack Fingleton

Brightly Fades The Don
Jack Fingleton

Cricket Country
Edmund Blunden

Odd Men In
A.A. Thomson

Crusoe on Cricket
R.C. Robertson-Glasgow

Benny Green's Cricket Archive

Please enclose cheque or postal order for the cover price, plus postage:

UK: 65p for first book; 30p for each additional book to a maximum of £2.00. Overseas: £1.20 for first book; 45p for each additional book to a maximum of £3.00

Pavilion Books reserve the right to show new retail prices on covers which may differ from those previously advertised in the text or elsewhere and to increase postal rates in accordance with the Post Office's charges.